Preston Dennett

UFOs Over Arizona

A True History

of Extraterrestrial Encounters

in the Grand Canyon State

Schiffer Publishing Ltd

4880 Lower Valley Road • Atglen, PA 19310

Copyright © 2016 by Preston Dennett

Library of Congress Control Number: 2016949369

Designed by RoS
Cover design by Matt Goodman
Cover art image by Kessara
Type set in Agency FB/Arno Pro

ISBN: 978-0-7643-5166-2
Printed in The United States

Published by Schiffer Publishing, Ltd.
4880 Lower Valley Road
Atglen, PA 19310
Phone: (610) 593-1777; Fax: (610) 593-2002
E-mail: Info@schifferbooks.com
Web: www.schifferbooks.com

For our complete selection of fine books on this and related subjects, please visit our website at www.schifferbooks.com. You may also write for a free catalog.

Schiffer Publishing's titles are available at special discounts for bulk purchases for sales promotions or premiums. Special editions, including personalized covers, corporate imprints, and excerpts, can be created in large quantities for special needs. For more information, contact the publisher.

We are always looking for people to write books on new and related subjects. If you have an idea for a book, please contact us at proposals@schifferbooks.com.

I'VE BEEN FLYING NOW FOR 44 YEARS, AND I'M THE LAST GUY THAT'S GOING TO SAY I DON'T BELIEVE THEY'RE UP THERE. I'VE NEVER SEEN ONE, BUT WHEN AIR FORCE PILOTS, NAVY PILOTS, AIRLINE PILOTS TELL ME THEY SEE SOMETHING COME UP ON THEIR WING THAT WASN'T AN AIRPLANE, I HAVE TO BELIEVE THEM . . . I AM INDEED INTERESTED IN UNIDENTIFIED FLYING OBJECTS. I FRANKLY FEEL THAT THERE IS A GREAT DEAL TO THIS AND I HAVE DISCUSSED IT OFTEN WITH MANY AIR FORCE OFFICERS.

—BARRY GOLDWATER, ARIZONA STATE SENATOR

IN 1997, DURING MY SECOND TERM AS GOVERNOR OF ARIZONA, I SAW SOMETHING THAT DEFIED LOGIC AND CHALLENGED MY REALITY. I WITNESSED A MASSIVE DELTA-SHAPED CRAFT SILENTLY NAVIGATE OVER SQUAW PEAK, A MOUNTAIN RANGE IN PHOENIX, ARIZONA. IT WAS TRULY BREATHTAKING. I WAS ABSOLUTELY STUNNED . . . AS A PILOT AND A FORMER AIR FORCE OFFICER, I CAN DEFINITIVELY SAY THAT THIS CRAFT DID NOT RESEMBLE ANY MAN-MADE OBJECT. I'D EVER SEEN.

—FIFE SYMINGTON, GOVERNOR OF ARIZONA

THE TYPE OF UFO REPORTS THAT ARE MOST INTRIGUING ARE CLOSE-RANGE SIGHTINGS OF MACHINE-LIKE OBJECTS OF UNCONVENTIONAL NATURE AND UNCONVENTIONAL PERFORMANCE CHARACTERISTICS, SEEN AT LOW ALTITUDES, AND SOMETIMES EVEN ON THE GROUND. THE GENERAL PUBLIC IS UNAWARE OF THE LARGE NUMBER OF SUCH REPORTS COMING FROM CREDIBLE WITNESSES. WHEN ONE STARTS SEARCHING FOR SUCH CASES, THEIR NUMBERS ARE QUITE ASTONISHING.

—DR. JAMES MCDONALD, SENIOR ATMOSPHERIC PHYSICIST, UNIVERSITY OF ARIZONA

Contents

Introduction 6

Chapter One: The 1947 Super–Wave 8

Chapter Two: Sightings—1960–1989 26

Chapter Three: The Phoenix Lights and Beyond 54

PHOTO GALLERY 73

Chapter Four: Landings and Humanoids 84

Chapter Five: Onboard Experiences 110

Chapter Six: UFO Crashes 149

Chapter Seven: Contemporary Cases: 2000–2015 159

Epilogue 178

Appendix 180

Endnotes 181

Sources 185

Index of Place Names 191

Introduction

As early as 25,000 BC, the area now known as Arizona was inhabited by Native Americans, mainly the Navajo, Hopi, and Apache. Today evidence of ancient canals, aqueducts, and fortifications can be found throughout the state. The first European explorations were done by the Spanish in the sixteenth century. Mexico claimed the area, and reports of mineral wealth encouraged further explorations, many of which were discouraged by hostile Native Americans. It wasn't until the Mexican-American War in 1848 that the area was ceded to the United States.

One year later, the California gold rush caused a stampede westward. Many hopeful prospectors never made it to the Golden State and, instead, remained in Arizona where rich copper deposits were being discovered. The industry quickly flourished and Arizona (then part of the New Mexico Territory) became known as the Copper State. Only later would it earn its official name as the Grand Canyon State.

When the Civil War began in 1861, the area joined the southern Confederacy. But when the war ended and the Confederate troops were taken, most of the other settlers also left, leaving Arizona again populated almost solely by Native Americans.

The Homestead Act of 1862 encouraged settlers back. During this time, Arizona epitomized the Wild West era, particularly in cities such as Tombstone, which became famous for its gunfights and lawlessness. At this time, the population was around 10,000.

As the western population grew, strife increased between settlers and the Native American population. Apaches, in particular, defended their homeland battling against ranchers and cattlemen.

It wasn't until 1886 and the defeat of Geronimo that "the Indian Threat" was removed. By this point, the population hovered just under 100,000.

In 1912, Arizona became the forty-eighth state. Its name was derived from the Native American word "Arizonac," meaning "place of the small spring." At this time most of the state was still undeveloped. However, following the construction of the Roosevelt Dam, the state began to thrive. In 1910, the population was 204,000. Twenty years later, it had doubled. By 1950, the population was 750,000. As of 2014, the population was nearly seven million.

Today Arizona produces more than half the nation's copper. It is also rich in gold, silver, oil, and timber. Farming, ranching, and especially tourism provide much of the state's industry.

Arizona contains the United States' third largest Native American population. The federal government owns approximately forty-four percent of the state.

The geography of Arizona is unique. The sixth largest state (114,000 square miles), the northeast section is part of the Colorado Plateau, while the remaining is largely desert basins and gentle valleys and mountains. Altitudes range from seventy feet above sea level (near Yuma) to 12,633 feet at the top of Humphreys Peak north of Flagstaff. The Colorado River is the state's main source of irrigation. Because of the arid climate, Arizona has always struggled with inadequate water supplies. The major lakes, including Powell, Mead, Mojave, and Havasu were all created by damming the Colorado River.

The Grand Canyon (with gorges a mile deep) is the state's number one tourist attraction and is visited by more than three million people each year.

It should come as no surprise that Arizona also has a rich and exciting UFO history, producing some of the world's most famous and influential encounters.

Arizona's top three encounters are easy to identify. The Kingman UFO crash in 1954 is the state's most famous UFO crash/retrieval incident and one of the first UFO crashes to be publicly revealed. The 1975 abduction of woodcutter Travis Walton in Snowflake in full view of five of his coworkers is arguably one of the most investigated and best verified abduction cases in US history. But the hands-down grandfather of all Arizona cases, and perhaps any sighting in the entire world, occurred on March 13, 1997, and is known as the Phoenix Lights. On that evening, thousands of people witnessed a miles-wide craft move slowly over Phoenix, headed south across the state and then curving around and heading back where it came from.

Of course, these are not the only Arizona encounters to become famous. Sedona has become internationally known as a UFO hotspot and attracts thousands of visitors every year.

Also, Arizona was the location of some early prominent UFO researchers including James McDonald, an atmospheric physicist who investigated several high-quality Arizona cases and one of the first mainstream scientists to investigate UFOs scientifically, and Coral and Jim Lorenzen, who founded the first successful citizens UFO investigative group in which they called the Aerial Phenomena Research Organization (APRO). The Lorenzens pioneered UFO research, and APRO became the model for all other UFO organizations to follow. Because of the Lorenzens, many cases in Arizona and across the world were investigated and recorded for posterity.

Combining the statistics from the National UFO Reporting Center (NUFORC) and the Mutual UFO Network (MUFON), Arizona has more than 3,000 recorded encounters. In this book, we shall cover the entire history of UFOs over Arizona, from sightings and landings to abductions and UFO crashes. We will explore little-known cases, famous cases, and some cases that have never been published before.

Cases have been drawn from a wide variety of sources including books, magazines, newspapers, UFO reporting centers, radio shows, television documentaries, firsthand witness interviews, and more. With literally thousands of cases, this book can only provide a small glimpse into the actual number of cases.

So come along on an incredible journey that is sure to change the way you feel about UFOs over Arizona.

Chapter One

The 1947 Super-Wave

While evidence shows that UFOs have been visiting our planet for millennia, it wasn't until 1947 that the modern age of UFOs began. In 1947, our planet experienced a massive super-wave of sightings largely unprecedented in human history. Across the United States and the world, strange objects were being seen in staggering numbers.

As the military struggled to understand the activity in our skies, ordinary citizens were left to fend for themselves.

Because Arizona had relatively low population levels at this time, only a few cases predate the modern era of UFO history. One early case occurred about thirty-five years before the UFOs arrived in large numbers.

In 1913 or 1914, game warden Gene Holden was riding horseback in the Tonto Rim area in Winslow when he saw a low-flying object approach overhead. It was glowing and appeared to be a huge "silver tin plate" so bright that it hurt his eyes. It moved overhead about a hundred feet up and soared off into the distance. Holden had no idea what it might be until years later in 1947, when the term flying saucer first came into use.

Another early case occurred on September 30, 1946, to fourteen-year-old Morgan (pseudonym), who lived in the tiny town of Dome, twenty-three miles east of Yuma. At that time, there was no running water in his house, and it was Morgan's duty to retrieve it each night. The trip was about 300 yards each way, and he had never had a problem.

On this evening, however, he had just started when he saw a brilliant flash. "It was bright enough that it cast very black shadows in front of my body," explained Morgan. "I stopped, turned, and saw what appeared to be a very large object on fire at about forty-five degrees above the horizon." There were no visible wings, no windows, and no tail.

It appeared to be about ten miles away, but even at that distance he could see what looked like "structural beams" on the object. As he watched, it moved across the sky disappearing behind Castledome Butte.

Says Morgan: "I told my mother what I had seen, and she said it was maybe an airplane, but I had never seen a plane that looked like that."[1]

The Super-Wave Begins

Around 11:00 p.m. on June 10, 1947, Coral Lorenzen (who would form the UFO group APRO), stepped outside on her porch. She noticed a glow forming to the south. It increased in brightness until it became a ball of light that immediately zipped upward at high speed until disappearing into the distance.

Lorenzen had witnessed many balloon and missile launches and had never seen anything like this. She later wrote that "fantastic as it might seem, there was only one explanation for the thing I had seen: there might be intelligent life on other worlds, and their ships were the strange things people had reported in the heavens from time to time through the years."

One month later, on July 7, 1947, around the same time as the Roswell UFO crash, amateur photographer William Rhodes of Phoenix was drawn outside by a strange sound. Hoping to photograph a jet, he was surprised to see what appeared to be a flying disk. It was semi-circular, flat, and circling the area about 2,000 feet away.

Rhodes quickly snapped two photos of the object, which veered and flew off quickly to the west. Realizing he had just captured two pictures of the "flying saucers" that the newspapers were talking about, he rushed to his laboratory and developed the film.

The two photos came out perfectly. He offered them to the *Arizona Republic*, who published them on July 9, 1947, under the headline, "Saucer Flits in the Sky at Unbelievable Speeds."

The story doesn't end there. Kenneth Arnold viewed the photos and seeing that they portrayed what he had seen earlier that year over Mount Rainier, he publicly declared his belief that Rhodes' pictures were genuine. Arnold's endorsement caught the attention of air force and the FBI.

According to Rhodes, the FBI showed up within forty-eight hours of the photograph being published. Two men presented themselves as Lieutenant Colonel Beam (from Hamilton Field, CA) and FBI agent Mr. Ledding. They interrogated Rhodes about the sighting and the photographs. Says Rhodes: "They confiscated the negative and said I could get it back soon. But that never happened." In 1948, Rhodes was asked to come to Wright-Patterson AFB in Ohio for an interview, but he declined. Shortly later, further military and government officials arrived at his home to interview him again. Says Rhodes: "Years later when I called the FBI, they denied all knowledge of the incident."

The bombshell occurred on March 5, 1985, when the air force declassified Air Intelligence Report #100-203-79. Formerly "Top Secret," the report (originally dated December 10, 1948) presents an analysis of the current UFO situation at that time, reporting on different types of UFOs and speculating on their possible origins and intentions. The report concludes that "some sort of flying object" has been observed. What are these flying objects? The report takes a decidedly hesitant stance: "It is not known at this time whether these observations are misidentifications of domestically launched devices, natural phenomena, or foreign unconventional aircraft."

Important here is the appendix, particularly Appendix C: "Selected Reports of Flying Object Incidents." Several current cases are mentioned, including the sighting by William Rhodes, which the air force conveniently "forgot."

The report says that William Rhodes "allegedly saw a disk circling his locality during sunset and took two photographs. The resulting pictures show a disk-like object with a round front and a square tail . . . These photographs have been examined by experts who state they are true photographic images and do not appear to be imperfection in the emulsion or imperfections in the lens."

Today some researchers have speculated that Rhodes may have photographed one of the actual UFOs that crashed at Roswell.

As the 1947 UFO super-wave swept across the United States and the world, Arizona continued to have its share of high quality cases.

On July 8, Mrs. Ray Wilder and Mrs. Earl Moore, both residents of Douglas, observed a disk-shaped object move across the sky, glinting in the sun and appearing to change shape.

Also on July 8, three Arizona State Highway Department workers had an experience they would not soon forget. At 8:15 a.m., Henry Hodges and R. N. Villa were in Yuma when they saw two identical-looking, silver-colored, saucer-shaped craft following one another at a high altitude above them. They called out to their coworker, Henry Varela, who also observed the two objects, which moved soundlessly and at very high speeds. Impressed by what they saw, the workers reported their sighting to the US Weather Bureau, who told the witnesses that perhaps they had seen "a misidentification of the planet, Venus."

A third sighting on July 8 occurred in Tucson when three men, William Holland, William Harman, and Lewis Zesper (a former air force pilot) observed an oval-shaped metallic object about twenty-five feet in diameter move at an altitude of 4,000 feet above the mountains to the east. The object wobbled as it moved from north to south.

The next day, on July 9, Henry Vardela of the Arizona State Highway Department reported that he saw two disks fly in single-file formation over the mountains near Yuma.

That same day in Nogales, Western Union office manager Guy Fuller, police Sergeant Pete Mincheff, Sam Marcus, and Arthur Doane all observed objects that they described as "flying tortillas" a local-term used to describe the flying objects that were being seen across the state.

Day after day, the sightings continued. Just before noon on July 10, Mrs. L. B. Ogle saw a small glowing orb about seven inches in diameter, hover and wiggle back and forth immediately outside their downstairs window.

At 2:30 a.m., July 11, Anna Potts of Yuma, was woken up by her barking dog. She went outside to comfort him, and instead saw a disk-shaped object zoom overhead. It was moving at high speeds and rotating. No sound could be heard, and the object was in view for only about five seconds, but long enough for Potts to be convinced that she saw a genuine flying saucer. She later reported her sighting to the *Daily Sun*.

That evening, Mrs. W. P. Hopkins of Douglas observed a disk-shaped object hover directly over Fifteenth Street Park, in direct view of a large group of floodlights.

The wave ended two weeks later when about twenty-five residents of Douglas watched a small cluster of lights, which zipped around the town, circling it ten times at high speed until turning away and disappearing in a burst of acceleration.[2]

The Start of Project Blue Book

During the 1947 super-wave, the air force formed Project Sign, a small group of officers dedicated to studying the saucer reports. Project Sign evolved into Project Grudge, which was renamed Project Blue Book. Blue Book would study UFOs on an official basis for the next two decades.

Despite the huge number of sightings, only thirteen Arizona cases investigated by air force Project Blue Book intelligence officers were labeled unidentified. The first of these occurred on October 14, 1947, the same day that Chuck Yeager broke the sound barrier, reaching a record speed of more than 760 mph. On that day, two army officers (one a fighter pilot, and the other a pilot and air force gunner) were working in a mine at Cave Creek, eleven miles north of Phoenix, when they observed a black wing-shaped object moving overhead at an estimated altitude of 8,000 feet and a speed of 350 mph. Both men were familiar with all types of aircraft, and yet neither was able to identify what they had seen. Blue Book intelligence officers assigned to the case were equally baffled, and noting the high credibility of the witnesses, declared the case unidentified, case #95.

It wasn't only the air force who was beginning to look into the strange phenomena taking place; some prominent civilians were also taking an interest. On August 15, 1948, Walt Andrus (a graduate of the US Navy Electronics Technician program, pilot and amateur radio operator) and his wife were in downtown Phoenix when they saw four disks flying in formation in the daylight sky.

The sighting began when Andrus's five-year-old son shouted out, "Daddy, look, silver balloons."

Andrus looked up. "Four round, dull silver objects were floating slowly in the northwest at an angle of forty-five degrees above the horizon, moving straight west," explains Andrus. "Three were flying in geometric formation, while the fourth was lower and considerably behind the first three."

Andrus noticed that the formation was opposite that of fight aircraft, where one protects the other directly below it. They flew in complete silence. Says Andrus: "Everyone on our side of the street stopped to watch these objects as we followed them across the sky. Moving directly west, the objects arrived at a point nearly straight north of us when the lead object disappeared in the clear sky."

The rest of the objects followed, each disappearing in the same spot. As a weather observer, Andrus had released weather balloons on a daily basis. He is positive that the objects were not balloons.

They continued to watch the sky, and to their surprise, three of the objects reappeared in the distance, still flying in formation. They were visible for only a few seconds before moving away, but he observed them long enough to see that they were circular, thin disk-like objects. "You remember it vividly," says Andrus. "It makes an impression in your mind that you never wipe out."

Andrus was stunned, and this sighting led to a lifelong interest in UFOs inspiring him to join APRO and, twenty years later (in 1967), become one of the founding members of the Mutual UFO Network (MUFON.)

At 5:45 p.m. on April 28, 1949, a group of witnesses in Tucson observed a silvery cigar-shaped object move overhead at an estimated speed of 300-600 mph. The object looked metallic and appeared to be revolving or rotating. It was totally silent and in view for twelve minutes.

Researcher Bruce Maccabee PhD writes that this case "was a real challenge to the Project Grudge investigators . . . The Project Grudge personnel had no other choice than to leave this one unexplained." (Blue Book case #361)

Only a small portion of cases investigated by Blue Book intelligence officers were declared unidentified or even adequately investigated. According to J. Allen Hynek, the reverse was true. Blue Book officers paid little attention to the best cases and instead paid attention to cases that seemed to have obvious prosaic explanations. They did their best to not label cases unidentified. However, sometimes they were unable to avoid it. A large number of the unidentified Blue Book cases were labeled as such in large part because the witnesses were military personnel whose credibility could not be easily dismissed.

On the afternoon of May 9, 1949, Master Sergeant Troy Putman from the 43rd Air Refueling Squadron at Davis-Monthan AFB was laying on his deck outside his home in Tucson when he saw two strange aircraft overhead. They were round and had a shiny mirror-silver surface. They moved at an estimated altitude of 10,000 feet at about 750-1,000 mph. The objects first traveled in a level flight, banked left and then right, and disappeared over the Catalina Mountains.

Putman reported his case to his superiors and it was routed to Blue Book, which declared the case unidentified (Blue Book #384), mainly because of the credibility of the witness. Researcher Michael David Hall writes:

> IF THIS WITNESS HAD NOT BEEN SUCH A HIGHLY RELIABLE OBSERVER AND ACCUSTOMED TO SEEING ALL SORTS OF AIRCRAFT IN A VARIETY OF CONDITIONS, IT IS DOUBTFUL THAT THE GRUDGE OFFICERS WOULD HAVE STAMPED THE CASE UNIDENTIFIED.[3]

Pilot Chases Disk

As reported by the *Los Angeles Daily Mirror*, on February 2, 1950, an air force pilot from Davis-Monthan AFB was cruising over the Tucson area in a B-29 when he observed "an unidentified object" ahead of him. He gave chase to the object, which easily outdistanced him, leaving a "long black plume of smoke." The object eventually disappeared behind a distant range of mountains. Queries to White Sands Proving Grounds in New Mexico revealed that there had been no rocket launches on that day. The next day, Davis-Monthan released an official statement, explaining the sighting as "vapor trails from a high-flying American airplane."[4]

Astronomer Sees UFO

Despite allegations of skeptics, there are many accounts on record in which professional astronomers have observed UFOs, such as the following reported by famed astronomer Seymour L. Hess of Lowell Observatory in Flagstaff.

At 12:20 p.m., May 20, 1950, Hess was at Lowell Observatory when he saw a disk-shaped craft moving slowly against the prevailing wind at an altitude of about 12,000 feet. Hess observed the object through binoculars and became convinced that it was a powered vehicle of some kind. Says Hess: "It was extremely prominent and showed some size to the naked eye; that is, it was not merely a pinpoint."

He heard no noise as the object moved across the sky and disappeared into a large cloudbank. He estimated that it was no wider than five feet, and moved at about 200 mph.[5]

Mysterious Fireball

In the late 1940s and early 1950s, New Mexico was targeted by hundreds of mysterious green fireballs. The fireballs were unlike meteors in that they traveled parallel to the ground and after exploding left no debris or damage. While

New Mexico experienced the majority of the activity, the surrounding states, including Arizona, were not spared.

One of Arizona's most dramatic incidents occurred on November 2, 1951, when more than 165 people over a wide area observed a green fireball that "blazed more bright than the moon and appeared much larger." As was typical of the mysterious fireballs, it moved parallel to the Earth and finally "exploded in a frightful paroxysm of light without making a sound."

Search parties were sent to the area, but they found no evidence of any debris.[6]

The 1952 Blue Book Cases

The air force's Project Blue Book investigated several thousand UFO cases, but only a very small portion of them were given the label unidentified. Arizona has only thirteen such cases, eight of which occurred in 1952. This year turned out to be one of Arizona's busiest so far.

One of the first major cases occurred on April 3, 1952. Chick Logan, a civilian flight commander, was on the runway at Marana AFB (in Benson) waiting for a radio transmission from one of his students when he noticed an oval light. He didn't pay much attention to it, but then several other people noticed it and said that it wasn't moving. Chick Logan decided to take off and intercept it. He climbed up to about 14,000 feet but was not equipped to go any higher. The object appeared to be at least 40,000 feet up. Logan described it as about five times the size of a B-29 Superfortress. "It was not like a disc," said Logan, "but more oblong . . . It was real bright and shone like polished aluminum. I'll tell you, I have been flying for twenty-five years, and I have never seen anything like it."

The object remained over the base for nearly an hour before disappearing. Research revealed no weather balloon launches that might have caused the sighting.

The third Arizona case to be declared unidentified by Blue Book occurred on April 17, 1952, at Yuma Test Station. It was 3:05 p.m. when a group of army weather observation students (some of them graduate engineers) observed a circular white object fly overhead. Although the sighting lasted about seven seconds, it was long enough to impress the witnesses and attract the attention of Blue Book. After interviewing the witnesses and investigating, Blue Book officers labeled the case #1127 unidentified.

Ten days after the above incident, on the evening of April 27, Sergeant G. S. Porter (an airport control tower operator) and his wife were outside their home in Yuma when they observed a bright red disk-shaped object fly overhead. It appeared to be about as large as a fighter plane and was cruising below an 11,000-foot overcast.

Shortly later another disk appeared. It was followed by another, and others, until the two of them observed a total of seven disks. Minutes later they saw two more disks fly overhead in formation.

The series of sightings occurred over a period of about two hours. Porter reported his case to authorities who routed the case to Blue Book. After interviewing Porter, Blue Book officers were unable to come up with an explanation and declared it case #1163, unidentified.

The next Arizona sighting to shake up the air force occurred only four days later, on May 1, 1952. Says J. Allen Hynek: "This case is a classic."

On that day, air force intelligence officer Major Rudolph Pestalozzi was standing at the steps of the base hospital at Davis-Monthan Air Force Base when he and another airman saw two round metallic objects approach a B-36 plane that was flying over the base. The two objects raced forward at about four times the speed of the aircraft, then slowed down and took formation around it.

One object flew about twenty feet behind the port side while the other flew between the right engine and the leading edge of the tail. For the next five minutes, the two objects paced the aircraft, then took off. One of the disks stopped and hovered and then followed the other.

Thoroughly shaken-up, the crew of the B-36 (which was en route from Carswell AFB in Texas to March AFB in California) requested permission to make an immediate landing at Davis-Monthan.

Permission was granted. Major Pestalozzi, as the intelligence officer, interrogated the crew of the B-54 and learned that all ten men aboard had closely observed the objects which, they said, had a convex top and bottom, were about twenty-five feet in diameter and about twelve feet thick.

Despite the nearness of the objects, the plane suffered no malfunctions. Pestalozzi was impressed by the sighting, which he himself witnessed. He prepared a file about the incident that he called "the thickest report I'd ever filed on a UFO."

After investigating the incident, Hynek labeled the case unidentified. Blue Book officials, to his dismay, disagreed. Writes Hynek, "Despite the detailed description of the maneuvers of two shiny, silent objects, Blue Book dismissed this case as 'Aircraft.'"

Years later, in 1966, Dr. James McDonald heard about the case and decided to investigate. Contacting Blue Book, he learned that the files were mysteriously missing. Unable to get any cooperation from Blue Book, McDonald contacted the witnesses himself. He then sent a long letter to Major Hector Quintanilla, the head of Project Blue Book, detailing everything he had learned. Hynek writes:

I RECALL THAT AT THE TIME DR. MCDONALD WAS REGARDED BY BLUE BOOK PERSONNEL AS AN OUTSTANDING NUISANCE. THIS WAS PARTLY BECAUSE HE WAS INTERESTED IN A SCIENTIFIC STUDY OF THE "TRUE" UFOS, AND PARTLY

BECAUSE HE WAS SO OUTSPOKEN. HE SPOKE HIS MIND FORCEFULLY, AND
DIDN'T HESITATE TO CRITICIZE BLUE BOOK METHODS WHENEVER POSSIBLE..
. IT IS DUE TO THE INDUSTRY AND PERSEVERANCE OF DR. JAMES MCDONALD
THAT THIS EXCELLENT CASE WAS RESURRECTED AT ALL.

Across the country, a massive UFO wave was in progress. On June 19, 1952, the UFOs returned. On this occasion, USAF pilot John Lane observed a round white object fly on a straight and level course. He reported his case to Blue Book, who declared it unidentified, case #1310.

Also in June of 1952, Lieutenant Commander John C. Williams (retired) was with his wife, Josephine, and their guest outside their home in Tombstone. They had ventured outside to watch the sunset. Commander Williams and the others were surprised to see "a huge circular object" swoop down and fly directly toward them.

Commander Williams had graduated from the Naval Academy in 1919, completed flight training in Pensacola in 1922, and then spent the next ten years flying for the navy. He was familiar with all kinds of aircraft and had never seen anything like it. He estimated that it was at least 300 feet in diameter, possibly larger. Says Commander Williams:

SUDDENLY IT STOPPED IN MID-FLIGHT, SEEMED TO HOVER, THEN REVERSED
ITS DIRECTION AND RETRACED ITS COURSE. IN A MATTER OF SECONDS,
HOWEVER, IT RETURNED, STOPPED AGAIN, APPEARED TO OSCILLATE AND
TILT FROM ONE SIDE TO ANOTHER. AGAIN IT REVERSED ITSELF AND
APPARENTLY RETURNED IN THE SAME STRAIGHT LINE.

The object repeated this strange maneuver three times before finally zooming away at high speed. Four years later, Commander Williams wrote a letter to the Director of NICAP (National Investigative Committee into Aerial Phenomena) saying in part:

WE HAD A PERFECTLY CLEAR VIEW OF THE OBJECT, WHICH LOOKED
SOMETHING LIKE A CUP AND A SAUCER, OR A DERBY HAT. ITS SPEED WAS
UNBELIEVABLE. IT DIMINISHED TO A TINY SPECK AND THEN OUT OF SIGHT
IN ABOUT FOUR SECONDS.

Based on what he had heard from other sources and upon his own sighting, Commander Williams became firmly convinced that UFOs were in fact, extraterrestrial in origin. "I don't know where they come from," he says, "but I have the feeling we are being observed and studied by these outer-space beings."

When it came to declaring a UFO incident unidentified, the air force strongly preferred military witnesses. The next case declared unidentified occurred at 2:20 a.m. on August 4, 1952, over Phoenix. USAF communications officer W. F. Vain (and another witness) observed an object that had a straight and level trajectory but changed shape as it flew overhead. It first appeared as a large yellow ball, then lengthened and narrowed until it was shaped like a plate. The object was in view for five minutes, but Vain was still unable to identify it. Neither were Blue Book officers who labeled it unidentified, case #1812.

Two months later, on August 13, 1952, Captain Stanley W. Thompson (USAF retired) observed nine UFOs in three separate V-formations moving over Tucson. While Project Blue Book failed to investigate his case, NICAP sent civilian researchers to record Thompson's testimony.

Eleven days later, Blue Book officers interviewed Mr. and Mrs. George White. On August 24, 1952, the Whites were in Tucson when they observed a large metallic sphere glowing with a bright white light. At first it flew slowly, but then sped up and moved in a dancing, wavering motion. They watched it for a full minute but were unable to identify it. Again, neither could Blue Book officers, who labeled it case #1964, unidentified.

The next three Blue Book cases all occurred in September 1952 in Tucson.

On the morning of September 3, two civilian pilots (McCraven and Thomas) were flying over Tucson when they saw a shiny, dark ellipse make three broad, curving sweeps over a period of one and a half minutes. Blue Book Officers declared it unidentified, Case# 2038.

When it comes to UFOs, a common cliché is that aliens will land before a stunned witness, exit their craft, and say the immortal words: "Take me to your leader." In a few cases, this nearly happened, such as the following, which took place on September 6, 1952.

At precisely 4:55 p.m., ex-Congresswoman Isabella King and Bill McClain observed an orange tear-shaped object overhead. It first whirled on its vertical axis, then descended very quickly, stopped, began whirling in the opposite direction, and retraced its path upward. After interviewing the witnesses and investigating the incident, Blue Book officers were stumped and the incident became Case #2048, unidentified.

The final case of the year occurred on September 17. It was twenty minutes before noon when Ted Hollingsworth and his wife observed three objects described as "large, flat, and shiny" flying in a tight formation slowly across the sky. Moments later it was followed by a second formation of objects, this time moving more quickly. Blue Book officers were alerted to the case, but unable to find an explanation, they added it to their list of unidentifieds, case #2105.

While the credibility of the witnesses seemed to be the deciding factor of whether or not a case was declared unidentified, even this guideline wasn't always followed. Conspicuously missing from the 1952 Blue Book unidentifieds is another 1952 Tucson sighting, only this one was directly over Davis-Monthan Air Force Base. Two metallic-looking disk-shaped objects were seen for several minutes by multiple witnesses on the base. An intelligence officer and a sergeant each took about forty photographs. Strangely, both sets of photographs showed only "black ovoid blobs" instead of the metallic object viewed by the witnesses. Presumably, some radiation emitted from the objects interfered with the photographic process—a phenomenon that has occurred in many other photographic cases. The question remains: why did Blue Book officers fail to label this case unidentified? One possible reason is that some of the best cases never made it to Blue Book and were routed instead to the Air Technical Intelligence Command, (ATIC). Considering the photographic evidence, it's possible this case was deemed too sensitive even for Blue Book.[7]

CIA Targets APRO

While the air force was dealing with a sudden onslaught of sightings, the CIA turned its attention to its own citizens. One of the first citizen-based UFO investigative groups had just formed and it was apparently causing concern. APRO (the Aerial Phenomenon Research Organization) was cofounded by Coral and Jim Lorenzen in 1952.

In the summer of 1953, the Lorenzens discovered that the US government was spying on them. Coral watched two men drive up to their house, stop, and approach. They claimed to be paint contractors and wanted to paint the house. Coral told them that they were renters. The "painters" then tried to engage Coral in casual conversation. They returned to their car and drove away, not stopping at any other house.

Coral told her husband Jim. They later shared the story with others and made a shocking discovery. The treasurer and the secretary of APRO reported that they both were also visited by the same two mysterious gentlemen. In both cases, the gentlemen seemed more interested in talking to the APRO members than about a paint job.

After the CIA incident, the Lorenzens discovered that other government agencies were also looking into APRO. Writes Jim Lorenzen:

> AN ASSOCIATE OF MRS. LORENZEN WHOSE HUSBAND WORKED IN THE OSI (OFFICE OF SPECIAL INVESTIGATION) TOLD HER THAT THE LOCAL OFFICE HAD A SIZABLE DOSSIER ON APRO AND THE LORENZENS.

APRO would continue strongly for more than thirty-five years, though in 1969, lost much of its membership to the newly formed group, the Mutual UFO Network (MUFON).[8]

Although only two more Arizona cases would be declared unidentified by Blue Book (both in early 1953), the year turned out to produce a large number of high-quality cases.

The first occurred on January 30, 1953, at 7:25 p.m. The main witness was Dr. Alan Webb, a chemical engineer and research chemist employed by the University of California. Webb was in a car with four other people driving along Highway 80. They were about seven miles east of Yuma when Webb observed a strange light ahead of them that "flickered and danced."

As they approached the object, they realized it was hovering over the Spain Flying Field. The object was incredibly low, hovering at about twice the height of the floodlights. It was stationary right above a small single-engine plane being serviced by a mechanic on the airfield.

Webb kept his eye on the object and was surprised to watch it suddenly ascend. "It rose slowly at first, then gathering momentum, it lifted rapidly." The light blinked several times, then "vanished among the stars."

Being a scientist, Webb was impressed. His friends had also seen the object and had no explanation. Webb and two of his friends returned the next day and located the mechanic who had been working on the plane. He denied seeing any object, but referred them to a US weather station a quarter mile to the east.

Webb spoke with a weatherman who said that he had released a weather balloon on that day, but that it had only a very small flashlight bulb, which remained steady and did not flicker. Nor would it have hovered that low in the area they had seen the object. Webb could see that the balloon explanation simply did not fit the facts.

The weatherman was convinced that Webb had seen a genuine UFO and apparently had good reason to. Says Webb: "He said that ours must have been a UFO, that such things were a great mystery but had nevertheless been seen frequently in the neighborhood by the personnel of the weather station and also of the nearby air force fighter base."

As we have seen, most Blue Book cases that were labeled unidentified involve witnesses of high credibility. This next incident is another good example. At 1:50 p.m. on February 4, 1953, US Weather Bureau observer Stanley Brown used a theodolite (a camera attached to a telescope) to track a "white oblong object" that flew straight up, leveled off, and was then joined by a second similar-looking object. The newly arrived UFO then flew away and returned, repeating this maneuver twice. Brown observed the objects for about five minutes until they were lost in the clouds. Blue Book officers labeled it unidentified, case #2388.

Again, some of the best cases never even made it to Blue Book. One month following the above sighting, on March 3, 1953, an extraordinary event took place over Luke AFB. It was 1:30 p.m. and Captain Roderick D. Thompson of the 3600th Fighter Training Group at Luke AFB was leading a group of three F-84 jet interceptors. They had reached an altitude of 20,000 feet and a speed of 500 mph when a 300–500-foot crescent-shaped object appeared above them. Thompson gave chase, flying up to 30,000 feet and increasing his speed to 560 mph. The object began to accelerate, so Thompson activated his gun camera and shot 30 feet of 16mm film as the object sped away. No word from Blue Book.

Three days later on March 7, 1953, a group of twenty air force officers at a gunnery met at a base in Yuma and observed about a dozen disk-shaped objects that dove and hovered over the base. This case was also ignored by Blue Book, though the civilian group NICAP did conduct an investigation and concluded that the objects were unidentified.

One month later, on April 18, 1953, Arizona's twelfth and final Blue Book unidentified case occurred over Tucson. Again, the witness was of high credibility. At about 5:45 p.m., Staff Sergeant V. A. Locey observed three anomalous orange lights for a period of about three minutes. After investigation, air force officers labeled it unidentified, case #2542.

Blue Book would continue for another sixteen years. Although they would investigate other Arizona cases, not a single one was labeled as unidentified.

Despite the air force's lack of response, the sightings continued. At 10:00 a.m. on May 5, 1953, Wells Allen Webb was seven miles east of Yuma when he saw a silver-white cloud-like UFO hovering in the sky. The object seemed to be changing from oblong in shape to circular. At the time, Webb was wearing Polaroid sunglasses, and he noticed a series of dark-colored concentric rings surrounding the object. He took off his sunglasses and observed the UFO with his eyes, but the rings were no longer visible. However, when he put the sunglasses back on, the rings could be easily seen.

Researcher Marc Davenport believes he might have the answer to this mystery. "The fact that Webb observed dark rings surrounding the UFO only when he was wearing polarizing lenses implies that an invisible something was causing at least partial polarization of light at intervals around the craft. The sunglasses apparently allowed him to 'see' normally invisible 'lines of force' in the same way fine iron filings sprinkled on a sheet of paper allow one to 'see' magnetic lines of force from a magnet held beneath the paper."

A few weeks later, on May 21, 1953, veteran private pilot Bill Beers was outside his home with two others in Prescott when they saw eight disk-like objects maneuver overhead. According to Beers, the objects "swooped around in formation, peeled-off, and shot directly up and down in a manner that could not be duplicated by a plane."[9]

The 1954 Cases

While the early 1950s produced many high-quality reports, activity slowed down slightly in 1954, which produced at least three high-profile cases.

On the evening of April 16, 1954, school superintendent Elbert Edwards and his friend John Goddard were camping above Havasu Canyon in the Grand Canyon when they saw a very bright light swoop down from the sky and approach. Goddard had a pair of 8X binoculars and observed the object for the next minute. He said it was cigar-shaped and had a row of five portholes or lights along the side. The bright light was coming from its tip. The object moved from north to south, vanishing over Mexico.

As investigated by Project Blue Book officers, on December 23, 1954, Kenneth Hite, a first lieutenant stationed at Davis-Monthan AFB, was flying a combat air patrol mission when he saw a UFO over Nogales. He was flying at 15,000 feet, while the object appeared to be 10,000 feet above him and ten miles ahead. Hite locked on to the object and pursued it to an altitude of 28,000 feet. The object continued to parallel Hite's path, always maintaining a distance of about 10,000 feet above him. It moved over Nogales, then headed towards Douglas, then turned south. Hite chased it a little while longer, but running low on fuel, was forced to turn back. Blue Book officers concluded that the pilot had seen a "ferret or snooper" flight from a country south of the United States.

In 1954 (exact date not given), four meteorologists, including atmospheric physicist James E. McDonald, were driving between Tucson and Nogales when they saw a metallic object hovering over the nearby Santa Rita Mountains. The object had a metallic aluminum appearance and was glinting in the setting sun. The four scientists observed the object for several moments, but none were able to identify it.

McDonald was a leading scientist with the University of Arizona, publishing more than a hundred scientific papers in journals like *Nature*, *Scientific American*, and the *Journal of Atmospheric Sciences*. Unable to forget what he and the other witnesses had seen, he contacted the Astronomy Department at the University in the hopes of finding an explanation. When none could be found, he contacted the air force, who thanked him for the report and called him "an expert observer."

Still McDonald couldn't let go. Within a few years of his sighting, he began to investigate UFO reports and eventually became one of only a small handful of prominent scientists who took the UFO subject seriously.[10]

A Loping UFO

One of the red flags that UFO investigators look for when trying to identify a genuine UFO is anomalous movement. Conventional objects generally move in straight lines, and if turning, move in slow gentle curves. However, UFOs are often described as moving in ways that seem to defy physics, including hovering, moving at right angles, and accelerating or stopping instantly.

A typical case occurred on March 28, 1955, and involved a UFO seen over Joseph City. The witness described the object as elongated and said that it passed overhead with a "loping or rocking motion."[11]

Blue Book Identified?

While officers in Project Blue Book labeled thirteen cases "unidentified," many cases that were probably legitimate were labeled "identified." J. Allen Hynek, who worked on Blue Book, stated that often attention was more directed towards cases with conventional explanations, while good cases were often ignored. A good example of Blue Book's approach to UFO cases is this next case, which occurred on October 17, 1955. An observer, described as "a military source," observed a V-shape containing about twelve yellow pale lights move at high altitude very quickly overhead and off into the distance. Blue Book officers labeled the case: meteor.[12]

UFO Attack

There are a number of cases in which planes have nearly collided with a UFO. In a smaller number of cases, planes have actually collided with a UFO or disappeared inside it. The following case, if true, provides an unsettling example of a hostile UFO. According to researcher Brad Steiger, sometime in 1955, a private pilot and his friend were doing some prospecting by the Agua River outside Prescott. Looking up, they saw a military plane surrounded by two glowing objects. The two objects struck the plane with "some kind of strange beams" after which the plane exploded. Writes Steiger:

> WHEN THE AIRMEN JUMPED FREE OF THE BURNING CRAFT IN THEIR PARACHUTES THE UFO SWUNG BACK AND SEARED THE SURVIVORS WITH THE SAME DEADLY RAYS.[13]

A Mothership

On October 6, 1957, engineer Earl Sydow, from Tucson, watched a bright oval-shaped object hovering overhead. He retrieved his telescope and trained it on the object. Through the scope, he watched the object emit five smaller objects. Each of the objects flew away, followed by the large mothership. Six other witnesses were also present and made the same observations. Sydow reported his case to NICAP, which conducted an investigation but was unable to identify the object.[14]

A Black Wingless Object

One month later, in November 1957, mechanical engineer Jack Craig of Bisbee observed "a black, wingless object" about 100 feet across and fifteen feet thick. It flew about 300 feet high, emitted a small amount of white smoke, then climbed up into the sky and moved south over Mexico. Craig reported his sighting to James McDonald, who was intrigued by the sighting, particularly because of the credibility of the witness.[15]

Disks Over Davis Dam

Researchers have long noticed that power stations, nuclear installations, dams, and other similar structures are magnets for UFO activity. Are the UFOs monitoring our technological development? Or is there another reason?

Before he died, one witness to such a case told his son about a series of dramatic encounters over Davis Dam in the late 1950s. Says the son of the witness:

> MY FATHER WORKED AT A SMALL DAM CALLED DAVIS DAM IN ARIZONA ON THE COLORADO RIVER, ACROSS FROM WHAT IS NOW LAUGHLIN. IT IS BETWEEN HOOVER DAM AND PARKER DAM. HE WOULD TELL OF UFOS COMING AT NIGHT TO GET POWER FROM THE DAM. HE AND ANOTHER MAN WOULD BE OUT ON THE TOP OF THE DAM AND WOULD SEE THE UFOS.

The father told his son that the objects appeared often. They were saucer shaped and covered with lights.[16]

Mass Sighting Over Tucson

Early on the morning of April 1, 1958, hundreds of people in the Tucson area observed a group of five or six silvery objects floating leisurely eastward over the city. As calls flooded into local news stations, the reports soon found their way to researcher James E. McDonald, who began a formal investigation.

McDonald was able to locate and interview more than eighty witnesses who observed the objects from locations more than seventy miles apart. After collecting and analyzing all the data, he was able to triangulate the reports. He contacted the local air force bases and weather stations and was able to rule out atmospheric phenomena, weather balloons, and conventional aircraft. He tried to obtain radar information but was told that "radar information is classified."

Finally, a full picture of the incident emerged. His investigation showed that at around 6:00 a.m., a group of five or six oval-shaped silver-colored objects an estimated twenty-five miles high moved overhead. All the witnesses described the same thing. After the objects left, a group of six air force jets appeared, moving in the direction of the UFOs.

McDonald interviewed multiple groups of people who observed the objects together, including a group of weathermen, several residents, a navy seaman, a military pilot, a group of Greyhound bus passengers, and more. He made numerous inquiries trying to find the identity of the jets, but received the runaround from the air force. It was this treatment that first convinced McDonald that the military was withholding information about UFOs.

He eventually prepared a forty-page report on the sighting, which unfortunately was never published. His investigation, however, had opened doors and he soon became inundated by new witnesses who had heard about his interest in the subject.[17]

Blue Book Visits Mesa

On April 8, 1958, two men in their twenties observed what they first thought was a shooting star. The object dropped rapidly out of the sky until it was about 1,500 feet over the town of Mesa, and then slowed down. At this point, the men saw that the light was actually a solid object with windows around it emitting orange light. After dropping down, the object immediately climbed into a near vertical ascent, and then accelerated away, disappearing out of view in about ten seconds. The witnesses were amazed and utterly convinced that they had seen a genuine UFO. Investigating Blue Book officers disagreed and despite the fact that there is no known aircraft that can perform the maneuvers described by the witnesses, wrote: "It may have been a military aircraft on a classified mission."[18]

A Square UFO

While many people describe their sightings as "flying saucers," the truth is that UFOs come in a wide variety of shapes and sizes. On June 29, 1959, a young witness in Phoenix saw his first UFO.

I WAS 10 OR 11 WHEN I SAW THIS OBJECT IN THE SKY RIGHT ABOVE US. IT WAS NOT SPHERICAL BUT SQUARE TO RECTANGULAR AND MADE OF WHAT RESEMBLED PLUMBING JOINTS JOINED TOGETHER TO FORM A RECTANGULAR SHAPE WHICH WAS HOLLOW IN THE CENTER . . . I DON'T KNOW HOW TO BETTER DESCRIBE IT. IT WAS SILVER IN COLOR AND HOVERED ABOUT 200 FEET ABOVE US AS WE WERE PLAYING IN THE STREET. IT HOVERED THERE FOR A COUPLE OF MINUTES AND THEN WENT STRAIGHT UP INTO THE SKY AND DISAPPEARED FROM SIGHT. THERE WERE NO LIGHTS, NO SOUNDS, JUST THIS OBJECT IN THE AIR ABOVE US.

Years later, wondering if anybody has ever seen a similar-looking object, he reported his sighting to NUFORC.[19]

"You Are Never to Speak of This"

One evening in 1959, a family of nine was driving outside Phoenix near South Mountain on Baseline Road, when they saw a very bright light sweeping down from the mountain on their right. To their shock, it was a "saucer-shaped object." It flew alongside their car ahead of them, then dipped down in front of them on the road and took off upwards to the northeast until it was pinpoint in size. At this point, it darted left abruptly, "disappearing like a shooting star."

Says one of the witnesses:

THE SPEED AND ABRUPT MOVEMENT WERE LIKE NOTHING I'D EVER SEEN. WE WERE USED TO SEEING AND HEARING JETS IN AND AROUND PHOENIX BUT NEVER AT NIGHT. JETS FREQUENTLY BROKE THE SOUND BARRIER OVER PHOENIX DURING THAT TIME SO WE WERE USED TO SEEING THEM AND THIS WAS NOT ONE OF THEM. THERE WAS MUCH COMMOTION IN THE CAR AND MY PARENTS, WHO WERE NORMALLY CALM AND SERIOUS, SOUNDED ALARMED AND SCARED, WHICH SCARED ME. THE TERM UFO WAS NOT USED; WE ALL USED THE TERM "FLYING SAUCER" TO DESCRIBE IT. MY FATHER ABRUPTLY TOLD ALL OF US THAT WE WERE NEVER TO SPEAK OF THIS AGAIN BECAUSE THE CHILD WELFARE PEOPLE WOULD THINK THEY WERE CRAZY AND UNFIT PARENTS AND TAKE US AWAY. WE NEVER REPORTED THE INCIDENT TO ANYONE.

Fifty years later, after confirming that her parents and siblings all remembered the sighting, the witness reported it to NUFORC. As she says: "I'm reporting it now because I thought there should be some record of the incident for posterity."[20]

A Cigar-Shaped Object

Sometime in the late 1950s (exact date not given), Kenneth Harayda and his friend were in Nogales when they observed a large cylindrical object with portholes moving at a low altitude over a small hill. The object then moved south disappearing over the Mexican desert. James McDonald investigated the case personally and often pointed to it as one that he could not explain, and a reason that UFO reports should be taken seriously.[21]

Chapter Two

Sightings: 1960–1989

The next few decades produced countless high-quality sightings. Only a few received much publicity beyond local newspapers while the vast majority went completely unrecorded. Many sightings are typically brief and involve unexplained lights at night. The following sightings represent the more extensive kinds of sightings, both high-profile cases, and others that are lesser known.

When one person comes forward to report a sighting, often several others will come forth with confirmation, especially if the first witness is of high credibility, such as in the following case, which occurred on August 26, 1960, in Mesa.

At the time, Mr. Clete L. Miller was the science department head and chemistry teacher at Mesa High School. He was a pilot and served in the Army Air Corps from 1942 to 1946. At around 8:00 p.m., Miller and his wife saw a brilliant object hovering in the southeast sky. It was emitting four separate beams of light, while a bright beacon-like light flashed from the top of the object.

At one point, the object disappeared and reappeared much farther to the north, at which point Miller heard a rumbling noise. He called nearby Williams Air Force Base and was told that there were no unusual aircraft in the area that they were aware of. Miller then contacted local newspapers, who printed his story the next day. As a result, several other people in the area called the newspaper to say that they had seen the same thing. The case was eventually investigated by NICAP.[22]

A Disabled UFO?

On June 26, 1962, UFO researchers Jim and Coral Lorenzen received a UFO report coming from their hometown of Tucson. The witnesses were two brothers, John and James Westmoreland, who were camping out in the backyard of their home with their friend Ronnie Black. John was fourteen years old, and James and Ronnie were both age eleven.

Around 9:00 p.m., they noticed what appeared to be an unusually bright star. It seemed to move and slowly become lower in the sky, but when it remained stationary, they lost interest.

The object remained in place for more than two hours. Around 11:45 p.m., it began to descend again, moving close enough to discern a triangular shape. It emitted three smaller green objects that darted away. At the same time, another swooped down and hovered in place above the first.

The boys were amazed and watched the first object emit another three green objects that went into the second object. Next the second object moved close enough that the boys could see what appeared to be some type of landing gear. The second object retrieved one more smaller object from the first, and then it slowly faded away.

Now a third object appeared, this time close enough to see a white, cone-shaped superstructure above a round aerofoil. The boys watched as a small door opened from underneath and three objects were emitted. It moved lower and a cable was lowered for about five minutes and then drawn back up into the craft carrying a large dark object. The door closed and the object moved upward and to the east until it was out of sight.

The Lorenzens questioned the boys extensively, and concluded that the third and closest object was about eighty feet in diameter and a quarter-mile from the witnesses. They also concluded that the object seen being pulled back up into the object was the same size as the smaller ships that they had seen. Was this a disabled UFO being retrieved by a mother ship? The Lorenzens considered this a real possibility.

IN VIEW OF PRESENCE OF THE SMALLER OBJECTS, WE CAN THEORIZE AT SOME TIME OR ANOTHER, ONE HAD BECOME DISABLED AND LOST, A SEARCH WAS INITIATED, AND A RECOVERY EVENTUALLY AFFECTED. THE LATTER PHASE OF THE OBSERVATIONS, IN WHICH A DEVICE WAS LOWERED TO THE GROUND AND RETRACTED TO THE THIRD SAUCER AT THE END OF IT, COULD HAVE BEEN THAT 'RECOVERY.' THIS IDEA MAY BE FURTHER SUPPORTED BY THE SAUCER'S PROMPT DEPARTURE AFTER THE OBJECT WAS TAKEN ABOARD. THE RECOVERY OF THE OBJECT FROM THE WASH MAY HAVE BEEN THE SOLE PURPOSE OF THE PRESENCE OF THE SAUCERS THAT NIGHT.[23]

M*A*S*H Star Sees UFO

Actor Jamie Farr is perhaps best known for his role as Klinger on the hugely successful television series, M*A*S*H. Unknown to many, he is also one of Arizona's most famous UFO witnesses. In the early 1960s, Farr and his fiancée Joy were driving through Arizona after midnight when they observed a light zigzagging at high speed. They watched it stop in midair, hover, then take off again. At one point, the object approached within 100 yards of their car. Farr drove down the highway at around 60 mph while the UFO paced his car. The couple could see what appeared to be a dome with a light at the base. Also, the UFO seemed to stir up the dust on the ground below it. Joy wanted to pull over, but Farr was frightened and insisted on continuing. The UFO took off at high speed and vanished. Farr, a former skeptic, is now convinced that UFOs are real. He also reports that his vehicle never worked the same after the incident.[24]

Like Geese Fly

In April 1963, a family living on the south side of Tucson, about one mile from the Papago Indian Reservation, had a memorable sighting of a formation of UFOs. One of the children went outside before school to feed the pigeons when he saw a group of disks, each about thirty feet in diameter, flying at an elevation of only about 100 feet, in a perfect V-formation—"like geese fly." The witness called out his brothers and mother, all of who witnessed the formation of objects. Says the witness:

THEY WERE TRIANGULAR, WITH ROUNDED EDGES [AND] GRAY IN COLOR. THEY PROCEEDED TOWARDS THE RESERVATION SLOWLY UNTIL THEY CAME TO A SMALL MOUNTAIN WHERE THE RESERVATION HOSPITAL IS LOCATED ... THEY THEN STOPPED AND HOVERED FOR A BIT, THEN DISAPPEARED BEHIND THE MOUNTAIN.

The next day, they searched for further evidence where the objects had hovered, but found nothing.[25]

The 1965 UFO Wave

Throughout 1965, a massive UFO wave swept across the United States. On September 7, 1965, a Tucson liquor-store clerk saw six whitish-yellow, oval-shaped objects flying so low overhead, it looked like they were about to land. Two of the objects flew side-by-side, while the remaining four were clustered together. Each object had windows that emitted a pink light. The clerk—who told investigators that she had hypersensitive hearing—could hear a high-pitched hum coming from the objects. She heard them coming before she saw them, and says the sound hurt her ears and gave her a headache. The objects moved off to the southeast and disappeared over the mountains.

Despite the fact that the objects were oval-shaped and made a strange humming sound, Blue Book officers assigned to the case noted that there was an airport nearby and that the witness had seen conventional aircraft.

On October 25, 1965, a man described only as "a military official" was in his home located nine miles southeast of Luke AFB in Glendale, when he saw a bright object in the southwest sky that he first thought was a planet. As he watched, it began to change in color from white to orange and back again. Then it started to move at high speed, first going south, then north, then southeast, and finally toward the east. Then it changed elevation and disappeared. One hour later, the military official saw that the object had returned. It again moved erratically and at high speeds before disappearing. Project Blue Book officers interviewed the official. Despite the movements of the object, the officials labeled the case "Venus and Jupiter."

A final case, also investigated by Project Blue Book, occurred on November 26, 1965 and involved three witnesses: a husband, wife, and son. The husband was an astronomer and a retired air force officer from World War II whose job was aircraft identification. The family was outside when their attention was drawn to some sort of explosion in the skies over their Phoenix home. Looking up they saw a "perfect circle of blue star-like objects."

They estimated that there were about thirty to fifty objects. They stayed in circular formation for fifteen seconds, then suddenly broke apart and then began "swarming like bees, resolving into two undulating V-formations." The glowing blue objects then broke apart and re-formed into a single V, and flew off to the south. Despite the almost perfect credentials of the witness, Blue Book officers labeled the case: "Birds."[26]

Young Mother Sees Spaceship

The following case was reported to NUFORC by a young woman who was traveling with her boyfriend and baby from Tucson to Mexico sometime in 1966. Writes the mother:

MY THREE-YEAR-OLD SON WAS ASLEEP ON THE BACK SEAT OF THE CAR. IT WAS AFTER DARK AND I HAD FALLEN ASLEEP WHEN MY FRIEND STOPPED THE CAR, PULLED TO THE SIDE OF THE ROAD IN THE MIDDLE OF THE DESERT NOT FAR FROM THE MEXICAN BORDER. HE WOKE ME UP AND SAID, "LOOK AT THAT." WE GOT OUT OF THE CAR AND THERE IN THE SKY IN FRONT OF US HOVERED A SPACESHIP. IT WAS CLOSE ENOUGH TO SEE WHAT APPEARED TO BE WINDOWS ENCIRCLING THE MIDDLE SECTION. CIRCLING THE MIDDLE SECTION WAS ALSO WHAT LOOKED LIKE LIGHT BLUE AND GREEN COLORED VAPOROUS LIGHTS SWIRLING AROUND THE WINDOWS. THE SPACE SHIP WAS SHAPED LIKE TWO HUGE SAUCERS PLACED TOGETHER

IN A V SHAPE AND IT MOVED SLOWLY IN A CIRCULAR DIRECTION. WE
WATCHED IT FOR AWHILE AND THEN IT JUST INSTANTLY VANISHED.

I HAVE ALWAYS BEEN OPEN MINDED AND MY MALE COMPANION WHO
LIVED IN THE FOOTHILLS OF THE TUCSON MOUNTAINS, SAID THAT HE
HAD OFTEN SEEN UFOS THERE. STILL, ALL I COULD THINK OF WAS THAT
SOMEONE WAS FILMING A MOVIE ABOUT SPACESHIPS OUT THERE IN THE
MIDDLE OF NOWHERE AND THAT WAS WHAT I WAS SEEING. IT LOOKED
EXACTLY LIKE WHAT I HAD ALWAYS THOUGHT A SPACESHIP LOOKED LIKE.

The witness was extremely impressed by her sighting. As she writes:

I HAVE OFTEN MENTIONED THIS SIGHTING TO OTHERS AND NO ONE
SEEMED TO DOUBT WHAT I HAD SEEN. PERHAPS THERE ARE MORE PEOPLE
IN THE WORLD WHO DO NOT DISBELIEVE IN THEIR EXISTENCE THAN
ONE WOULD IMAGINE. I HAD NEVER SEEN ONE BEFORE NOR SINCE, BUT
I KNOW WHAT I SAW. I DO NOT KNOW FROM WHERE IT CAME OR EVEN IF
IT MAY NOT HAVE BEEN CREATED BY SOMEONE ON OUR EARTH PLANET.
THIS IS THE FIRST TIME THAT I HAVE WRITTEN THIS DOWN AND 46 YEARS
LATER, IT IS STILL QUITE CLEAR IN MY MIND. I EXPECT THAT I JUST TOOK
IT ALL FOR GRANTED AND THE ONLY REASON THAT I AM WRITING ABOUT
IT NOW IS THAT ON JUNE 20, 2012 I HEARD THE GUEST SPEAKER, PETER
DAVENPORT ON *COAST TO COAST* SAY THAT IT WAS NECESSARY TO SHARE
THIS INCIDENT WITH AN ORGANIZATION SUCH AS THE ONE THAT HE
REPRESENTS.[27]

UFOs Over Luke AFB

Sometime around 1966, seven year-old Scott Jansen (pseudonym) had an
experience that he would remember for the rest of his life. At the time, his
father, an air force pilot, was stationed at Luke AFB and lived on the base
housing grounds. One evening while Scott walked home from a friend's
house, moving from the non-commissioned officers' side to the officers' side,
he suddenly felt that something was wrong. For some reason, he looked up.
To his shock, there was a large object that appeared to be watching him. "I
remember it seemed to be hovering just above tree line straight above me,"
said Scott. "It displayed moving colored lights."

As he realized that it was unusual, he became frightened and ran home.
He doesn't remember if he told his parents. For decades after the experience
he told almost nobody about what happened. Only recently did he reveal
his encounter, writing:

I KNOW THE EXPERIENCE WAS REAL. I KNOW MY FEELINGS WHILE IT WAS HAPPENING, AND TRUST WHAT INSTINCT AND INTUITION I HAD AT THAT TIME. I KNOW IT WAS AN EVENT THAT I WILL REMEMBER FOR THE REST OF MY LIFE, AND THAT CHILDREN DON'T REMEMBER EVENTS ALL THROUGH THEIR LIFE UNLESS THERE IS GOOD REASON. I BELIEVE TO THIS DAY THAT I SAW SOMETHING THAT WAS TECHNOLOGICALLY IMPOSSIBLE FOR THAT TIME . . . TO THIS DAY I BELIEVE I SAW A UFO AT VERY CLOSE RANGE.

Explaining why he finally decided to go public, Scott wrote:

I FELT COMPELLED TO WRITE SOMETHING ABOUT MY EXPERIENCE NO MATTER IF IT FELL INTO THE ABYSS SOMEWHERE OR NOT.[28]

UFO Tracked on Radar

A particularly well-verified sighting involving multiple eyewitnesses and radar confirmation occurred at 10:00 p.m. on January 13, 1967. At that time two pilots in separate planes (a National Airlines jet and a Lear jet), each observed a mysterious red flashing object that appeared to be elongating and increasing in size. In addition to these two witnesses, an aircraft controller in nearby Albuquerque was watching the object on his radar screens and was also in communication with both pilots. The radar operator noticed a curious fact: whenever the pilots reported the light flashing off, the object would disappear from his scope. And when the pilots saw the light flash on, the object would reappear on his screen.

The object was in view for more than twenty-five minutes. J. Allen Hynek (who investigated the incident in depth) writes: " . . . As the tower warned the jet that the object was getting closer, it seemed to play a cat and mouse game with the jet, involving some rapid accelerations."

During the incident, the following conversation ensued. The controller in Albuquerque asked the National Airlines jet: "Do you want to report a UFO?"

The pilot of the National Airlines jet replied: "No."

Albuquerque control then asked the Lear Jet: "Do you want to report a UFO?"

The pilot of the Lear jet replied: "No. We don't want to report."

Finally, the object took off at a thirty-degree angle upward and accelerating at super high speed; it was out of view in less than ten seconds.

J. Allen Hynek pointed out this case as an example of how attitudes toward UFOs can affect the reactions of a witness.[29]

"The Size of a Grapefruit"

UFOs come in all shapes and sizes. Most often they appear to be disk-shaped and about the size of a large vehicle, or even larger. Much more unusual are tiny UFOs. In the following case, which occurred on June 27, 1967 over Glendale, witnesses observed a mysterious glowing object the size of a grapefruit. They were able to gauge its size nearly exactly because they saw it at very close range.

It was around 11:00 p.m. as Chris (pseudonym) returned from a night of bowling. She stood on her porch talking to her sixteen-year-old neighbor, the babysitter of Chris's children, who were now asleep. Both women noticed something strange: a small white glowing object moving silently across the nearby street directly toward them. Moments later, it hovered only a few feet before them and stopped. Says Chris: "It came right up to our faces, with a motion forwards and backwards as if examining us. It felt as though it were alive or intelligent. Then it retreated over my street, Flynn Lane, changed directions and moved east."

The two witnesses hopped in Chris's car and tried to chase the object, but it moved quickly and was gone. The witness believes she saw something unexplained, and writes, "I have never seen anything like it before or after."[30]

Solid Craft

On January 8, 1968, thirteen-year-old Jason (pseudonym) was in the back seat of his parents' car as they drove through old Tucson. Suddenly he saw a "craft" rise up from the left side of a small hill to their left. It appeared to be about 150 feet away, round-shaped with blue, red, and yellow lights around the perimeter. "It came up over the hill," Jason says, "then paused as if it saw us too and then went back down behind the hill to the left again." He saw it only for a few moments, but long enough to sear into his memory. Fearing that his parents wouldn't believe him, he remained silent.

Another impressive case of a solid craft occurred a few months later over Lake Havasu. The witness doesn't recall the exact date, but the event itself remains vivid. As he reported to NUFORC:

IT WAS A HOT DAY AND A CLEAR BLUE SKY. I HAD JUST SHOT UP A THREE-STAGE MODEL ROCKET WITH A LIZARD PAYLOAD AND WAS WALKING THROUGH THE DESERT TRYING TO RECOVER IT. I SAW A FLASH OF LIGHT COME FROM BEHIND ME. WHEN I TURNED AROUND, THERE WAS A CHROME CIGAR SHAPED OBJECT WITH NO LIGHTS OR MARKINGS JUST HANGING THERE RIGHT IN FRONT OF ME. IT WAS SHAPED KIND OF LIKE A TINY TWO-MAN SUBMARINE. IT WAS TOTALLY SILENT. I STARED AT IT FOR ABOUT TEN

SECONDS THINKING MAYBE IT WAS A BALLOON. THEN IT DIPPED TO ONE SIDE (NORTH) AND DISAPPEARED IN AN INSTANT. IT WAS TOO CLOSE TO BE AN ILLUSION. I REMEMBER SAYING TO MYSELF: "THAT WAS NOT OF THIS EARTH!" I DIDN'T TELL ANYONE OR EVEN REMEMBER THIS UNTIL THE LATE '90S. NOW I REMEMBER IT VERY CLEARLY. HAVEN'T HAD ANYTHING LIKE THAT HAPPEN EVER AGAIN.

This case is only one of many on record in which toy rockets (not to mention actual rockets) have provoked the appearance of a UFO.[31]

Cottonwood UFOs

It was mid-June in 1968. The sun had just set and Larry (pseudonym) was out on the porch with his family trying to escape the pervasive heat. They were looking at the Mingus Mountains, which faced their porch when "an odd light" appeared above the mountains. It rose up slightly, then, as Larry says:

> IT SUDDENLY LIT UP THE WHOLE VALLEY . . . IT WAS OVAL SHAPED, AND JUST HOVERED THERE FOR ABOUT HALF AN HOUR. THEN THE LIGHT WENT OUT SLOWLY UNTIL IT WAS A SMALL LIGHT AND DARK OUT. ALL OF A SUDDEN TWO MORE LIGHTS MERGED WITH THE OTHER AND HOVERED THERE FOR A COUPLE OF SECONDS AND THEN SHOT OFF TO THE NORTH.

The family was left stunned and convinced that they had seen something very unusual. "It was a beautiful sight," Larry later wrote. "I won't forget."

Only one month later, on July 29, 1968, Dr. James E. McDonald, senior physicist at the Institute of Atmospheric Physics at the University of Arizona, would testify before the US House of Representatives. At the time, McDonald was researching several cases of UFO sightings. He testified that UFOs were real and required further research. During the congressional hearings, McDonald said, in part:

> THE TYPE OF UFO REPORTS THAT ARE MOST INTRIGUING ARE CLOSE-RANGE SIGHTINGS OF MACHINELIKE OBJECTS OF UNCONVENTIONAL NATURE AND UNCONVENTIONAL PERFORMANCE CHARACTERISTICS, SEEN AT LOW ALTITUDES, AND SOMETIMES EVEN ON THE GROUND. THE GENERAL PUBLIC IS UNAWARE OF THE LARGE NUMBER OF SUCH REPORTS COMING FROM CREDIBLE WITNESSES. WHEN ONE STARTS SEARCHING FOR SUCH CASES, THEIR NUMBERS ARE QUITE ASTONISHING. ALSO, SUCH SIGHTINGS APPEAR TO BE OCCURRING ALL OVER THE GLOBE.[32]

A Beeping UFO

In early July 1969, three-year-old Jacklin and her family experienced a close-up sighting of a solid metallic UFO over their secluded ranch in Payson. Jacklin was just being put to bed when the entire family noticed a very bright object hovering low in the sky above their home.

Jacklin's grandfather said, "What the hell is that?" and rose from his chair. Jacklin ran for the door, but her grandfather stopped her. Together they watched the disk-shaped object. It had large square windows or portholes around its side, each of which was illuminated by a lemon-yellow light. Every second or so, the object emitted a high-pitched beeping sound. It moved in a slow, gliding manner, cruising leisurely upward.

"It was a dark night," said Jacklin, "but we could see that it was disk-shaped by the illumination of its own light . . . and apparently that created enough light to cast around the object and allow us to see it."

Jacklin's father yelled, "Oh my God, oh my God! It's a UFO!" and began screaming for the other members of the family to come outside and watch. If Jacklin's grandfather hadn't been holding her, Jacklin says she would have run toward it. By the time the rest of the family arrived, it was moving away. They rushed outside and searched the area, but all traces of the object were gone.

Even though she was only three years old, Jacklin remembers the event vividly. Years later, she received confirmation of the event when she went to visit her grandfather. Writes Jacklin:

> I WAS VISITING HIM IN HIS APARTMENT IN CA WITH MY MOTHER WHEN SOMEONE BROUGHT UP THE UFO SUBJECT AND I MADE THE CASUAL REMARK "LIKE THE ONE THAT GRAMPS AND I SAW." AND AT THAT INSTANT THE EIGHTY YEAR-OLD MAN JUMPED UP AND WENT NUTS YELLING "YOU REMEMBER! YOU REMEMBER!"

Later Jacklin received further confirmation when she located a photograph of a UFO that looked exactly like the one she saw. She also realized the reason that yellow was her favorite color: it was because of that lemony light shining out of the portholes of that strange object all those years ago.[33]

"It Was Not from This World"

A somewhat spooky encounter occurred along an unidentified desert highway in Arizona to a young couple in mid-August 1969. At the time, they had rented a U-Haul truck and were moving their possessions from California to Dallas,

Texas. It was late in the evening when they saw a "glowing yellow-gold object" about nearly 300 feet in diameter ahead of them on the road. For a second they thought it might be the moon, except it was too bright. They realized then that the object was large, close, and moving directly toward them on a collision course. Says the witness:

> I STOPPED THE TRUCK. THE OBJECT STOPPED. IT JUST HOVERED THERE WITHOUT MOTION OR ROCKING. IT WAS ABSOLUTELY STILL. WE GOT THE IDEA THAT IT WAS WANTING TO TAKE US WITH IT. WE BOTH FOUND OURSELVES MUTTERING WORDS LIKE, "GO AWAY, WE DON'T WANT TO GO." SUDDENLY IT TOOK OFF AS THOUGH IT WERE SHOT FROM A SLINGSHOT GOING STRAIGHT OUT INTO THE NIGHT SKY AS FAR AS WE COULD SEE.

There was no noise, and the witnesses noticed no detail on the object. They know only that they saw something very unusual. Says the witness: "It scared us. It was not from this world."[34]

UFO-Car Chase

One of the strangest behaviors of UFOs is their penchant for chasing cars down remote highways. Another case occurred in April of 1970, as a young man drove alone along Highway 40, moving from Colorado to California. At some point, he noticed an unusual singular light in his review mirror. Whatever it was, it followed his car "steadily" for a short time. The object zoomed up to the right side of his car, pacing him exactly. Says the witness: "It traveled in a very smooth and steady manner."

He kept his eyes on the object as best as he could while still driving. Then it was gone. But looking in his rearview mirror, he saw that it was still following him. He had a very strong feeling that whoever was inside the object, they were looking at him very closely.

The witness lost track of time. The next thing he knew, his car's electrical system failed. Luckily he was near a small town where he pulled into a gas-station that was closed for the night. The object that had tracked him for miles was now gone. In the morning, the witness discovered that the alternator of his 1967 Chevy Chevelle had failed, presumably as the result of his close encounter.[35]

"We Don't Talk about It"

The weekend of July 4, 1971, two friends were driving home after camping in the Colorado River area. It was about 3:00 a.m., and their kids slept in the back seat. They both observed strange bright green lights ahead of them on the highway. They pulled over to watch as they knew there were no towns or stoplights or structures in this area. The lights blinked in a strange "checker-shaped" pattern, moving from left to right. After about ten minutes, the objects suddenly zoomed toward the witnesses, then turned right and floated in complete silence over the nearby ridge. When they pulled into a gas station several miles ahead, they asked the man at counter about what they saw. He said, "Yeah, we see stuff our here, but we don't talk about it."[36]

Two Low-Level Sightings

UFO sightings are not random: they are here for a purpose. In other words, they're after something. These next two cases are good examples. In the first the UFO appeared to be surveying the Pima mine, presumably interested in the minerals and ores. In the second case, the UFO appeared to be hunting for something else: people.

Just after midnight on July 22, 1971, an anonymous witness observed a strange "flat disk" with a "teardrop-shaped tail" and a bluish-glowing light around its exterior. The craft moved at a leisurely 45 mph, directly over the west side of the waste dumps of Pima mine, about thirty miles south of Tucson.

The witness was about 100 feet away and watched the craft rock back and forth, clearly under intelligent control, until finally darting off to the north. Only one week earlier, the witness saw another (or the same) craft moving from south to north, turn at a right angle and move off to the east where it disappeared. He speculates that the craft are attracted to the area. "There are several very high voltage high power lines supplying power to the mine plus a continual thermal updraft from the open pit copper mine."

About one year later, in June of 1972, a young eighteen-year-old man (who wishes to remain anonymous) was stationed at Fort Huachuca, in the Electronic Warfare School. One evening he was driving around off-base with his girlfriend (later to become his wife) when they saw a "round bright object" crest the hill behind them about 300 feet away. The object hovered about thirty feet high and was pacing their vehicle alongside and behind them. It was extremely bright and appeared to be about fifty feet in diameter.

"It was hard to tell exactly how large as it was so bright," says the witness. "It lit up the road. The light was a white light, very brilliant. I could not make out any detail as it glowed so bright."

His girlfriend began screaming for him to leave. He stepped on the accelerator, at which point the object zoomed closer. Seeing it approach, the witness pulled onto a side-road, spun the car around and raced in the opposite direction. The object zoomed across the desert "as if to cut us off."

The witness pulled another U-turn, heading directly back to the fort and safety. As he says:

We were both shaken up. I had never seen anything like it before. I did not tell anyone as they would not believe us. What I remember most that frightened me is the feeling I got. I can't explain it, but I felt it was hunting us—maybe the wrong word but I knew that I could not stop and had to keep driving. I do not want my name used or my identity revealed.[37]

UFOs Over a TAC/MAC Base

On November 18, 1972, two witnesses were in their car outside an unnamed Tactical Air Command/Military Airlift Command base (TAC/MAC), most likely Monthan-Davis, AFB, which is known for this type of activity.

As they drove along the perimeter of the base, they both saw a large triangular-shaped object hovering about thirty-five feet off the ground. It was "flat black" in color and had no visible markings, though it did seem to shimmer along the edges. Both heard or felt a deep droning sound and watched the object traverse the road in front of them about 100 feet away.

Without warning, a bright beam of light shot down from the object and swept from left to right across the road, as if searching for something. Dust appeared to rise in the beam. Says the witness: "We experienced an ill, nauseous, dread feeling."

The beam retracted and the object moved toward the military base. As soon as the object was gone, the feeling of dread left them. It was then that they noticed something else:

The airbase came alive, i.e., search lights, sirens and military police vehicles ranging along the security fence. We saw this due to our being on a slight rise. We left in our car, and decided to check if the base was shut down; the main gate was closed and MPs were not allowing anyone to enter. The next day the word was that a coyote had set off the perimeter alarm.[38]

Beamed by a UFO

On the evening of March 27, 1974, four adult friends were returning from Las Vegas, Nevada to Kingman. One of the people in the car mentioned that he heard Kingman had been having UFO activity recently. A short time later, they pulled over at a viewpoint to change drivers when somebody shouted, "God, what is that?"

Mrs. A., (one of the passengers) explains what happened next:

We all got out and were scared speechless. There was no sound whatsoever as a huge form, platter-shaped, silver, and as big

AS A FOOTBALL FIELD WITH THREE HUGE SPOTLIGHTS BEAMING DOWN, APPROACHED, STOPPED, AND HOVERED OVER OUR CAR. MY HUSBAND AND I STARTED PRAYING. IT HOVERED OVER US FOR FIVE MINUTES AND THEN TOOK OFF (THANK GOD) AND LEFT BEHIND A STEEL-BLUE HAZE ALL AROUND WHERE IT HAD HOVERED.[39]

The UFO and the Cloud

UFOs have often been reported hiding above, behind, or even inside clouds. In some cases UFOs are seen surrounded by mist or fog. This next case provides an unusual example.

On June 1, 1974, a man was driving on his motorcycle about forty miles southwest of Tucson when he noticed a small cloud in the sky. It was the first cloud he had seen that day, and it seemed unusual. It was moving toward him and expanding in size. Without warning, the cloud stopped and a large metallic, cylindrical-shaped object appeared from behind it. It made no noise, but darted away quickly and out of sight, leaving the strange cloud behind. The witness got off his motorcycle and whipped out his binoculars. The object was gone, but the cloud was now rising swiftly upward. Soon it was out of sight.

About five minutes had passed and the witness was still searching the sky when the cloud reappeared in nearly the exact same spot it had been. Moments later, the metallic object approached from the south, slowing down as it appeared to enter the cloud, which quickly rose upward and disappeared. The witness went straight to Tucson and contacted local air force bases and radio stations about his sighting. He is convinced he saw a UFO. Reporting his sighting to NUFORC, he wrote, "I was shook up for weeks by what I saw."[40]

Probed in Snowflake

In 1974, Steven Paulson and his girlfriend decided to go camping. They drove outside their hometown of Snowflake and onto a logging road off the main highway. They found a nice secluded spot and set up their campsite. After preparing something to eat, they sat together under a pine tree and watched the stars. Steven's girlfriend was dozing on his lap when all at once the ground around him became illuminated.

Looking up he saw a star-like light almost straight up. The light suddenly dropped down until it was only four feet away from him. It now appeared to be a small sphere of light, like a ball of energy. Writes Steven:

I REALIZED I WAS WITNESSING SOMETHING FROM OUT OF THIS WORLD . . . I BECAME FROZEN-LIKE, WITH TINGLING ON THE BACK OF MY NECK

AND BACK. MY BREATHING BECAME ERRATIC. I TRIED TO TOUCH IT WITH THE END OF MY RIFLE.

The object was just out of reach. Steven felt like it was looking at them and analyzing them. "It was definitely zeroed in on us for some reason," he says.

It hovered there for about two minutes when it slowly rose upwards and dissipated. At that moment, Steven's girlfriend jumped up, grabbed his arm and said, "What the hell was that?" Steven was doubting his own eyes, but knowing that his girlfriend saw it proved that it was real.[41]

The Childs Sightings

According to the International Center for UFO Research (ICUR) in Scottsdale, throughout the 1970s the small town of Childs was deluged by sightings. The town is located along the Verde River along the Mongollon Rim. The only thing remarkable about the town is the hydroelectric plant, where many of the local residents work.

Childs quickly began to draw attention when a series of sightings occurred almost nightly, usually involving lights that hovered over the hydroelectric plant. Says Brian Myers, president of ICUR:

ONE OF THE MOST AMAZING WAS A REPORT WE HAD OF A LARGER CRAFT THAT WAS HOVERING AND A SMALLER CRAFT THAT CAME OUT OF IT. THEN THERE WAS A PROBE-LIKE LIGHT THAT CAME OUT OF THE SMALLER CRAFT AND FOLLOWED A POWER-LINE ALL THE WAY DOWN TO WHERE THE HOUSES WERE.

The sightings soon attracted the media, which brought crowds of curious people hoping to see the lights. The sightings eventually stopped, or the residents—tired of the publicity—stopped talking.[42]

Followed by a UFO

Late one evening in July 1974, two friends drove along a desert highway outside Phoenix. There was no traffic and they sped along at a brisk 80 mph. Suddenly the driver slowed down because a car was approaching from behind them about a quarter mile back. It moved quickly and soon the light from it became so brilliant that the driver had to cover the rearview mirror with his hand.

The object moved closer until it was right on their bumper. At this point, the lights were blindingly bright. Strangely, it was utterly silent. The friend in the passenger seat turned around to see what it was when he saw it move sharply upwards and disappear. They screeched to a stop and jumped out of the car. But the object was gone. Says the witness: "I don't know what it was, but I know it was not a car, plane or a helicopter."

Puzzled, the two friends looked at each other in shock and drove off. Says the witness: "This happened forty years ago, but it feels like a minute ago."[43]

Luke AFB Lied?

AS A FORMER STAFF SERGEANT IN THE USAF, AND A TOWER CREW CHIEF AT LUKE AFB CONTROL TOWER, A FORMER PHOENIX FIREFIGHTER AND ENGINEER, A BUSINESS OWNER, A JET AIRCRAFT MECHANIC FOR LOCKHEED MARTIN AND NASA, A HUSBAND, FATHER AND AN AMERICAN PATRIOT, I PROMISE YOU THESE COMMENTS ARE TRUE AND HONEST.

So goes the testimony of an anonymous gentleman as he relates his testimony of a dramatic UFO sighting at Luke AFB on August 10, 1974.

The gentleman was working as the Tower Chief when a colonel from Luke AFB Command Post phoned him on the hotline saying that he had a civilian resident from Sun City who was looking at a UFO at that very moment. The colonel told the Tower Chief to take the call.

The chief answered the phone and spoke with the resident, a lady, who said that there was a bright object hovering over the White Tank Mountains. "Do you see it?" she asked him repeatedly.

Says the chief: "The UFO was real and clearly visible. It glowed orange to red and seemed to move all about an approximate two to ten degrees each time it moved."

"Do you see it?" the lady repeated again.

The chief replied, "No."

"I wish to point out at this time that we lied to the lady," explains the chief. "We saw the object all too well. But due to the extremely heavy amount of paperwork we would have to undergo, not to mention a psychological assessment, we answered her, no, and that was a lie. To this day, I regret lying to this lady."

The chief and four other officers in the control tower observed the glowing object for forty-five more minutes when "suddenly and in the blink of an eye, it shot up and off to the right."[44]

UFOs Over San Carlos Reservoir

This next case was investigated by Jim and Coral Lorenzen of APRO who called it "one of the most unusual objects which we have encountered in twenty-seven years of examining UFO reports."

At 2:00 a.m. on February 26, 1975, Mr. G., a forty-five-year-old cement mason from Phoenix, slept on top of a camper on the bank of the San Carlos Reservoir, in the San Carlos Indian Reservation. Two others slept inside the camper.

Mr. G. woke up to see "a strange structured object" hovering about ten feet away from the camper and four feet off the ground. It was fifty feet wide and thirty feet high, black in color, and was moving silently at a walking pace northward along the edge of the reservoir.

Mr. G. banged on the top of the camper to wake up his friends. Meanwhile, the object changed directions and moved toward another camper about a mile away. At the same time, the fiberglass fishing poles down in their fishing boat were tapping mysteriously against the sides of the boat. Also, large groups of fish were jumping out of the water in a manner Mr. G. had never seen before.

Finally, Mr. G.'s friends came out, but by then the object was gone, and everyone went back to sleep.

One hour later, at 3:05, Mr. G. woke up to see a bright light shining through the blanket covering his face. Sitting up he saw an object about forty to fifty feet in diameter with a brightly glowing domed superstructure. The object flared its light at Mr. G. and then went dark, though he could still see the object plainly in the moonlight. He noticed several rings of light situated along the circumference of the craft. Again, the fishing poles were all shaking and the fish were jumping strangely.

The object began to move away, so Mr. G. again woke his friends. They all rushed outside, but again the craft had moved away. Mr. G.'s friends did see the vibrating fishing poles and the jumping fish.

The Lorenzens are convinced that the cement mason saw a genuine UFO. Writes Coral Lorenzen:

> WE FEEL THAT MR. G. IS A SINCERE AND HONEST MAN AND HE CERTAINLY WAS DETERMINED TO TELL SOMEONE ABOUT HIS STRANGE EXPERIENCE. HE DROVE ALL THE WAY FROM PHOENIX TO TUCSON (A ROUND TRIP OF 240 MILES) JUST TO REPORT WHAT HE HAD SEEN.[45]

A Tiny UFO

While most people think of UFOs as craft carrying alien beings inside them, some UFOs appear to be much smaller objects. Some researchers speculate that these are miniature probes sent down to investigate our planet. Often they take the form of small balls of light. In other cases, they appear to be metallic, as in the following.

On June 10, 1975, two brothers were outside smashing aluminum cans for recycling when a small "thing" flew down out of the sky and hovered only a few feet away, making a loud humming noise. Thinking at first that it was a hummingbird or very large insect, they saw instantly that it was some sort of machine. They both felt that it was watching what they were doing.

"It was round-shaped like a hockey puck," said one of the brothers, "a black-dark grey dull surface . . . like the color of a gun barrel, but not as smooth. The object hovered, moving smoothly toward us, then backward. It moved quickly back and forth, left and right. I was slightly fearful, unsure of what it was and afraid it might hurt us. My brother started throwing rocks at it, trying to knock it out of the air . . . The object easily avoided being hit, zipping away, then back again almost as if playing with us!"

For the next fifteen minutes, the brothers tossed rocks, trying to knock the thing down. Finally the object retreated. "It took off quickly," says the witness, "flying low through the desert, easily avoiding the native brush as it flew. It came back three times, each time moving so fast, it was very difficult to keep track of. The last time it flew off, it flew low and then upward, quickly disappearing into the sky."

The brothers were amazed by the experience and realized that they had seen a genuine UFO.

Two months later, the object returned. The brother was alone riding his bike home when the same object flew down and began to pace him. "It hovered around a foot from my face," says the witness. "I was terrified. I tried to go faster, but of course it easily stayed with me. It didn't do anything but simply hover and fly along with me as I biked home. Again I felt like it was observing me."

Realizing that he was still a good distance from home, he "freaked out." He felt very unsafe, so he looked away from the object and focused on getting home as fast as he could. Finally, it left him alone. "I don't know exactly when it took off," he says, "but when I got to the driveway and looked up, it was gone." Thankfully, the probe-like UFO has not returned.[46]

Fighter Jets Chase UFO

In June of 1975, an anonymous gentleman was stationed at the Douglas FAA Flight Service Station. One evening during his graveyard shift, he went outside to conduct his hourly weather observation, which included taking temperature and dew-point readings.

Looking up, he saw a light blue spherical object moving slowly over the mountains toward Fort Huachuca. The object glowed with a fluctuating intensity that ruled out conventional aircraft.

He watched it for several moments until it stopped directly over Fort Huachuca, at which point it began to dart back and forth. Realizing that he was observing a genuine UFO, the witness took action. As he says: "I went back inside the station and rang Davis-Monthan AFB in Tucson on our interphone line requesting them to verify a target at that location.

Davis-Monthan confirmed a target over Fort Huachuca, and their height-finder radar indicated an altitude 'above 90,000 feet.' The size of the object as it appeared, and at that altitude, must have been huge. Davis-Monthan scrambled 2 F4s.

"I went back outside," continues the witness, "and in minutes could see, approaching from the northwest, two aircraft moving towards the object and the glowing trails of their afterburners going full bore told me it was the F4s. When the aircraft were approximately ten or twenty miles from the object, it zoomed away at high speed towards the southwest and disappeared over the mountain horizon, leaving the F4s orbiting around the area."

The witness returned inside to find that Davis-Monthan was looking for more information. He provided whatever details he could and then told them jokingly, "Congratulations, you just confirmed a UFO."

Says the witness: "They were not amused."[47]

UFO Probes Police Officer

On the evening of August 17, 1975, a patrol officer was on duty in Keams Canyon (north of Holbrook), when he saw a brilliant light beam down from the sky behind his vehicle, illuminating the entire area around him. The officer immediately slowed his vehicle and looked upward to see a dark shape. Red and green lights rotated around it while the beam of white light came down from the bottom side.

He exited his patrol van, at which point, the object extinguished its lights. The officer returned to his patrol van and drove for about three minutes when—without warning—the van lost its lights, the engine shut off and the radio failed to work. The entire electrical system was down.

It lasted for only thirty seconds and suddenly restarted. The UFO was nowhere in sight. The officer reported his encounter to headquarters. He later found out that he wasn't the only one seeing UFOs on that night.

About twenty-five minutes following the officer's sighting, three other officers also saw what appeared to be the same object, except they saw two separate craft. The UFOs moved at a very low altitude before streaking away.

A few minutes later, four additional objects appeared, again flashing red, green and white. They flew at around 5000 feet toward Keams Canyon, the location of the first officer's encounter.

Later that evening in Tuba City, the UFOs returned. Both citizens and police officers viewed two separate incidents, again involving strange colored objects moving at high speeds.

Ground Saucer Watch (GSW—a civilian UFO investigative group founded by William Spaulding) first heard about the sighting when they were contacted (they said) by the 26th Air Division of NORAD.

GSW sent a team, headed by David Bates, to investigate. They examined the patrol van and found higher than normal residual magnetic readings. The engine revealed nothing unusual. There was no evidence of faulty wiring. The team did find what appeared to be burned scrub and trees where the UFO had hovered. They checked with Luke AFB and Holloman AFB (in New Mexico), both of whom said that they had no aerial missions in that area during the sightings. Writes Spaulding:

GSW FULLY BELIEVED ALL THE OFFICERS EXPERIENCED BONA FIDE UFO SIGHTINGS, AND AS OUR TESTING DATA IS PROCESSED IT IS EXPECTED THAT THIS WILL SUBSTANTIATE THIS BELIEF.[48]

Daylight Disks

One summer in 1976, a young student and his two younger siblings were playing near their campsite in the Prescott National Forest. The youngest of them noticed a "large cigar-shaped metallic object" that hung silently about 200 feet overhead.

"It was really close," says the student. "I instantly felt like we were being watched. I got scared, grabbed my brother by the arm and yelled for my sister to follow me back to our camp. We all ran . . . not looking back."

Frightened by what they had seen, they told their mother. Together, they all returned to the area, but the object had gone.

Another case occurred on July 10, 1976, over downtown Phoenix. The witness was sitting in the back seat of a car. Her father was driving, her mother was in the front passenger seat and her niece sat in the back passenger seat to the left. The witness was looking out the right window when she saw a "shiny silver disc-shaped object" hovering perfectly still about 200 feet above a vacant corner lot. It was nestled in the midst of a group of tall office buildings.

"It was a highly polished, aluminum-looking disc-shaped craft, round, about the size of a third of a city block. It covered the entire vacant lot. The best way to describe it would be that it had the appearance and proportions of a fat silver dollar with rounded edges, but absolutely smooth."

The witness watched it for about six seconds when she turned to her family and said, "What is that?"

At that exact moment, a private plane was swooping over the freeway and everyone thought she was talking about that. When she turned back to the UFO, it was gone. She searched the sky, but it was nowhere to be seen. To this day, she is certain she saw a UFO. As she says: "There was no question in my mind that this was an extraterrestrial craft."[49]

"That's Not the Moon!"

On May 22, 1977, there was a lightning storm over the Tortilla Mountains. At that time, a man was staying at the Owl Head Ranch with several other people. Due to the storm, the power failed and the ranch was without electricity. A few hours after the storm, the power was still out when somebody pointed out that the moon was rising up from behind the mountains. It soon became clear, however, that it was not the moon. It rose too quickly and was much brighter. Somebody shouted out, "That's *not* the moon!"

Everybody gathered to watch. Says one witness:

IT WAS A VERY BRIGHT ORB IN THE SKY, MOVING QUICKLY TOWARD US AND DANCING AROUND IN JERKY MOVEMENTS. TWO OF US RAN OUTSIDE TO SEE BETTER. IT CAME CLOSER, WAS VERY BRIGHT AND GAVE OFF SHADOWS, BUT NO NOISE. WE STOOD THERE AWHILE, I DON'T KNOW HOW LONG. THERE WAS A FEELING OF AWE AND PEACE, BUT AFTER AWHILE IT CAME REALLY CLOSE. THE COLOR WENT FROM ORANGEY TO WHITISH BLUE.

After some time, the object slowly left. Says the witness:

THE THING WITHDREW AND DANCED OFF INTO THE DISTANCE, THEN MOVED ERRATICALLY AND WENT STRAIGHT OUT [AND] AWAY. THE CLOCK WAS STOPPED, ALL POWER STILL OFF, SO WE DON'T KNOW HOW LONG THIS TOOK. IT WAS REALLY WEIRD AND HAS STAYED WITH ME ALL THESE YEARS.[50]

UFO Abducts Cactus

In one of the more unusual encounters, on July 22, 1978, at around 6:00 p.m., a man was sitting outside his Phoenix home with a friend when they heard a thunderous sound. Suddenly there was a brilliant flash of light. Looking up they saw two "rotating silver craft" that quickly transformed into black triangular shapes. Then something unbelievable happened. "The first craft emitted a beam that lifted a forty-foot cactus out of the ground and fixed the sand so the earth looked untouched." Both craft then disappeared as they had arrived, in a brilliant explosion of light. The witness, who moved to New York because of the incident, reported his case to NUFORC, writing, "I still keep in contact with my friend, and this always comes up in conversation."[51]

UFOs have often shown an interest in human technology, as these next two cases illustrate. The first occurred in the summer of 1980 in Bisbee. The witness (a former rocket scientist who worked as a telemetry collector and analyst for the NSA) was at a gas station only a few hundred yards distant from the Lavender Pit copper mine. He had a strange feeling that something was hovering above. Looking up, he saw a large metallic object about 250 feet up, glinting in the setting sun. It appeared to be a metallic oblate spheroid, like a squashed sphere, about 100 feet in diameter. There were no signs of any rivets or seams and looked absolutely perfect. It was rock-solid stationary in the sky. "Do you see that?" he exclaimed to the gas station owner.

"I sure do!" the gas station owner replied.

They both stared in awe at the object, which was silent except for a low humming noise. It was so low to the ground that the witness considered throwing a stone at it, but decided that his actions might seem "unfriendly." Both he and the gas station owner felt that they were being observed by the occupants of the craft.

Several cars drove by, slowing down as they saw the object and then racing away along the road which led along the circumference of the pit mine. Says the witness: "Nobody stopped, although they could be seen leaning down and forward briefly to get a better look."

After several moments the craft wobbled slightly then moved at a slow pace directly over the mine for about a mile, then accelerated at extremely high speed upward toward the Queen Mine near Old Bisbee and took off to the west. Shortly later, the witness left the gas station and was driving toward Old Bisbee when a jet fighter plane appeared, flew over the mine at a few hundred feet and followed the exact pathway of the UFO. Says the witness: "Our government knows about these things. Who is kidding who here?"

Were the ETs looking for copper? The second case (which occurred less than 200 miles away and a few months later) is remarkably similar. On October 23, 1980, five men in Morenci observed a large dull-black boomerang-shaped object approach the smokestacks of the Morenci copper smelter plant, the US's largest producer of copper. To their surprise, the object hovered over the smokestacks, sending down a brilliant beam of light into each one. At one point it dropped a small fireball into one of them. After about five minutes, the object moved quickly to the southwest.

One of the men, Joe Nevarez, wished that the object would return so he could see it better. At this point, the men were shocked to watch the object perform an instant reversal. It approached again, this time hovering over the slag dump of the smelter before moving north.

Researcher Richard Haines points out this case as an example of a CE-5, meaning the object's behavior was affected by the witnesses, in this case, by Nevarez's mental command for the object to return. The incident received national publicity.

According to the International Center for UFO Research (ICUR) in Scottsdale, throughout the 1980s, a huge boomerang-shaped object nearly a half-mile wide appeared repeatedly over the small town of Morenci. One sighting in particular was seen by hundreds of the residents. The object hovered in place for long enough so that everyone who was outside was able to see it. More than a hundred members of the Morenci High School observed the object, and described it as being "several football fields" in size. People throughout the town also watched it. The witnesses all agreed that it was covered with red and white lights on the underside which swept back in a boomerang shape.

Brian Myers of ICUR says that the same craft has also been reported frequently over the Hopi and Navajo reservations in the northeastern part of the state.[52]

Two Police Sightings

On October 15, 1981, at around 9:00 p.m., a retired police officer was camping with two friends (T. C. and M. C.) at Apache Lake. They packed up their camp, attached the boat to the trailer and had just started down the road when they looked up to see a huge object hovering very low above the road ahead of them. They slammed on the brakes and stared in wonder.

Says the officer: "It was shiny like crumpled aluminum foil, and as it changed colors from the sparkling of the sun, we noticed it was vibrating and making no sound."

T. C. told the officer to exit the vehicle and see what it was. The officer refused and told T .C. to do it himself. T. C. pulled out his gun, but the officer and M. C. told him to put it away. Says the officer: "We were frightened and felt that we were being watched by the UFO. We rolled up the windows and locked the doors and watched it in astonishment, afraid to do anything. We watched it for about ten minutes, like it was a Mexican standoff, trying to figure out how to leave without driving under it."

They decided to retreat and back up. At that moment, it took off straight up "faster than the eye could see."

Says the officer: "I was scared to the point that I could hardly move, talk, and felt like vomiting. I am willing to take any type of lie detection test to verify the truth of our sighting."

The witness reported his sighting to NUFORC twenty-eight years following the incident after being diagnosed with Progressive Multiple

Sclerosis, writing, "I wanted to report this to someone before my disease takes my life, and because of all the naysayers and scientists saying people who see unknown flying objects are crazy. It's hard to deny when you see one in broad daylight."

The second police encounter occurred one evening in December 1981, when a Mesa police officer and his wife exited the door of their home to see a large red, glowing object hovering about 500 feet high near their home. The object appeared to be dripping little droplets of red flares. The wife said, "What is that? It looks like it's on fire!" She was instantly worried that the vehicle was about to crash.

Instead the object remained in place for nearly two minutes before drifting to the east and gliding lower over the rooftops of the neighboring homes. The officer immediately reported the sighting to the Mesa Police Station, and later to the UFO Bureau at Davis-Monthan AFB. He and his wife later learned that at least two other residents in Chandler and Mesa had also observed the object.[53]

Luke AFB Tracks UFOs

According to researcher Bill Hamilton, in 1982, he interviewed a lady whose daughter-in-law worked at Luke AFB in Glendale. One evening (date not given) a formation of objects flew over Phoenix and were tracked on radar. The daughter-in-law says that the records from the radar-returns were recorded on magnetic tape and immediately stored in a locked vault. The next day, a general from the Pentagon arrived, picked up the tapes, and left.[54]

MPs Encounter a UFO

For anyone who doubts that the military is actively covering up UFO sightings, this next incident, involving an MP duty officer at the US proving grounds in Yuma, should provide compelling evidence.

While on duty in February 1982, the MP patrol supervisor called the duty officer on the phone and said that two MPs had just witnessed a UFO over the Cibola Range, north of Martinez Lake Road, and he needed advice as to what action to take. The MP duty officer told the supervisor to bring the men in for questioning. Says the duty officer:

I INTERVIEWED THE TWO MPs AND TOOK STATEMENTS FROM BOTH. THEY STATED TO ME THAT AT APPROXIMATELY 2330 HOURS, 15 FEBRUARY, 1982, THEY HAD BEEN ON A ROUTINE MOTOR PATROL ON THE CIBOLA RANGE WHEN THEY OBSERVED A LARGE ORANGE BALL APPROACH FROM THE NORTH AND COME TO A REST ON TOP OF A LARGE RADIO TOWER LOCATED

IN THE CENTER OF CIBOLA. AT THIS POINT THE DRIVER OF THE MP VEHICLE STOPPED HIS VEHICLE SO THAT THEY COULD BETTER OBSERVE WHAT THEY WERE OBSERVING. THEY WERE APPROXIMATELY 500 METERS EAST OF THE TOWER. AS THE DRIVER PLACED THE VEHICLE IN FORWARD GEAR MOVING TOWARD THE TOWER, THE BRIGHT ORANGE BALL CAME DOWN FROM THE TOP OF THE TOWER TO GROUND LEVEL AND BEGAN MOVING TOWARD THEIR LOCATION. THE DRIVER STATED TO ME THAT HE HAD NEVER IN HIS LIFE HAD CURIOSITY TURN TO FEAR SO QUICKLY. THE DRIVER THEN TURNED HIS VEHICLE AROUND AND ATTEMPTED TO DEPART THE AREA. BOTH MPS STATE THAT THE BALL APPEARED TO BE AROUND 100 FEET IN DIAMETER. [IT] CLEARED THEIR VEHICLE AND PROCEEDED OVER THE MIDDLE MOUNTAINS GOING EAST AT A VERY HIGH RATE OF SPEED.

Further questioning revealed that the MPs tried to contact the station dispatcher, but were unable to do so as their car radio mysteriously failed. So they drove straight to the base to report the incident in person to their supervisor.

The duty officer did more research and discovered another witness who had observed the glowing orange object over the proving grounds. He put together his report. Says the officer:

I PRESENTED SAME TO MY COMMANDER. HE REQUESTED TO KNOW JUST WHAT MY MPS HAD BEEN SMOKING AND HAD ME DESTROY THE REPORT AND ALL STATEMENTS. TWO WEEKS LATER BOTH MPS INVOLVED IN THIS INCIDENT WERE SENT OVERSEAS ON ORDERS AND I NEVER SAW THEM AGAIN.[55]

Fishing for UFOs

On September 4, 1984, two brothers were fishing at Alamo Lake. It was around 9:00 p.m. and a moonless night, when they both saw what appeared to be a strange vehicle approaching the north side of the lake. This caught their attention as they both knew there was no road on the north side. At the time, they were in complete darkness and yet the object seemed to head directly toward them, hovering an apparent three feet above the ground, lighting up the vegetation along the shore of the lake.

Once it reached the edge of the lake it continued to move above the water right toward their boat. Overcome with fear, the brothers threw down their fishing poles and drove away at full speed. The craft immediately began to pace them. The motor mysteriously died and the object stopped along with them. The witness's brother screamed, "What are you doing?"

"The motor died," he said. The object now hovered about sixty feet away and seemed to watch them as they tried frantically to restart the engine. No matter how hard they tried, the engine wouldn't turn over. It had never done this before and only moments earlier had been working perfectly. They both kept trying until they were completely worn out.

The witness's brother became desperate. He stood up and waved at the object, screaming, "Quit f—king with us!"

Immediately, the lights on the object went out and the boat motor started on the first try. They immediately drove to the opposite shore and exited the boat, trembling in fear. They stayed along the shore watching until morning, but the object never reappeared.

Says the witness:

> MY GREATEST REGRET WAS: WHEN THEIR LIGHTS WENT OUT, I DIDN'T SHINE MY FLASHLIGHT AT IT TO SEE WHAT IT WAS. MY BROTHER AND I BOTH AGREE WE BELIEVE SOME OUTSIDE FORCE PUT THE GREAT AMOUNT OF FEAR IN US, UNLIKE WE EVER HAD BEFORE OR SINCE. ONE OTHER ASPECT WE NOTICED WAS NOT TIME LOSS, RATHER JUST THE OPPOSITE. WE SAT WATCHING THE LAKE WITH LIGHTS OFF FOR HOURS, BELIEVING THE SUN SHOULD BE COMING UP, ONLY TO WAIT HOURS MORE.[56]

UFOs on Radar

Perhaps Arizona's most significant sighting of the year, on October 7, 1985, an air traffic controller and a police helicopter pilot tracked more than sixty UFOs on radar. According to the *Arizona Daily Star*, there were fifteen groups of objects, each containing about four to six UFOs. The first group arrived shortly after midnight, followed shortly by the others. The objects traveled at 288 mph and were in view for ninety minutes.[57]

UFO Over Yuma

On March 7, 1986, Jack (pseudonym) and his friend Mike (both navy men) were traveling along Highway 8 about seventy miles outside Yuma. The sighting began when Mike pointed out what appeared to be a radio tower with blinking red lights to the southeast. Jack (who was driving) didn't pay it much attention until Mike, who was staring at it, said that the radio tower appeared to be moving and that it was coming closer.

Jack looked over and saw that the object wasn't a radio tower at all. Instead, it was a much smaller object—black and cylindrical with a red light at each end—and it was a lot closer than he first thought.

"It's going to cross the road," said Mike.

"We slowed down to a crawl," says Jack, "and I got as close to the thing as I could. We watched it float over the road in front of my car about twenty feet from being under it."

Jack estimates that the object was about twenty feet tall and three feet wide. Both ends tapered to a point where the lights were located. The surface was "like a black hole, non-reflective."

It floated about ten feet above the road, moved down to the other side and lowered itself until it was about three feet above the ground. Then, a four-inch razor-sharp beam of light shot from the craft. The beam proceeded to "scan around the desert floor as if it was looking for something. It moved around the plants and it was the most graceful thing I have ever seen. Mike and I watched it go off into the desert until it was out of sight."[58]

Sedona Sighting

On May 11, 1986, minister and private pilot Robert H. Henderson was flying with his wife, Nann, in a Cessna 172. They were at 8,500 feet in clear weather over Verde Valley in Sedona when they saw a bright flash of light ahead of them. The light approached quickly on what appeared to be a collision course. Henderson was preparing to take evasive action if necessary when the object—described as a "modified half-sphere with the flat side down"—passed at very high speed to the left and below the plane. Henderson was unable to explain the object as any conventional craft because it moved much faster than anything he had ever seen. Unknown to Henderson, Sedona was in the middle of wave activity.[59]

UFO Wave Over Sedona

In the late 1980s, researcher Tom Dongo investigated dozens of sightings in the Sedona area. A well-known flap area, Sedona seems to have more UFO encounters than other areas. The late 1980s proved to be particularly active.

One case involves an anonymous woman who lived in an outlying section of Sedona. One evening while preparing dinner, the entire area around her house became illuminated by brilliant orange light. Rushing outside, she saw a disk-shaped object larger than her house only a few hundred feet overhead. It moved up a nearby canyon before suddenly disappearing.

Another case occurred to three Sedona residents who observed a "slow-moving, hat-shaped, grayish-silver UFO" that flew directly over the local airport. It then moved over the town and behind Capitol Butte.

Throughout 1986, "Stan" saw a red- and white-colored object hovering over his home in the Loy Butte area. Usually the object was off in the distance. One evening, however, it flew directly toward him, stopping close overhead. Looking up, Stan could see that the red part of the UFO was actually a spherical light attached underneath it. At this point, the red light detached and swooped down, circling several times over his home as though probing him. The object then flew back up to the larger white object, which promptly flew away to the west.

In 1986, a father and son were hiking on Airport Mesa when they saw a large silver cigar-shaped object hovering between the thunderclouds overhead. They watched it for ten minutes as it remained perfectly stationary, until it became lost in the clouds.

That same year, a resident of Cottonwood saw a formation of six glowing objects hovering in formation over the Cottonwood power company substation. After several minutes, they moved away to the south.

Around the same time as the above incident, another Cottonwood resident was driving over Mingus Mountain when she saw a group of glowing orange spheres of light moving as if in procession. Seconds later she saw three military helicopters chasing the objects. The entire incident lasted only about ten seconds.

On December 19, 1986, a family in Sedona was driving near Doe Mountain when they saw what appeared to be a helicopter. The helicopter transformed into a brilliant sphere emitting a rainbow array of prismatic colors. The sphere then rocketed upward until it was only a point of light, at which point it disappeared in the clouds at high speed.

Only a few years earlier, the father in the above case had been drawn outside his home by a loud humming noise. The noise increased and he saw a gigantic "flying wing" that appeared to be nearly a half-mile wide. It left a "vaporous trail of glowing particles" as it passed.

In 1986, a couple and their friend were driving at night near the Mongollon Rim when their headlights failed. At that moment they saw a glowing triangular-shaped UFO hovering about five hundred feet above their car. The disk remained in place for about five minutes before moving away to the west.

In July 1988, a resident of the Les Springs development watched a small orb of light from her window as it zigzagged near Steamboat Rock.

A few months later, in the fall of 1988, four tourists were hiking on Bell Rock when they saw three disk-shaped objects hovering in formation overhead. They allegedly took photos of the objects, which quickly darted west to the Apache Mountains.

In the spring of 1989, two visitors staying in a hotel in Sedona watched a UFO from their hotel room window as it flew over Schnebly Hill. The object stopped, and then ejected a glowing red sphere that danced around the larger object. After several moments, the red object attached itself to the larger object and the strange UFO darted away.

In the fall of 1989, two local residents observed a "glowing, low-flying object" move at super high speeds directly over downtown Sedona at around 4:00 a.m.

In the winter of 1989, two women were driving through Sedona late at night when they saw a dull silver-colored object reflecting off the light of a full moon. Shortly after they saw it, the object darted away at high speed.

One of the last sightings of the wave involved a married couple who were discussing and observing an odd egg-shaped cloud hovering over the town when three large glowing green spheres dropped from the cloud and moved away in three separate directions.[60]

Buzzed by a UFO

It was around 1:30 in the morning on July 7, 1989, and Steve (pseudonym) was driving east along Interstate 10 just outside Blythe. He thought he was alone on the highway when what he assumed was a diesel truck appeared to his immediate left as if to pass. It was only inches away, and nearly ran Steve off the highway. He swerved into the other lane, but the truck, instead of passing, seemed intent on pacing him down the highway at around 70 mph. Angry, Steve looked at the truck and was surprised to see that it had no running lights or markings of any kind, just a flat black metallic surface. It began to move faster.

Then it did something incredible. Says Steve: "It was accelerating as if passing until I watched it go up into the sky, off the ground . . . I looked out my front windshield to watch it elevate into the sky, up over my car . . . I watched it fly from me to the southeast, banking at about 200 feet over the desert valley floor."

The object had no apparent wings, rotors, or wheels. It was rectangular in shape. He could now see a row of red lights along the side. It was completely silent as it accelerated at high speed toward the top of a nearby mountain. Steve skidded to a stop, jumped out, and watched the object reach the mountaintop and drop down behind it. He was an aviation enthusiast and had been to countless air shows. He never saw anything that could maneuver like this object.

He hopped back in his car and drove two hours home to Phoenix. He told his father, who revealed that he had the same kind of experience years earlier.[61]

Chapter Three

The Phoenix Lights and Beyond

While the last few decades had been very active, the nineties brought a new flood of high-quality cases. One case in particular would become Arizona's most widely viewed sighting ever and would thrust the entire state into the international limelight. Meanwhile, sightings occurred at a fairly regular rate. Some areas, however, seem to have a disproportionately large amount of UFO activity. These areas are called UFO hotspots, or flap-areas. Tucson is definitely one of Arizona's UFO hotspots, particularly the area over the Catalina Mountains.

One morning in late April 1990, Johnny X. was driving through northwest Tucson when his children yelled, "Look, Daddy, there's a flying saucer."

Johnny pulled over and saw what he first assumed was a lenticular cloud. Looking closer, he saw that it was actually a huge silver object with a perfect ring around the circumference. It hovered stationary in the sky and was perfectly silent. Johnny's wife exited the car and snapped a photograph. They continued to watch the object for about twenty minutes after which it "faded away."

After developing the photo, Johnny and his family were convinced that they had captured a genuine UFO. Johnny gave a copy of the photo to his neighbor Joe, who showed it to his wife Ada.

Ada was shocked because she had seen the same object, also in late April 1990. She watched the object move slowly over the Catalina Mountains. Afterwards, she decided to contact officials at Davis-Monthan AFB. She drove to the base and was ushered into an office with three air force officers. They put the photo on a projection screen and asked Ada, "What are you looking at?"

"I'm looking at a flying saucer," she said.

According to Ada, the officer replied, "That's what it is. Don't ever show the picture to anyone, and don't talk about it, because you might cause a riot."

Ada saw the same object fly over the Catalinas again in October 1990. She also says that many of her neighbors have also seen weird flying objects over the Catalina Mountains.

Writes researcher T. Harvey, "There are rumors around Tucson about an underground base in the Catalina Mountains. There are many old mines scattered all over the region . . . Maybe one of those mines leads to a base?"

Harvey isn't alone in his speculations. Roger Scherrer of Southwest UFO Research says that people have seen lights and solid craft entering and exiting the Catalina Mountains, not to mention reports of unmarked black helicopters.

Just over 100 miles away and one month later, in November 1990, the Marcellino family observed a bluish metallic object moving downward over the Superstition Mountains outside Phoenix. The object emitted a buzzing sound and observers were able to "feel" it as it passed. At one point the object radiated a blue light, apparently causing a local power failure. Electricity was quickly restored, but was disrupted again when the object returned.[62]

Sedona Saucer

According to researcher Dr. Patricia Rochelle Diegel, a woman by the name of Doriel was driving home along the back roads of Sedona around 1990 (date approximate) when she saw a disk-shaped object flying only a few yards in front of her low above the road. Her husband Gary drove behind her in a separate car, but was now out of sight. Fearful, she slowed down hoping Gary would appear; at the same time the UFO also decreased its speed. She slowed down even further; so did the object. By now she had nearly arrived at their home in Oak Creek. She saw Gary's headlights appear. Simultaneously, the UFO took off straight up and disappeared.

When Gary arrived, Doriel told him about what happened. He told her that he had seen the UFO, too. At first he thought it was a shooting star, except for the fact that it was going straight up.

According to Dr. Diegel, this experience is not unusual for Sedona. She has investigated thirty-six similar cases involving people who encounter UFOs along the back roads of Sedona. Says Diegel:

THEIR DESCRIPTIONS OF THE ENCOUNTER ARE REMARKABLY SIMILAR TO DORIEL'S. THE FLYING SAUCERS FOLLOW THEM, HOVER OVER THEM, MOVE ON AHEAD OF THEM—AND THE MINUTE ANOTHER CAR APPEARS, THE OBJECT WILL ZOOM ALMOST STRAIGHT UP AND THEN DISAPPEAR.[63]

Lights Over Mongollon Rim

During the summer of 1991, a forest service employee was invited by friends to their home on the shore of a lake near the Mongollon Rim. They were just about to eat dinner when the house generator mysteriously quit working. While the owner of the house went to check on the generator, the forest service employee was looking out over the lake. Suddenly the lake lit up in brilliant light. The source, he saw, was about 150 feet above the lake and only 400 yards away. Then it began to approach.

The owner of the house appeared and, seeing the light, grabbed his friend and ushered him quickly into the house, pushed him in the bathroom, and made him crouch down. He ordered his friend not to speak. The light approached and was soon shining into the bathroom window. The owner of the house was terrified, but the Forest Service employee felt "only scared." Five minutes later, the light moved away. The owner of the house then revealed that the strange light had appeared before. On prior occasions, he was struck by the light and afterward suffered "a flu-like illness," which he believes was caused by the light.[64]

Tucson Summer Sightings

As investigated by Ray Maurer, then-director of the Arizona State MUFON Chapter, a gentleman was driving along a lonely stretch of highway between Tucson and Casa Grande at around 1:00 a.m. in July 1992 when he saw a strange object performing "a bunch of strange maneuvers." Maurer is convinced that the witness is credible and that he saw something unusual. Says Maurer: "If it wasn't a UFO, it had to be a very high-tech experimental craft the military has come out with."

About one month later, on August 19, 1992 at 1:00 a.m., a thirty-one-year-old man was driving near Tucson when he saw "a strange light" in the distance. He was puzzled because the object approached with odd swooping movements, similar to a falling leaf. Moments later, it descended, moved over a nearby field, and began to hover. Then it sent out a conical beam of light, illuminating everything beneath it. The witness could now see the object, which (according to MUFON field investigator Kathy Woodward, who interviewed the witness) was about thirty feet in diameter and looked "like a manta ray with a dull black matte finish." A ridge ran down the center of the craft, and a band of whiter lights encircled the front.

The witness pulled over and exited his car to better observe the object, which immediately approached to within 300 feet of the witness. It was silent and close enough so that the witness could see the moonlight reflecting off the surface. When the craft continued to approach, moving directly over his car, the witness became frightened, dashed into his vehicle, and drove off.

As he drove away, he saw the object move off and stop about fifteen feet above a nearby farmhouse. Again it sent down a conical beam of light, illuminating the entire house and the area around it for about twenty seconds. It then moved away from the house and sent down another beam of light over a grove of trees behind the house.

The witness was still driving away when the object zoomed back toward his car, approached to about fifty feet, then moved off to the southwest. The witness estimates that the encounter lasted about fifteen minutes.[65]

Cave Creek UFOs

As investigated by MUFON UFO Field Investigators J. M. Leakes and Bill Tice, on March 24, 1993, two young men (Pat and Scott) fishing at Horseshoe Reservoir near Cave Creek were startled by three multicolored objects that were "bobbing up and down" only a few miles away. The objects appeared to be either triangular-shaped or possibly disks with domes on top. They emitted a white aura and had a row of rotating blue lights in the middle and a row of steady yellow lights at the base. Two brilliant white lights shined from the lower corners of the objects. Occasionally each object emitted a bright beam of light downward, sometimes toward the witnesses. The closest object remained for more than five hours while the other two occasionally disappeared and then returned. Pat and Scott were frightened at first, but stayed up most of the night to watch the display. By the end, they were both convinced that the occupants of the craft were aware that the men were watching them.[66]

Prescott Valley UFOs

Jerry Moss (a retired pilot) first saw UFOs over his home in Prescott back in 1966. But it wasn't until September 1993 when Moss's son came to visit that they both had an incredible sighting. They were both outside when they looked up and saw "a silver thing in the sky about 2,000 feet up." Moss dashed inside, retrieved his video camera and began to film the object.

"I've been a pilot," says Moss. "I see a lot of planes, but I knew this wasn't a plane. It was a silver sphere. It made absolutely no sound. It was going off toward the Mingus Mountains. The strange part about it is that it moved around a lot. It was hard to keep my camera focused on it."

Moss had seen a similar object hovering over Glassford Hill, an extinct volcano west of Prescott Valley, but this one was much closer. He filmed it for fifteen minutes, while it disappeared and reappeared in a different location, and also transformed from a disk shape to a triangle, and then back to a disk. Moss says simply: "It does some strange things."

Two weeks later, the object returned over the Bradshaw Mountains. Again Moss took videotape footage, which shows what appears to be a fifty-five-gallon oil drum-shaped object with smoke coming from the top of it. Says Moss: "I'm not easily fooled by things, but I'm completely baffled by these. I just can't explain what they are."

UFO researcher Lyle Vann reviewed Moss's tape and calls it some of the best UFO video footage he's seen.[67]

UFO Visits the Phoenix Zoo

Kenneth Synnott had worked as a security guard at the Phoenix Zoo for eight years and never saw anything like what he saw after midnight one evening in 1993. He was working the night shift, and drove around in his security truck patrolling the 124 acres of zoo grounds. As Synnott wrote in a letter to *Fate* magazine, "I noticed an extremely bright light in the air directly above the lion and tiger exhibit. The light was oval, and so bright it hurt my eyes to look at it."

Synnott called his partner on the radio. Before Synnott could speak, his partner asked if he could see the strange light. "At that point," says Synnott, "the light was moving over my truck . . . As the light passed over me, the truck's motor stopped and the lights went out. I sat motionless, more frightened than anything else . . . As soon as the light passed over the truck, the light and motor came back on."

The UFO moved on, occasionally sending down a brief beam of blue light. Wherever the UFO went, the animals below would react "making sounds that were very unusual for that time of night." Synnott kept his eye on the UFO, which moved west off the zoo ground, over to the baseball stadium across from the zoo and stopped. He watched it for several more minutes. Then the light winked off and he heard the sound of jets approaching from the direction of Luke Air Force Base. The jets flew over the baseball stadium, but by then the object was gone.

Synnott joined up with his partner, who had observed the entire incident from the front gate entrance of the zoo. They immediately checked all the animal exhibits and found nothing out of order. They called the head animal keeper, and—fearing how other employees or the public might react—collectively decided to keep the event a secret. Synnott told only his immediate family.

Ten years later, Synnott decided to go public with his encounter. He no longer works at the zoo and is retired in Las Vegas. Says Synnott: "I never saw a light as bright as the one over the zoo."[68]

Phoenix Lights Precursor

On the evening of February 6, 1995, Lynne D. Kitei MD was in her Phoenix home with her husband Frank, also a doctor, when he called frantically to her to observe the strange lights outside their window. Says Kitei: "Less than a hundred yards away from our property, three objects hung in midair, about fifty to seventy-five feet above the ground. I immediately looked underneath and around them to see if anything or something or someone was creating the spectacle, but I saw nothing . . . The soothing amber light contained within each orb looked different from any light I had ever seen. It didn't glare at all and was uniform throughout, reminding me of a holiday luminary that shines from within, without the light extending beyond its edge. Frank and I were in awe, mesmerized by the extraordinary scene."

Kitei snapped a photo, thrilled and amazed that she had seen a UFO. And for those who didn't believe her, she had the photo, which clearly showed the strange glowing object.

Almost two years later, on January 22, 1997, Kitei was going to bed when she saw that the UFOs had returned. Writes Kitei, "Three huge amber orbs hung there in a stationary row, strangely similar to the three orbs outside our window in 1995."

Kitei called to her husband, but he wasn't interested. She watched the orbs for several minutes until they slowly faded away.

The next evening, on January 23, the orbs appeared again. This time, Kitei filmed a half-minute of moving footage. She showed her husband when he came home, at which point, the lights returned again. This time there were six glowing orbs stretched along for at least one mile in front of the South Mountain.

Kitei called the *Arizona Republic* newspaper. As she spoke to them, the lights immediately disappeared. The next day she called Luke AFB and spoke to a female lieutenant who told her, "I can tell you that they did not come from Luke and they did not come into Luke. We had nothing to do with them."

She called the local airport and found a firsthand witness, an aircraft controller who was in the tower at the time of the sighting. The controller confirmed the sighting, saying, "We looked on radar, but nothing showed up. We then thought maybe they were lights carried by skydivers. But that would be unlikely because it was too late and they were in perfect formation. They couldn't have been flares either. Flares drift downward. They stayed right in place."

Another air-traffic reporter who present that night confirms the sighting, saying, "There must have been five of us up there and we all saw these lights."

The lights returned on January 24, and Kitei was again able to film them. Soon Kitei found herself going outside at night to watch for the strange orbs. She saw them again on January 30, March 4, 6, and 10.

What, Kitei wondered, was flying over Phoenix? And why wasn't anybody noticing?

Kitei was not alone in noticing the increase in activity.

On March 7, Herb Moran (an aviation industry worker and private pilot) observed a group of amber lights hovering for thirty-five minutes near the Palo Verde Nuclear Generating Station. Later that evening he saw another light over the Estrella Mountains.

On the same day, Steve of Ahwatukee (south of Phoenix on the other side of South Mountain) was with his family in Gila Bend when they observed and videotaped "strange orange lights" over the local Indian Reservation.[69]

Dragoon Mountains UFO Wave

According to the Cochise County Chapter of MUFON, a wave of sightings occurred throughout late 1996. One of the first sightings of the wave occurred on August 5, 1996, when witnesses saw an "erratic nocturnal light" about four miles south of Willcox. One month later, on September 14, witnesses observed a hovering light over Sierra Vista. The light returned again five days later on September 19. While MUFON concluded that the witness probably was viewing Venus, other sightings started to be reported. On September 18, a witness observed multiple objects fly over the Middle March Pass. Yet another sighting occurred on October 21, when witnesses saw a "large well-illuminated triangle" flying overhead about two miles south of Tombstone. Investigators at MUFON state that these sightings are only a few of a larger number of sightings which have been occurring over the Cochise County area for the past two years.[70]

The Phoenix Lights

March 13, 1997 began like any other day in Phoenix, with no hint that one of the largest-viewed UFO events in modern history was about to occur. The first indication of anything unusual began early in the evening when the National UFO Reporting Center in Washington State received a flurry of calls coming from Nevada and Arizona. The initial call came at 8:16 p.m. from a retired police officer in Paulden (sixty miles north of Phoenix). He called NUFORC to report a cluster of five red lights heading south.

Two minutes later, a witness from Prescott phoned in his sighting. This was immediately followed by more calls from nearby Wickenburg, Tempe, Scottsdale, and other areas. As he fielded the deluge of calls, Peter Davenport quickly realized that something very significant was happening in the skies of Arizona.

All across the state people were seeing UFOs. More calls came from Chino Valley, Dewey, Cordes Junction, Cave Creek, and other cities. By the time the object moved over Phoenix itself, the phones at the UFO Reporting Center were ringing off the hook. At the time, thousands of residents of Phoenix, Prescott, Scottsdale, and nearby areas were witnessing an incredible display.

Traffic stopped on streets. Ballgames stopped in mid-play. People ran out of stores and homes to stare at the spectacle.

All witnesses agree that the object or lights spanned a huge portion of the sky, some felt a few miles in length. All agreed that it was low in the sky, only a few thousand feet at most. All agreed it was moving at a slow, leisurely pace. All agreed that it was silent, except for a very low hum heard by only a few witnesses.

Meanwhile, at Luke Air Force Base chaos reigned. As the objects approached, they flew directly over Luke AFB and into Phoenix. According to people outside the base, Luke quickly scrambled several jet fighters flying after the object passed overhead. At the same time, the switchboards of the base lit up with callers inquiring about the objects.

Simultaneously, police stations and radio stations across Phoenix were also flooded with calls. The whole city was quickly becoming electrified.

Later, investigators would learn that there was either multiple craft or at least, several different events throughout the evening.

Cement truck driver Bill Greiner was hauling a load of cement south on Interstate 17 when he saw two glowing objects move overhead. For the next two hours, he paced the objects as they approached Phoenix. The lights were still with him when he entered the west valley. To his surprise, he saw three F-16 fighter jets take off from Luke Air Force Base to intercept the lights. As the jets approached, the lights took off straight up at high speed. "It was crazy. I know those pilots saw it. . . I wish the government would just admit it. It's like having 50,000 people in a stadium watch a football game and then having someone tell us we weren't there. . . I'll never be the same again. Before this, if anybody'd told me they saw a UFO, I would've said, 'Yeah, and I believe in the tooth fairy.'"

Shortly after 8:00 p.m., an anonymous pilot watched as the lights appeared over Squaw Peak and moved slowly off to the southeast.

At 8:15 p.m., General Kelly (retired) and his wife were in Glendale when they saw a large V-shaped formation of seven lights. They parked the car and watched the object for several minutes, noting that it made no sound as it passed overhead.

Around 8:25, a psychiatrist, his wife, and their child were driving along the I-10 near the Gila Indian Reservation when they observed a formation of lights about 300 yards across pass over their car at an altitude of about 1,500 feet. There was no noise. Each member of the family reported feeling like they were telepathically told not to worry about what they were seeing.

At 8:30 p.m., Mike Fortson and his wife, of Chandler, observed the object pass in front of the full moon. Fortson observed the object for nearly two minutes. He estimates that it was at about 1,200 feet altitude, moving at a speed of 35 mph and was about a mile in length. It had a dark black surface that seemed to become almost translucent as it passed in front of the moon. He also noticed that the edges of the object seemed to ripple or distort. Says Fortson: "During the whole sighting we never moved our feet. There was no question in our minds that what we saw was not of this Earth."

Mike is sure that he saw something unusual. "People say, 'Mike, you know, maybe you saw a B-2 Bomber. My response was: we could land all forty of our B-2 bombers on the wing of this craft."

Bruce Gerboth of Ahwatukee says that he observed the lights around 8:30, and was convinced that the five amber orbs were connected to a triangular-shaped object. One hour later, he was surprised to see what he believes were the same lights moving over Gila Bend.

Phoenix resident Mr. Berry told reporters, "Pretty incredible what I saw. I didn't know what it was. I just saw lights in the sky in the shape of a big V and ran in and got my binoculars. It did not look like an aircraft. It was moving pretty slow. . . It was big."

Eleven-year-old Boy Scout Tim Macdonald observed the object for three minutes. "It looked like a stealth bomber. It was in a triangle and it had three lights. It was there for two or three minutes. When it disappeared, I thought it was a UFO," he told newspaper reporters.

Don and Grace of Phoenix saw the object and said that it was definitely solid. It appeared to be a large V-shaped object. The underside had seven lights and was constructed of gray panels. To their amazement, one of the orbs detached from the structure, flew to the right, then returned and re-attached itself to the object. Seth Adams said:

> IT WAS ONE OF ONE OF THE BIGGEST THINGS I'VE EVER SEEN THAT MOVED LIKE THAT. I MEAN, IT WAS JUST ENORMOUS. I DON'T KNOW IF IT WAS AS BIG AS AN AIRCRAFT CARRIER. IT MIGHT HAVE BEEN, BECAUSE I'VE NEVER SEEN AN AIRCRAFT CARRIER FLY.

Stacy Roads and her mother saw a gigantic triangular shaped craft as it flew over the freeway. Both witnesses were certain that they saw a metallic mass between the lights. She estimated the craft was two miles wide. "The object we saw," she said, "if we opened up a newspaper, you could not block out the object that we saw . . . it was gun-metal black. It wasn't shiny, it wasn't invisible. It was more of a dull bluish-black color."

Her daughter Emily says: "We both just stayed there and looked at it for a couple of minutes, and it was completely silent."

Around 9:30 p.m., in Carefree, a couple watched the giant triangular craft light up and move overhead. Says the witness: "My feelings at the time were only of excitement and not trepidation. The ship was not acting in a threatening manner. . . if anything, it seemed to have an agenda that it wished to execute as efficiently as possible. But its size, its spectacular shape seemed to represent a powerful presence. . . it was hovering near the nuclear power plant."

Tim Ley (a fifty-four-year-old management consultant) had just arrived home and was exiting his car when he saw the object. He ran inside and got his wife Roberta. They both stood outside and watched the object move directly overhead. "It was astonishing," said Ley, "and a little frightening. It was so big and so strange. You couldn't actually see the object. All you could see was the outline, as though something was blotting out the stars."

It was the lights that Ley found most fascinating. "They weren't bulbs," he said. "They looked like gas. There was a distortion on the surface. Also, the light didn't spill out or shine. I've never seen a light like that."

Erin Watson says:

I CAME OUT A SECOND AFTER MONICA, AND I REMEMBER LOOKING; IT WAS
COMING OVER THE MOUNTAIN, AND IT WAS ALMOST AS WIDE AS ONE OF THE
HUMPS, AND IT WAS VERY LOW... IT WAS JUST GLIDING, AND THEN IT STOPPED,
AND THEN THE SIDES RETRACTED A LITTLE AND IT WAS GONE, SHEW!

Her husband also observed the object. "There was no noise the whole time," he said.

Damien Turnidge watched the object pass overhead and says: "It was actually five lights that were a V, one in front and two on each side, and it was a perfect triangle."

Real-estate agent Max Saracen and his wife, Shahla, were driving along Deer Valley Road when the lights appeared. They pulled over to watch. "It was very spooky," said Saracen, "this gigantic ship blocking out the stars and silently creeping across the sky. I don't know of any aircraft with silent engines."

Dr. Bradley Evans, a clinical psychiatrist was with his wife Kris driving north on Interstate 10 toward Tempe. They saw the lights approach in a diamond formation. They watched the lights for the next twenty minutes as they passed silently overhead at an estimated altitude of 1,000 feet. The couple was in awe of the sighting and wondered if it might be military in origin.

Trig Johnston (a retired commercial airline pilot) and his twenty-two-year-old son were outside their home in Scottsdale. Like others that night, they went outside to see if they could see Comet Hale-Bopp. Instead, Johnson could hardly believe his eyes. "It was the size of twenty-five airliners moving at about 100 knots at maybe 5,000 feet," he said, "and it didn't make a sound. I've flown 747s across oceans and not seen anything like I saw that night. I don't expect anybody to take my word for it. This was something you had to see for yourself to believe."

Several air-traffic controllers actually observed the lights. Says one of them: "The object was turning—whatever it was. There was no variation. Perfect alignment. The lights were about 1,000 feet off the ground . . . " All who were present agreed that the objects were definitely not air force jets or flares.

A few people were able to videotape the lights. Chuck and Karla Raiden watched the lights pass over their home and also captured them on video. While the video clearly shows unusual lights, Chuck Rairden says: "The video doesn't do it justice."

Dana Valentine, a laser print technician observed the lights with his father (an engineer) from their Phoenix yard. They estimated the object was about 500 feet above them. "We could see the outline of a mass behind the lights, but you couldn't actually see the mass. It was more like a gray distortion of the night sky, wavy."

Around 10:00 p.m., UFO researchers Tom King and Bill Hamilton went to Gila Bend because a family reported that the strange lights from three days earlier were back. King and Hamilton were interviewing the witnesses when the object returned. This time they were able to videotape it.

Hamilton counted six orbs of very bright light traveling in front of the Estrella Mountains. All the witnesses were certain that the objects were not flares.

As the wave of objects approached Phoenix, one of the first to become aware of them was Luke AFB. According to multiple witnesses, jets were seen taking off from Luke AFB in pursuit of the objects. Almost immediately the base began receiving calls from concerned witnesses. Witnesses were told that the air force does not handle UFO reports and were referred to NUFORC.

The next day, a Luke AFB public information officer released an official statement saying that they knew nothing about the sightings. They had no radar reports. They had no airplanes in the sky that night. Commercial airports also reported no unusual radar readings. And they had received no calls.

Peter Davenport then revealed that many of the callers he received that night had been referred to NUFORC by Luke AFB, in direct contradiction to the official statement.

Tom King also revealed that he called Luke AFB after the event and was told that no jets had been launched after 7:00 p.m., again in direct contradiction to the statements of numerous witnesses.

Strange Universe producer Arte Shamamien called Luke AFB and was told by a colonel that witnesses probably saw a rogue pilot flying with a light rig designed to fool people.

At first they released an official statement saying that no jets were scrambled and nothing unusual occurred. Later, they admitted that they did have jets in the sky that night, but that the jet lights could not account for the alleged sightings. They denied dropping flares or having any knowledge of the flares.

Then in July, about two months after the incident, the Air National Guard admitted that they had sent jets from Davis-Monthan AFB in Tucson to conduct training exercises involving flares. The jets dropped the flares over the Barry Goldwater Gunnery Test Range, fifty miles southwest of Phoenix. Spokesman for the Air National Guard, Lieutenant Colonel David Tanaka told reporters, "Those flares that were seen could have been our flares."

This explanation fails to account for the evidence for several reasons. First, what people saw did not resemble flares. Second, the reports continued before and after the time that the Air National Guard was over the nearby test range. Third, the lights were not seen over the test range, but over Phoenix itself, hardly the location for a training exercise.

Months after the incident, officials at Luke AFB revealed that they continued to receive a barrage of calls from people asking about the Phoenix Lights. Lieutenant Colonel Mike Hauser told the *USA Today* newspaper, "They're calling us liars. I take great exception to that. I've answered every question. We have nothing to hide. But the fact is that we don't investigate UFOs."

In the *Arizona Republic,* Lieutenant Colonel Hauser was quoted again, saying, "We just know it was not one of our planes. Everybody is telling me that we have UFOs stashed all over the air force. I'm not taking issue with what people saw. Lots of things can make lights."

Lynne Kitei spoke with a public information officer who admitted that the sighting took place but had nothing to do with Luke AFB. He told her, "We don't know anything, that's the bottom line. There was something there, but what it was, that's the question. No one knows. Until someone finds out what they were, God only knows. It definitely wasn't a Luke F-16."

Kitei also spoke with a lieutenant colonel at Davis-Monthan who told her that their unit had been sending off flares for the entire week before. This meant that flare explanation didn't fit. If the Phoenix Lights were flares, the calls should have been coming in every day, not just on March 13.

Researcher John Greenwalde submitted an FOIA (Freedom of Information Act) request to Luke AFB asking for the release of any documents related to the incident. Luke replied promptly saying that they had no response regarding the Phoenix Lights and that it wasn't them.

To complicate matters, many residents were still seeing unexplained lights.

One of the first government officials to mention the incident was city council member Francis Barwood. It all began when she was on her way to a city countil meeting on May 6, 1997. She was stopped on the steps by a television crew who begged her to speak about the Phoenix Lights and told her that they had been turned away by virtually every level of government. Barwood told them that she knew nothing about the so-called lights, but she would make an inquiry.

Surprised that nobody had looked into the sighting, she asked City Manager Frank Fairbanks whether anyone was investigating the incident. Nobody was, so Barwood tried to unite the city council to ask Luke AFB for answers. The council refused and when Barwood continued to press the issue, she became the object of media ridicule.

But she didn't give up. She immediately received a flood of calls from witnesses looking for answers. Says Barwood:

> THERE WERE THIRTY-SEVEN THE FIRST DAY. AFTER THAT IT CLIMBED INTO THE HUNDREDS. I GOT CALLS FROM DOCTORS, LAWYERS, CELEBRITIES. A LITTLE LEAGUE COACH CALLED TO SAY BOTH TEAMS AND THEIR FAMILIES HAD SEEN THIS. MOST WANTED THEIR NAMES KEPT OUT OF IT, BUT THEY WANTED ANSWERS. HECK, IF I HAD SEEN IT, I'D WANT ANSWERS TOO.

Another call that impressed Barwood came from a man who was throwing a Hale-Bopp viewing party at his home. He told Barwood that he and all twenty of his guests observed the lights.

Barwood found herself the center of media attention. She was both ridiculed for her interest in the Phoenix Lights, and was conversely sought-after for interviews. Barwood soon realized what a sticky situation she had.

She called the mayor's office, the governor's office, and the office of Senator John McCain. None were able to offer any information. Barwood told reporters, "It's like a hot potato; no one wants to touch this. Do we have a bunch of wimps who are afraid to look into this?" Barwood also speculated that perhaps the air force was covering-up. "Or was it that they knew what it was and they didn't want to say?"

She said in another interview:

IT WAS ABOUT THIS TIME THAT SOME VERY PECULIAR THINGS REGARDING THE LIGHTS AND THE GOVERNMENT'S REPORTS CONCERNING THEM BECAME OBVIOUS, AND THAT I WAS CAST AS A TOTAL FLAKE. THE REPORTS THAT BOTHERED ME THE MOST, AND PROBABLY SOLIDIFIED MY RESOLVE TO GET TO THE BOTTOM OF THIS, WERE THE CONTRADICTORY REPORTS OFFERED BY THE PHOENIX POLICE DEPARTMENT.

As an example, Barwood pointed out that a police spokesperson revealed in a television interview that the police station had been overwhelmed with calls on the night of the event. A few days later, however, an official memo stated that only five calls had been received. "That inconsistency itself," said Barwood, "was enough to make me believe that something was amiss." In January of 1998, she held a press conference saying:

THE ISSUE IS NOT WHETHER OR NOT THEY WERE FLYING SAUCERS. THE ISSUE IS WHY THE GOVERNMENT HAS REFUSED TO TELL THE AMERICAN PUBLIC WHAT, EXACTLY, THOSE LIGHTS WERE. WHAT IS JUST AS FRUSTRATING, IF NOT MORE SO, IS THE FACT THAT THE INFORMATION WE DO GET EITHER KEEPS CHANGING OR CONTRADICTS WHAT WE WERE TOLD PREVIOUSLY.

Despite all the attention, Barwood was voted out of the office of the city council. "The government never interviewed even one witness," she said. "All I wanted to do was investigate this. I never said anything about extraterrestrials . . . How could they possibly not know about these craft flying low over major population centers? It's inconceivable, but it's also frightening."

Barwood later admitted that she talked to many high-level military officials who "were afraid to say publicly what they saw because they were told it would be the end of their careers."

As a result of all the attention thrown at her from the Phoenix Lights, Barwood announced her run for Arizona secretary of state during which she promised to look into the "seemingly paranormal events" of the Phoenix Lights.

She said:

THIS IS A PUBLIC SAFETY ISSUE OF STATE AND NATIONAL SIGNIFICANCE
THAT SHOULD NOT, IN GOOD CONSCIENCE, BE IGNORED BY A RESPONSIBLE
CANDIDATE. WE NEED TO GET BACK TO WHAT'S REALLY IMPORTANT, LIKE
OUR CONSTITUTIONAL RIGHTS AND OUR STATE RIGHTS. WE HAVE TO
HAVE SOMEONE WHO'S WILLING TO STICK HER NECK OUT TO PROTECT OUR
FREEDOMS.

Again she was ridiculed, but Barwood stuck to her guns, saying, "Whatever it is, I want to know." She says, "You can't ignore that something happened. Something was out there . . . Why are so many people afraid of saying, 'Hey, let's get to the bottom of what happened?'"

Barwood received a lot of publicity. Articles were written about her in mainstream newspapers and UFO magazines. She even appeared on the *Art Bell Show*. She became known as the "UFO candidate," a moniker that caused both positive and negative publicity. In either case, after all the votes were counted, Barwood was not elected.

Meanwhile, the office of Governor Fife Symington did their best to deal with the flood of calls asking for answers. At the end of August, more than five months after the incident, Symington held a press conference during which he told the media that he would assign a special investigator to look into the incident and investigate what people had seen.

Then, days later, Symington called another press conference saying that he had found the culprit. Reporters were stunned as a person wearing an "alien" costume walked into the room. The result was disastrous.

Writes researcher Bill Byrnes:

FOR THOSE PEOPLE WHO BELIEVED THEY'D BEEN WITNESS TO A REAL UFO
EVENT, AND FOR MANY OTHERS WHO CLAIMED SOME SORT OF CONTACT
WITH ALIEN BEINGS, EITHER THROUGH ABDUCTION OR PREVIOUS SIGHTINGS,
GOVERNOR SYMINGTON'S NEWS CONFERENCE WAS AN INSULT . . . THE NEWS
CONFERENCE, IF IT HAD BEEN AN ATTEMPT TO THROW COLD WATER ON THE
RUMORS OF A UFO INVASION, ACTUALLY SERVED THE OPPOSITE PURPOSE.
OBSERVERS WERE NOW MORE CONVINCED THAN EVER THAT THERE WAS SOME
KIND OF OFFICIAL COVER-UP GOING ON. WITNESSES WERE PUT OFF BY THE
AIR FORCE DENIALS, THE APPARENT INABILITY OF LOCAL GOVERNMENT TO
COME UP WITH AN EXPLANATION, AND NOW THE DELIBERATE ATTEMPT TO
MAKE FUN OF THE EVENT. WHAT WAS GOING ON?

Meanwhile, Senator McCain's office was feeling pressure about the Phoenix Lights. After being contacted by Barwood's office, Senator McCain contacted the air force requesting an investigation of the incident. The air force declined, saying that they do not investigate UFO incidents.

McCain, like Barwood, found himself stymied. In a television interview, he said:

> I DON'T KNOW ANY GOOD ANSWERS TO IT EXCEPT TO SAY SO FAR WE HAVE FOUND NO EVIDENCE OF BLACK HELICOPTERS OR ALIEN INVASION OR ANYTHING OF THAT NATURE. BUT THERE HAS BEEN AN INABILITY TO EXPLAIN REPORTS THAT SOME HAVE MADE ABOUT THE PRESENCE OF LIGHTS.

Few other UFO events have rocked government officials like the Phoenix Lights. There are some rumors that even the White House was aware of the events. According to reporter Steve Wilson of the *Arizona Republic*, and researcher Jim Dilitesso, on the night of the Phoenix Lights, the government went on DEF-CON 3 alert. He says that Clinton disappeared from public view for a period of hours. Meanwhile, a satellite that was supposed to detect incoming missiles malfunctioned. To cap it all off, *Scientific American* printed a story that stated that strong bursts of gamma radiation were detected on March 13.

While Phoenix's political leaders fumbled to deal with the Phoenix Lights, most of the citizens and researchers who looked into the case have come away convinced. Kitei's book *The Phoenix Lights* and Bill Hamilton's *The Phoenix Lights Mystery* are the most comprehensive reports of one of the most incredible UFO sightings in world history. The event was also well-covered by UFO programs, most notably in the documentary *I Know What I Saw*, produced by Jonathan Fox.

Peter Davenport of NUFORC was impressed by the Phoenix Lights. He had never received so many calls for a single event. "The incident over Arizona was the most dramatic I've seen," says Davenport. "What we have here is the real thing. They are here."

In another statement, he said:

> THIS CASE IS NOT CLOSED BY ANY MEANS ... IN MY JUDGMENT, THE EVENTS THAT TOOK PLACE OVER ARIZONA [ON MARCH 13, 1998] REMAIN THE MOST DRAMATIC UFO SIGHTING REPORTS THAT I'M AWARE OF.

UFO researcher Bill Hamilton observed the lights and interviewed many other witnesses. Says Hamilton:

> MY CONCLUSION RIGHT NOW IS THAT THE OBJECTS SEEN ON MARCH 13 WERE UNCONVENTIONAL, THEY WERE UNIDENTIFIED, AND THEY'RE FROM AN UNKNOWN ORIGIN. I DO NOT BELIEVE THAT THEY ARE OUR OWN ADVANCED TECHNOLOGY AIRCRAFT OF ANY KIND. . .

Some researchers have presented the possibility that the Phoenix Lights was not an accidental sighting. The craft flew at very low altitude at a speed estimated about 30 mph. Writes Steven Greer, "This certainly suggests that the objects indeed wanted to be seen."

Remote viewer Ed Dames, who claims to have worked for the government as a psychic spy, caused an uproar when he said that the Phoenix Lights were caused by lasers powered by humans—and that the whole event was a hoax. Most researchers agree that this theory is even less viable than the "flare" theory. Researcher David Rapp, a laser specialist for the aerospace industry, wrote a scathing article for the MUFON *UFO Journal* in which he explained why the laser theory is untenable on multiple levels.

There were videotapes and photographs taken. Some of these were apparently flares. A study of the later flare event by photo analyst Bruce Maccabee concludes that these objects were flares, which agrees with reports from Davis-Monthan. However, many witnesses believe that air force officials were well aware of the Phoenix Lights and the controversy that would likely ensue, and so to confuse the issue and provide a scapegoat, they dropped flares.

But the other films appear to show the real thing. According to photographic analyst Jim Dilettoso, he reviewed multiple amateur videotapes taken on that night. He was able to determine that there were at least four separate flights over the city lasting for a period of nearly two hours. The video showed that the lights were uniform and didn't vary in intensity or brightness. He was unable to match it with any known aircraft.

In January 1999, Peter Gersten of the Citizens Against UFO Secrecy (CAUS) filed suit against the Department of Defense, claiming that the government failed to response adequately to his Freedom of Information request asking for documents relating to the Phoenix Lights. It was a thirty-minute hearing held to a "standing-room only" audience. Gersten held up the forms he received from the Department of Defense which stated "documents found." Unfortunately, the documents never arrived. Instead, the Department of Defense reversed its position and returned a form to Gersten saying "documents not found." Gersten provided voluminous evidence to support the Phoenix Lights, including eyewitness accounts, drawings, and photographs.

In March of 2000, Judge Stephen McNamee ruled in favor of the Department of Defense. In his decision, he stated:

THIS CASE IS NOT ONE OVER THE EXISTENCE OR NON-EXISTENCE OF UFOS, BUT WHETHER THE GOVERNMENT HAS CONDUCTED A REASONABLE SEARCH REGARDING INFORMATION ON SPECIFIC AERIAL MODES OF TRANSPORTATION. A FRUITLESS SEARCH IS IMMATERIAL IF DEFENDANT CAN ESTABLISH THAT IT CONDUCTED A SEARCH REASONABLY CALCULATED TO UNCOVER ALL RELEVANT DOCUMENTS REQUESTED FOR BY PLAINTIFF. DEFENDANT HAS

MET ITS BURDEN BY PROVIDING SUFFICIENTLY DETAILED AFFIDAVITS FOR THE COURT TO CONCLUDE THAT A REASONABLE SEARCH WAS CONDUCTED IN RESPONDING TO PLAINTIFF'S FOIA REQUEST FOR DOCUMENTS. PLAINTIFF HAS FAILED TO DEMONSTRATE SUBSTANTIAL DOUBT REGARDING THE REASONABLENESS OF THE SEARCH. THEREFORE, DEFENDANT'S MOTION FOR SUMMARY JUDGMENT IS GRANTED.

Then came the real shocker. Years later, Governor Fife Symington revealed that he not only believed the Phoenix Lights were real, he was an eyewitness. As he said in an official statement:

IN 1997, DURING MY SECOND TERM AS GOVERNOR OF ARIZONA, I SAW SOMETHING THAT DEFIED LOGIC AND CHALLENGED MY REALITY. I WITNESSED A MASSIVE DELTA-SHAPED, CRAFT SILENTLY NAVIGATE OVER SQUAW PEAK, A MOUNTAIN RANGE IN PHOENIX, ARIZONA. IT WAS TRULY BREATHTAKING. I WAS ABSOLUTELY STUNNED BECAUSE I WAS TURNING TO THE WEST LOOKING FOR THE DISTANT PHOENIX LIGHTS.

TO MY ASTONISHMENT THIS APPARITION APPEARED; THIS DRAMATICALLY LARGE, VERY DISTINCTIVE LEADING EDGE WITH SOME ENORMOUS LIGHTS WAS TRAVELING THROUGH THE ARIZONA SKY. AS A PILOT AND A FORMER AIR FORCE OFFICER, I CAN DEFINITIVELY SAY THAT THIS CRAFT DID NOT RESEMBLE ANY MAN-MADE OBJECT I'D EVER SEEN. AND IT WAS CERTAINLY NOT HIGH-ALTITUDE FLARES BECAUSE FLARES DON'T FLY IN FORMATION.

THE INCIDENT WAS WITNESSED BY HUNDREDS—IF NOT THOUSANDS—OF PEOPLE IN ARIZONA, AND MY OFFICE WAS BESIEGED WITH PHONE CALLS FROM VERY CONCERNED ARIZONIANS. THE GROWING HYSTERIA INTENSIFIED WHEN THE STORY BROKE NATIONALLY. I DECIDED TO LIGHTEN THE MOOD OF THE STATE BY CALLING A PRESS CONFERENCE WHERE MY CHIEF OF STAFF ARRIVED IN AN ALIEN COSTUME. WE MANAGED TO LESSEN THE SENSE OF PANIC BUT, AT THE SAME TIME, UPSET MANY OF MY CONSTITUENTS.

I WOULD NOW LIKE TO SET THE RECORD STRAIGHT. I NEVER MEANT TO RIDICULE ANYONE. MY OFFICE DID MAKE INQUIRIES AS TO THE ORIGIN OF THE CRAFT, BUT TO THIS DAY THEY REMAIN UNANSWERED. EVENTUALLY THE AIR FORCE CLAIMED RESPONSIBILITY STATING THAT THEY DROPPED FLARES.

THIS IS INDICATIVE OF THE ATTITUDE FROM OFFICIAL CHANNELS. WE GET EXPLANATIONS THAT FLY IN THE FACE OF THE FACTS. EXPLANATIONS LIKE WEATHER BALLOONS, SWAMP GAS, AND MILITARY FLARES.

I WAS NEVER HAPPY WITH THE AIR FORCE'S SILLY EXPLANATION. THERE MIGHT VERY WELL HAVE BEEN MILITARY FLARES IN THE SKY THAT EVENING, BUT WHAT I AND HUNDREDS OF OTHERS SAW HAD NOTHING TO DO WITH THAT.

I NOW KNOW THAT I AM NOT ALONE. THERE ARE MANY HIGH-RANKING MILITARY, AVIATION, AND GOVERNMENT OFFICIALS WHO SHARE MY

CONCERNS. WHILE ON ACTIVE DUTY, THEY HAVE EITHER WITNESSED A UFO INCIDENT OR HAVE CONDUCTED AN OFFICIAL INVESTIGATION INTO UFO CASES RELEVANT TO AVIATION SAFETY AND NATIONAL SECURITY.

BY SPEAKING OUT WITH ME, THESE PEOPLE ARE PUTTING THEIR REPUTATIONS ON THE LINE. THEY HAVE FOUGHT IN WARS, GUARDED TOP SECRET WEAPONS ARSENALS, AND PROTECTED OUR NATION'S SKIES. WE WANT THE GOVERNMENT TO STOP PUTTING OUT STORIES THAT PERPETUATE THE MYTH THAT ALL UFOS CAN BE EXPLAINED AWAY IN DOWN-TO-EARTH CONVENTIONAL TERMS. INVESTIGATIONS NEED TO BE RE-OPENED, DOCUMENTS NEED TO BE UNSEALED, AND THE IDEA OF AN OPEN DIALOGUE CAN NO LONGER BE SHUNNED.

INCIDENTS LIKE THESE ARE NOT GOING AWAY. ABOUT A YEAR AGO, CHICAGO'S O'HARE INTERNATIONAL AIRPORT EXPERIENCED A UFO EVENT THAT MADE NATIONAL AND INTERNATIONAL HEADLINES. WHAT I SAW IN THE ARIZONA SKY GOES BEYOND CONVENTIONAL EXPLANATIONS. WHEN IT COMES TO EVENTS OF THIS NATURE THAT ARE STILL COMPLETELY UNSOLVED, WE DESERVE MORE OPENNESS IN GOVERNMENT, ESPECIALLY OUR OWN.[71]

Kitei Sees More UFOs

On January 12, 1998, a year after the Phoenix Lights, Lynne Kitei MD and her husband saw another UFO; in this instance "two huge golden lights one on top of the other." They were motionless and silent. She attempted to film them, but a fog moved in quickly and made filming impossible. In the days that followed she saw more.[72]

Police Encounter UFOs

On August 28–29, 1998, a lighted object caused a sensation over Yuma. A MUFON field investigator trainee uncovered the case and actually saw the object herself. The object was seen by several witnesses in Yuma, including two police officers, over a period of two nights. The object was described as "both hovering and moving about for up to an hour at a time."

Dan Wright, the deputy director of MUFON Investigations writes that the case had the potential to "be one of the most important cases of the year." Unfortunately, the field investigator was still in training and didn't contact airport personnel or obtain recorded interviews with the officers. MUFON never officially investigated the case. Says Wright: "In short, an opportunity was lost."

A second, better-verified sighting occurred one year later over Phoenix. It was 2:20 a.m., on October 12, 1999, and two police officers were flying a police helicopter on routine patrol over the city at about 2,000 feet in altitude. The officers' attention was drawn to a "single brilliant green light" that moved northbound near North Mountain at about 5,000 feet. "I first thought it was an aircraft," said the pilot (who had 2,300 hours of flight time in the helicopter and 4,000 hours of military aircraft experience). But it wasn't long before he changed his mind.

He first attempted to radio the craft. When the craft didn't respond, the pilot turned upwards to the right in an attempt to approach the object.

The object, which had been moving forward, now stopped, then turned into an orbit above the helicopter. Both officers were convinced that the object was unusual. It was twice the brilliance of Venus and totally silent. The pilot turned the helicopter to get a better look. At the same moment, the object reversed its course and began to circle the helicopter in the other direction. Both officers felt that the object was reacting to their movements.

The green light circled the helicopter nearly a dozen times, then "shot up through the air like a high-speed elevator; hundreds of feet in just a few seconds." Next, it dived downwards, then made a sharp turn.

The pilot contacted two other helicopters in air over the city and inquired if they could see the green light. Neither saw the light, nor did Phoenix Sky Harbor Tower, which also showed nothing on radar. Meanwhile, the object continued to dart back and forth for a period of ten minutes right over a busy highway, at which point, the officers were forced to depart to answer another police call. When they returned to the area later, the green light was gone.

The officers kept their sighting private, but an unknown person leaked the story to the local radio station KFYI, which played a clip of the pilots' actual conversation as they reported their sighting. Within a few days, the clip was posted on several Internet websites, which prompted a television segment on the case.

Jim Kelly, Maricopa County state section director for MUFON heard about the case and tracked down the officers, who both agreed to an interview. Kelly conducted a thorough investigation. He contacted local police who confirmed the encounter. He contacted local airports. Oddly, Sky Harbor Tower first refused to release the audiotape from the pilots and then declared that they had no recording. Writes Kelly, "I was perplexed by this answer. Did the FAA actually check the tape . . . or did they simply wish not to tell me that the conversation had occurred?"

After the investigation was complete, Kelly concluded that the observers had seen something unidentified. Says the pilot: "This object was not another aircraft. I base my conclusion on my unobstructed observations of its rapid heading, altitude changes, and aggressive maneuvering in relation to my aircraft."

In a follow-up review of the investigation, Bob Sylvester, the state director for Arizona MUFON wrote, "Both witnesses were highly credible, reliable, and trained to make observations. The investigator was very thorough and should be commended for his work on what I consider a very important case."[73]

Photo Gallery

1: 1947_07_07_PHOENIX.
On July 7, 1947, around the same time as the Roswell UFO crash, amateur photographer William Rhodes was drawn outside by a strange sound. Hoping to photograph a jet, he was surprised to see what appeared to be a flying disk. It was semi-circular, flat, and circling the area about 2,000 feet away. Rhodes quickly snapped two photos of the object, which veered and flew off quickly to the west. The photos caused a sensation, and today researchers have speculated that Rhodes captured the type of UFO that crashed at Roswell. (MUFON CMS)

2: 2003_08_14.
On August 14, 2003, a man and his wife were driving through Sedona taking pictures of the beautiful red rock mesas with their Kodak CX6330. They saw nothing unusual at the time, but upon downloading the images into their computer saw what appeared to be "a small bubble-type craft." Later, the witness received confirmation of his sighting when three other witnesses claimed to have seen the craft land in the same area. (MUFON CMS)

3: 2005_03_01.
Sometime in March 2005, a gentleman decided to have his picture taken at a graveyard in Tombstone. Instead of a ghost appearing in the picture, it was a UFO. Says the gentleman, "I was at Boothill Graveyard, in Tombstone, Arizona. I stopped there before nightall and upcoming rain to check it out along with the OK Corral. I had a friend take my picture next to Les Moore's gravestone and when the pic developed, there was an object the background." Neither the photographer nor the gentleman saw the object, which appears to be a triangular-shaped something, moving over the graveyard. (MUFON CMS)

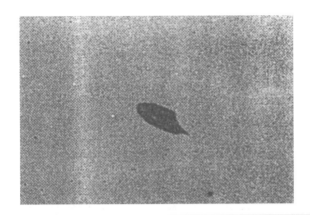

4: 2005_03_08.

This photo was taken by a warehouse employee in Chandler who says, "As I was leaving my workplace for the day, I noticed this strange object above the treeline. I thought it was some type of remote-control airship, but it was motionless and looked too sinister. A sudden chill ran up and down my spine. It was very eerie. I ran to my vehicle to get my camera. I snapped one picture as fast as possible. As I was going to snap another, it disappeared, almost like when you turn a TV switch off. Very strange. If you look almost in the center of the picture, you can see three construction workers unaware of the situation, going about everyday worklife." (MUFON CMS)

5: 2005_04_06.

"My family and I were on vacation in Tempe, Arizona and decided to go to Sedona for the day. While at the Catholic church, built in the rock in Sedona, I saw a flash in the sky, a reflection from the sun. I grabbed my camera and started taking pictures. I was only able to get one shot. I waited until now because this was my third sighting." (MUFON CMS)

6: 2005_05_14.
Researchers have noticed that there are an unusually large number of UFO sightings over cemeteries. Proof of this is the photo captured by a witness on May 14, 2005, over Mesa City Cemetery. The witness was visiting his deceased parents. As he left the cemetery, he decided to take a picture of the area. He noticed nothing in the sky at the time, however upon reviewing the photos was surprised to see two strange disk-like objects apparently hovering at a low altitude over the cemetery. (MUFON CMS)

7: 2006_04_30.
On the afternoon of April 30, 2006, a retired paramedic was out in the Sonoran Desert about forty miles away from Phoenix Sky Harbor Airport when he saw a jetliner with a large double contrail passing overhead. He knew this was a busy flight path for aircraft and didn't think much of it until he glanced up and saw something strange. "A black object had appeared between the jetliner's contrail," explains the witness, "and looked to be following it." (MUFON CMS)

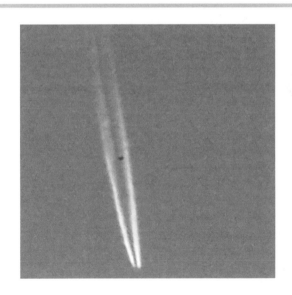

PHOTO GALLERY

8: 2007_06_03.

Phoenix has a live webcam that apparently has caught several images of anomalous objects. Says one gentleman, "I enjoy sky watching on several Live Web Cam sites and have gotten many unknowns over the past month on the East Coast. I have started viewing www.phoenixvis.net for about a week and caught an object hovering above the Superstition Mountain in Phoenix." This image is only one of many that he has managed to capture. (MUFON CMS)

9: 2007_06_11.

This image of two glowing anomalous lights was taken by Johnny Wheeler over the Camelback Mountains on June 11, 2007. (MUFON CMS)

PHOTO GALLERY

10: 2007_06_18.

This image of a cluster of glowing lights was observed by a mother and her five-year-old son, who were drawn outside their home in Yuma by their dog barking. She snapped a photo and tried to get more photos, but as the object came closer, both her digital camera and video recorder malfunctioned. She was only able to capture this one photo as the objects hovered at about 2,000 feet, then darted away. Says the witness, "I have never seen anything like this in my life." (MUFON CMS)

11: 2010_06_16_AZ.

On June 16, 2010, a man and his wife were driving from Las Vegas to their home in Arizona. It was daytime, and they were in Arizona when they stopped to take some photographs of some interesting rock formations. The witness saw a white object flit by quickly, and was surprised to see that he captured the image in his photo. (MUFON CMS)

12: 2013_12_25_MARICOPA.

On Christmas night in 2013, a family in Maricopa was eating dinner when they were drawn outside around 7:30 p.m. to see an "orange light" in the sky. All the members of the family observed the object float toward them for about five minutes at an altitude of only 1,500 feet. After it passed, it made a right turn, then faded and disappeared. Moments later, a second identical-looking object appeared and followed the same pathway as the first. This time, they captured a photo. (MUFON CMS)

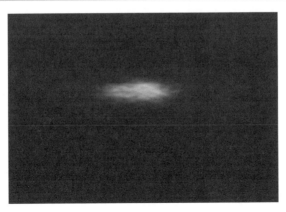

Chapter Four

Landings and Humanoids

Cases of UFO landings and humanoid sightings provide a link between simple sightings and extensive onboard experiences. While sightings are interesting, they are limited in the amount of information they offer to the observer. Conversely, with onboard experiences, abductees sometimes report missing time, or only partial and incomplete memory of the event—which is often accompanied by intense fear, further distorting their perception Sometimes memories are only retrievable through hypnosis.

However, cases involving landings and humanoids offer much more information than a simple sighting and are not shrouded in the controversy that surrounds abduction cases. Landings are also one of the rarest types of encounters.

This chapter covers more than forty cases throughout Arizona in which people have encountered a landed UFO and/or strange humanoids. Again, as few people ever report their encounters, the true number of Arizona UFO landings is likely several magnitudes larger. What follows, however, represents a good sampling of cases.

UFO Lands at Bisbee Copper Mines

On June 27, 1947 (only a week before the Roswell UFO crash), John A. Petsche, an electrician employed at the Phelps-Dodge copper mines in Bisbee observed a silver mirror-like, disk-shaped object move overhead. The object was silent and wobbled slightly as it moved. Two other men working with Petsche also observed the object, and all three agreed the object was unusual.

Meanwhile, a mile-and-a-half away, three other mine employees, including John Rylance (an electrician), I. W. Maxwell, and Milton Luna watched the object (described as oval-shaped) move lower and lower until it landed on a hill in the mine nicknamed Tintown. The object then took off, leaving a group of stunned miners. Reporters learned of the case and converged on the scene. Vernon C. McMinn, the gang boss for the group of electricians who had observed the object, told reporters that several other employees at the mine had also seen the object and described the same thing.

Unknown to the mine employees, Major George B. Wilcox of the US Army observed eight or nine light-colored disk-shaped craft move at a low elevation over the Bisbee area at the same time of the Bisbee mine sighting. The objects were evenly spaced in single file and moved with a dipping "rocking" motion.[74]

An Alien on the Road

Late one evening in early June of 1960, a young woman was driving her Cadillac through Globe on her way to California. Her husband Joe slept beside her in the passenger seat, and her two children were both asleep in the back seat.

As she pulled around the corner, the beam of her headlights caught a small figure about 100 yards ahead on the right side of the road. The figure was facing to her left. It looked like it was about to cross the road in front of her, so she slowed down. To her shock, the figure—which was about three feet tall—turned and faced her. Says the witness:

THE SECOND I SAW THAT THING, MY HEART CAME UP IN MY MOUTH AND MY STOMACH DID A FLIP-FLOP . . . [IT] WAS SMALL, BROAD-SHOULDERED, WITH LONG ARMS, DARK IN COLOUR, AND IT HAD A HEAD SHAPED SOMEWHAT LIKE A FLATTENED BALL—ALMOST LIKE A PUMPKIN. IN HIS HEAD WERE TWO YELLOWISH-ORANGE GLOWING "EYES." I RECALL THAT WHEN IT WAS IN SIDE-VIEW THERE WAS A LIGHT BEAMING OUT BEYOND THE FACE. I SAW NO NOSE, OR MOUTH, OR EARS. THE BODY WAS NOT AS WELL DEFINED AS THE HEAD, AND I GOT THE IMPRESSION OF HAIR OR FUR.

After staring at her for a few moments, the strange figure turned and ran off the road and into the brush. The witness slammed on the accelerator and sped away, screaming at her husband to wake up.

After he woke and she told him what she had seen, he wanted to return and look for it. She refused. As she says: "I told him that if he wanted to go back then he could go back by himself, but neither my children nor I were going back there on that lonely dark road."[75]

Landing in Tucson

On the evening of October 9, 1967, Richard, the thirteen-year-old son of a "prominent businessman," was riding his bike around his neighborhood when he came upon an eight-foot-tall metallic, cylindrical-shaped object resting on the ground about fifty feet away. It stood on two legs, each of which ended in a large circular pad. Wondering what the object was, Richard moved closer. At about thirty-five feet, the object made a "deep low-pitched hum" and took off straight upward and disappeared into the night sky.

Richard approached the area where the object was landed and saw obvious imprints in the soil. UFO investigator James McDonald was able to investigate the case. He photographed and examined the landing traces and determined that the two landing pads were 42 inches apart and 13.4 inches wide. They were made in "hard-packed" soil.

McDonald was so impressed by the case that he contacted air force officials at Davis-Monthan AFB and informed them about the incident. Blue Book air force personnel came in and conducted an initial investigation. One week later, they returned to re-examine the impressions. Unfortunately, it had rained and the landing traces were washed away. Air Force Colonel Raymond Sleeper later wrote a sixty-page report on the case, finally labeling it: Hoax. The Lorenzens and McDonald disagreed and believed that the boy had seen a genuine UFO.[76]

Near Landing in Hotevilla

In January 1969, Titus Lamson (a full-blooded Hopi) was drawn outside his home in Hotevilla one evening to observe a brilliantly lit object move in a westerly direction overhead. It was close enough for Lamson to see a saucer shape with a dome on top. As he watched, the object turned transparent. Inside Lamson observed the backside of somebody dressed in a gray-colored "ski-jump suit." The man had long blond hair down to his shoulders and was operating an instrument panel in front of him.

He watched the craft descend until it was only a few feet above the ground, at which point it took off over a nearby ridge. Lamson grabbed his flashlight and went to search for the object, but found no sign of it.[77]

The Saucer Man

One afternoon in August 1972, a young man was outside his home in Phoenix when he came upon a silver-white disk not far from the road near his home. The object was about forty-five feet wide and thirty-five feet tall. Says the witness: "Outside the craft stood a tall, lean male. He appeared to be about seven feet [tall], wearing a silver-grey military type uniform."

Other than his incredible height, the man appeared human-like. He spoke telepathically to the witness: "Return to your home. Do not come back out until morning."

Says the witness: "He was firm in his request, and compelling, though he did not present himself as threatening."

As the witness returned home, he heard sirens approaching the landing site. About two or three hours later, he was surprised to see the police arrive at the front door of his home and request that everybody stay indoors.[78]

UFO Landing in Phoenix

Sometime in the mid-1970s, a young military officer was driving from Williams AFB to Apache Junction. It was a clear and cloudless day, with no hint that something very unusual was about to occur. Says the officer: "I saw a saucer-shaped object rise out of the desert in front of me and slowly ascend into the air, straight up, until it was out of sight. At the time, I tried to guess the size of the object and estimated that it was at least as large as a high school football stadium. It was a dull silver color and looked like the flying saucers in old sci-fi movies. There was absolutely no sound associated with this sighting."

Because of the massive size of the object, the officer assumed that the next day, the newspapers would be filled with reports from other people. "I could not possibly have been the only one to see it," he said. Unfortunately, the newspaper mentioned nothing about UFOs. Not too surprising as the witness failed to report the sightings himself. As he says: "I did not tell anyone for years, thinking people would think I was a nut." To his credit, he finally reported his sighting to NUFORC.79

UFO Landing in Maricopa

In October of 1975, only a few weeks before the Travis Walton abduction, a young man and his girlfriend, and others living in the house, were drawn outside their home in Maricopa by what appeared to be a formation of four orange flares. But when two of the lights on either side simultaneously rose several hundred feet above the others, it became clear that they weren't flares.

Without warning, the orange lights disappeared to be replaced by three white lights in a triangular formation. The lights appeared to emit smoke or mist as they slowly drifted downward and landed about a quarter mile away in the backyard of a local ranch house, lighting up the entire area.

Further confirmation that the objects weren't flares came when they continued to move strangely. Says the witness: "We watched the objects on the ground and one of them kept going up and down, six to ten feet into the air. Reminded me of the dance of the bees . . . The objects were smaller than the house, perhaps twenty feet in diameter."

After several minutes, the lights disappeared. "About a week or two later," says the boyfriend, "one of the witnesses and myself walked up around the hill where the objects were first seen and found a mutilated steer that had not been touched by coyotes or buzzards, which were very numerous in the area. At the time we had never heard of cattle mutilations and did not seriously connect the two events. We were never able to approach the ranch house to ask what the hell went on that night as they had a very big dog that chased us away whenever we ventured too near."[80]

UFO Landing in Prescott

Also in the month of October 1975, four people observed a remarkable UFO landing outside the town of Prescott. The main witness was a teenager staying with friends. One evening the family dogs woke everyone in the house with their frantic barking. They all rushed outside expecting to see a bear or mountain lion. Says the witness: "What we saw scared the daylights out of us."

A strange circular object with lights rotating around the bottom perimeter had landed on the side of a small hill about a quarter mile away. Each of them observed the object from the house, too afraid to venture any closer. The object remained in place, perfectly still for about thirty minutes. Says the witness: "Then all of a sudden it just went straight up very fast and disappeared."

The next day, when it was bright daylight, they decided to ride over on horseback and investigate. Where the UFO had landed was rocky, but they found what appeared to be partial impressions of round footprints on the ground.[81]

The Invasion of Williams AFB

According to Tina Choate, (cofounder of the International UFO Research Center in Scottsdale), in 1978 and 1979, Williams Air Force Base came under a virtual UFO siege. UFO sightings were occurring with such regularity over the base that air force personnel there began to train themselves in preparation of imminent contact.

"They had them set down on the landing field," explained Choate, "and they had them appearing and disappearing on radar all the time."

The activity escalated to the point that authorities on the base believed that the aliens might be preparing for a face-to-face confrontation. Says Brian Myers (president of ICUR): "They were in a real state of panic down there. There was so much activity they thought there was going to be a landing like in the movie *Close Encounters*. They were even training people as a welcoming committee."

As far as is publicly known, no official contact was made and the sightings over the base eventually ended.[82]

Figures in the Windows

In November of 1980, George Parks was driving home late at night after working the night shift at the BHP Copper Mines in San Manuel when his life changed forever. Says Parks: "Coming around the bend at Oracle Junction, I saw a metallic craft hovering not far from the road. I saw seven windows. Behind every window stood a figure. An instant later, it flew off."

Parks was amazed by his sighting. He was in the military for more than twenty years and never saw anything like that. As a result of his encounter, he was inspired to join MUFON and, before long, became a field investigator. Following that he became the Pima County section director for MUFON, and later the Arizona state director. Says Parks: "I'm still looking for answers."[83]

Landing in Lukachukai

As researched by MUFON field investigator Richard D. Siefried (see MUFON Log#930618C), in mid-August 1982 at 1:45 a.m., Chris (pseudonym) was traveling with his father and his father's friend to the Lukachukai Rodeo. About ten miles north of town they saw a star-like object moving through the sky. Without warning, the object approached them. It came within a hundred feet when it sparkled and disappeared, leaving only a "hazy cloud."

Wondering if they had seen a meteor or something else, they drove for another five miles when they came upon a mysterious glowing light coming from inside a canyon that dropped off to the left of the road. They drove to the top of a hill and pulled over to take a look.

Despite standing on top of the truck, the source of the light was just out-of-sight, until Chris's father put Chris on top of his shoulders. Only then did Chris see an "object."

Intrigued, he wanted to hike down the canyon. But his father was nervous about hiking at night. Meanwhile, their friend had become frightened and retreated to the truck. They watched the glow for only a few minutes, and then drove away. In town, they pulled into a convenience store. Chris's father told the clerk, "You won't believe what I just saw."

The clerk listened, and then told them that an entire family had stopped by his store earlier and were "very frightened." They told the clerk that a strange object had landed on their property. The frightened family fled their home and went to the convenience store to call the authorities.[84]

Trucker Encounters Landed UFO

On September 12, 1983, a trucker and two teenagers had an unforgettable encounter with a UFO that landed right alongside the highway. Says one of the witnesses: "I was traveling East on I-10 as a passenger in a semi headed for Phoenix. It was nighttime and I was star gazing as I usually do when I saw this ball of fire heading straight for Earth. I was beside myself with excitement and I told my friend who was driving to stop the truck. I watched this thing as it was approaching and then it stopped dead in its tracks and just hovered there, a great glowing ball of fire. It was pulsating. Then it split into two spheres of fire. They started to move like the shape of an atom in-between each other, so fast. I couldn't move. All I could do was watch this most amazing thing that I have ever experienced. After I don't know for how long they formed together as one and landed on the ground."

The driver, a full-blooded Cherokee, was superstitious and wanted to leave, as did the other passenger. At the same time, another vehicle pulled over and also observed the landed object. After a short time, the object took off, leaving the witnesses "mesmerized."[85]

Alien on Highway 89

As reported to the MUFON Case Management System, on September 1, 1984, a family driving along Highway 89 in Kayenta had a bizarre experience they won't soon forget. It was a bright moonlit night and they were cruising at about 60 mph when a strange figure appeared only forty feet ahead of them in the middle of the road. It was "dressed in total white," according to the witness.

The father (who was driving) slammed on the car brakes and skidded to a stop, but "not in time to avoid hitting the person." There was no sound of impact. He got out of the car, checked the area, and found nothing unusual.

Confused he got back into the car and continued down the highway. About a half-mile later, the headlights failed and the car engine died. After coasting to a stop, he checked the car and discovered that the entire electrical system (interior lights, brake lights, emergency lights, and the radio) was nonfunctional.

The whole family exited the car and stood off the highway. Then the father returned to the car to get some blankets to keep his family warm. A few moments later, the interior lights of the car came back on. Everything else also functioned normally, so they returned to the car and continued their journey. Following this, their trip was normal.

As soon as he could, the father checked the car for damage and found nothing wrong, not even a burned-out fuse. The vehicle ran normally after the strange incident. The witness, realizing that he may have had a very close encounter with an ET, reported his experience to MUFON.[86]

An Alien Hitchhiker

According to Jan Harzan, executive director of MUFON, in 2004, he received an intriguing call from a retired airline pilot with 40,000 hours of flying time.

The encounter occurred around 1984 when the pilot picked up a hitchhiker about fifteen miles outside of Yuma. Writes Harzan: "He [the pilot] found it strange that this man was out in the middle of nowhere, literally out in the middle of the desert, standing on the side of the road with his thumb out. He normally did not pick up hitchhikers, but something told him to stop and give this guy a ride."

The hitchhiker told the pilot that he was looking for a ride to San Diego. Surprised, the pilot replied that he was heading to that city. As they spoke, the hitchhiker revealed something incredible: he was an extraterrestrial. He said that this was not his normal form, and he was in disguise. He had come to help humankind and was on his way to a research facility in San Diego.

According to the pilot, the gentleman was utterly sincere, and being next to the man, he felt a strange calmness. At the time everything the man said sounded "rational and reasonable."

Writes Harzan of this case: "I know, I know—sounds crazy . . . it would be even crazier not to get the facts. We'll see where this one goes."[87]

Dad's Time Machine

While the extraterrestrial hypothesis is the most popular to explain UFOs, it's certainly not the only one. Other theories include interdimensional beings or even time travelers, an explanation that seems to fit this next case.

On October 8, 1984, Jake (pseudonym) and his son, Sheldon, (twelve-years-old) were driving along Highway 89 to their home in Spring Valley after attending a funeral. Around 11:00 p.m., about five miles outside Yarnell, they pulled over to take a break from driving.

They began talking about UFOs. Says Jake: "I mentioned to my son that I think most UFO sightings are military-related or nonmilitary-related vehicles, possibly from the future like a time machine. I told my son that some day time travel could be possible."

Sheldon asked, "Can you prove time travel?"

Humoring his son, Jake replied, "Maybe, do you want to try it?" It was now 11:26 and the father and son marked the date and time and waited to see if anything would show up.

"Oh, my God!" Sheldon yelled. "What is that?"

Jake turned his head and was shocked to see a small flying object swoop down from the sky right toward them. It stopped about 50 feet high and 100 feet away. Says Jake: "We could see two people in the craft. They were looking at us. Sheldon looked at me, jumped into the car, and shut the door. I stood still and took it all in. After about five seconds, I waved and they waved back. I looked back at my son and he smiled. When I turned back to look at the craft, it was backing up. I waved again and they waved, too. The craft turned, picked up speed and altitude, and within a matter of seconds, was out of sight."

In complete shock, Jake returned to the car and looked in amazement at his son.

"That was you, Dad," said Sheldon. "That was you from the future. You did it! You proved time travel to me!"

The two of them drove home in a daze. According to Jake, his son was still shaken when they arrived home and told the rest of the family what they had seen. It was an event that neither of them will forget. Says Jake: "We have a plaque on the wall with the date, time, and place."

The experience itself caused Jake to think deeply about time travel. It affected them to such a degree that they are considering making a movie about it.[88]

Saved by a UFO

One evening in August 1986, Carolyn (pseudonym) found herself in a somewhat dangerous situation. She was at the Waweep Campground near Page, walking along the shore of Lake Powell. She was alone when, without warning, a bald-headed man attacked and tried to rape her. He forcefully threw Carolyn down so that she was half-in and half-out of the lake. Then he climbed on top of her and pinned her to the ground. Looking up, Carolyn saw a pair of shooting stars. One disappeared, but the other dropped down and "seemed to land at the end of the lake."

Carolyn assumed at first that it must be an airplane, but then it moved toward them. At the same time, the winds began to pick up. The "plane" now took on the appearance of a "big ball of fog." It approached closer and the wind became so strong it was lifting up small stones that struck both of them.

At this point, Carolyn's attacker stood up and looked at the object. He became frightened and ran away, yelling to Carolyn, "We better get out of here!"

Says Carolyn: "I looked at him and the ball of fog and decided I would rather go with the ball of fog. So I started walking out into the water towards the ball of fog. Then it just vanished. The water and wind calmed down and it was quiet again. I did not know what to make of this. I have not heard of many reports like this, but it seemed like it made a special trip down from the sky just to rescue me from this man."[89]

Pilot Sees Aliens

The following case was investigated by researcher Tom Dongo, who writes, "Regarding this incident, I must again be cautiously vague about identities."

The witness is a pilot for a major US airline. In 1986, he was driving south on Highway 89A from Sedona to Prescott. As he passed the Mingus Mountains, he saw strange flashes of light coming from a side canyon.

Writes Dongo: "He left his car to investigate the area, and in the side canyon, he saw a landed disc-shaped craft sitting on the ground and three humanoid beings walking around it. The three humanoids were aware of him immediately. One of them raised an arm high in a gesture of greeting. The pilot became rather unhinged at that point and made a dash for his car."

According to Dongo, the pilot jumped into his car and raced down the highway. The next thing he knew, the disk came swooping down, hovering in front of his vehicle as through trying to stop him. After a few moments, it quickly darted away.

The pilot drove to his home in Prescott and immediately called his friend, a well-known politician. After revealing his story, the politician asked if the pilot wanted to tell his encounter to the air force. The pilot agreed and soon found himself onboard a special air force jet heading toward Wright Patterson Air Force Base in Ohio. Upon arrival, he was placed inside a room for a half-hour until an officer arrived and told him that no questions would be asked of him. Without any other delay, the pilot was flown back to Prescott in another air force jet.[90]

Landing in Klondyke

In March of 1988, two witnesses were driving through Klondyke when they saw a silver object shaped like an upside down ice cream cone about 200 feet high and 100 feet wide at the base. It spun on its axis and made a soft humming noise. As they watched, it emitted bolts of electricity that struck the ground.

The object lowered down and began to land when an air force plane came from the northeast. The witnesses were surprised to see a man hanging out of the left side of the plane filming the incident with a large movie camera.

The object quickly evaded the plane by hopping about an eighth-mile to the south in less than a second, then disappeared.

The real excitement wouldn't happen until next morning. Says the witness:

[THE] NEXT MORNING WE SAW A HELMETED SPACE MAN HIDING IN THE SHRUBS LOOKING AT US. I MADE MENTAL CONTACT [AND] IT RAN OFF. IT HAD A BLACK CAPE THING AND WAS FOUR TO FIVE FEET TALL.

Following the sighting, the witnesses saw an official USAF car following them, which convinced them even further that they had seen something very unusual.[91]

"Just Passing Through"

While some alien encounters involve gray-type humanoids bent on abducting unwilling witnesses, some cases involve very different ETs with entirely different motives. The following encounter experienced by a young wife and mother involves an apparently unique type of being.

After seeing Peter Jennings' report on UFOs on television, she decided it was time to come forward with her story:

IN THE SUMMER OF 1988, MY THEN HUSBAND AND OUR CHILDREN SET OUT TO A LAW ENFORCEMENT TRACK MEET IN SHOW LOW, ARIZONA. MY HUSBAND WAS A DEPUTY AND WAS ON THE TRACK TEAM. AFTER THE MEET, WE RENTED A ROOM AT A LOCAL TWO STORY MOTEL. OUR ROOM WAS UPSTAIRS AND SORT OF IN THE MIDDLE OF THE BUILDING . . . THAT EVENING WE WERE ALL IN BED AND ASLEEP BY MIDNIGHT. MY THREE CHILDREN SLEPT ON THE BED THAT WAS CLOSEST TO THE DOOR AND MY HUSBAND AND I SLEPT ON THE BED NEXT TO THEM WITH ME BEING ON THE WEST SIDE OF THE BED.

SOMETIME IN THOSE EARLY HOURS, I AWOKE TO SEE TWO LARGE-SIZED ALIEN MEN WALK THROUGH THE WALL COMING FROM THE ROOM JUST SOUTH OF OURS. THEY WALKED THROUGH THE WALL, THROUGH THE DRESSER AND THE TELEVISION AND, AS THEY APPROACHED THE FOOT OF OUR BED, THEY STOPPED AND LOOKED AT ME. BY THIS TIME I WAS TOTALLY PARALYZED AND TERRIFIED. I COULD NOT SCREAM, MOVE, OR ALERT MY HUSBAND IN ANY WAY. I FEARED FOR OUR LIVES AND ESPECIALLY MY CHILDREN.

AS THESE BEINGS STOOD THERE WATCHING ME AND MY FAMILY, I COULD SEE THAT BOTH HAD TO BE AT LEAST SIX FEET, FIVE INCHES OR TALLER. THEY WERE VERY MUSCULAR BUT YET VERY LEAN—NO BODY FAT—[AND] BOTH WERE WEARING BODY ARMOR.

Strangest of all was the way their faces looked. Says the witness:

I NOTICED THEIR COLOR: ONE WAS A BLUISH GRAY AND THE OTHER WAS A REDDISH-GRAY COLOR. BUT THESE TWO ALSO HAD A FACE LIKE A HORSE, THEIR MOUTH AND NOSE CAME OUT JUST LIKE A HORSE OR A DOG. AS I LOOKED AT THE ONE THAT WAS REDDISH GRAY, HE LOOKED AT ME AND MENTALLY TOLD ME, "IT'S OKAY. WE'RE JUST PASSING THROUGH," AFTER WHICH TIME I THINK I PASSED OUT.

The witness reports that she blocked the incident from her conscious mind and didn't think of it or remember it for many years. She has never told her husband or her children. As she reported her sighting to NUFORC, she wrote, "I wonder am I doing the right thing."[92]

An Alien House Visit

Sometime in the late 1980s (exact date not given), Susan Bedell invited her niece Laura (pseudonym) to stay in her home in Sedona. Due to lack of space, during the visit Laura slept on the sofa in the living room. One evening Laura awoke to hear somebody banging around in the kitchen. Sitting up, she saw strange bright lights in the kitchen area.

"Susan?" Laura asked. Instantly the noises stopped. Fear swept over her. Was it a burglar?

Suddenly, six feet in front of her, a glowing light appeared. It expanded lengthwise and took on the form of a small humanoid creature.

According to researcher Tom Dongo who investigated the case, the creature had a "disproportionately large head, gray skin, large slanted almond eyes, and a body that seemed too frail to hold it up."

Laura stared at the being, and it stared back at her then slowly vanished in the same way that it had appeared.[93]

Landing in Sedona

One evening (date not given), a retired couple was watching television in their home in Sedona. Looking out the window, they saw a "blue-white light" fall to the ground near their property.

Living in a remote desert area and thinking that a plane had crashed, they rushed to the sight. Instead of finding a crash-site, however, they encountered a landed UFO. The object was large and disk-shaped. Around it were several small figures with large heads busily gathering samples from the surrounding area.

Paul Dongo investigated the case and writes:

THE WOMAN UTTERED SOME SORT OF CRY, A SOUND THAT ATTRACTED THE ATTENTION OF THE LITTLE MEN. REALIZING THEY HAD BEEN SEEN, THE COUPLE TURNED AND RAN AS FAST AS THEIR LEGS WOULD CARRY THEM. AS THEY STRUGGLED OVER THE CREST OF A LOW HILL, THEY WERE HIT IN THE BACK AND KNOCKED DOWN BY SOMETHING THAT CAUSED SEARING PAIN. THE COUPLE THEN LOST CONSCIOUSNESS. WHEN THE COUPLE CAME TO, IT WAS NOW MIDDAY AND THEY WERE THREE MILES FROM WHERE THEY HAD BEEN THE NIGHT BEFORE. TO THEIR FURTHER CONSTERNATION, THEY DISCOVERED THEY HAD FRESH SCARS AND MARKS ON THEIR BODIES.[94]

One morning in August 1988, journalist and artist Ron Quinn received a call from his friend "Sam," who he had known for nearly twenty years. Following the death of his wife, Sam had been traveling throughout southern Arizona taking pictures of ghost towns, graveyards, and abandoned mines.

The two men met and Sam told Ron that he had an "odd and frightening experience" that he wanted to relate. He handed Ron an envelope and told Ron that there was a picture inside of what he saw. "Prepare yourself for a big shock," he said.

Ron opened the envelope. His friend was right; Ron was shocked. "It was a photo of what appeared to be a 'space alien' taken from about seven feet away," explains Ron.

Ron stared at the photo. He knew that Sam was an honest and quiet man. There was no possibility that this was a hoax. Ron asked him to explain the photo. Sam said that on August 14, 1988, he was driving to an abandoned mining town outside Ruby, just north of the Mexican border. While taking pictures during the day, he heard a strange swishing sound followed by a sonic boom. Looking up, he saw nothing unusual, so he continued to take photographs.

About twenty minutes later, while hiking around the area, he saw the entity in the photograph. Writes Ron:

STANDING A SHORT DISTANCE OFF TO HIS RIGHT WAS A RATHER SMALL INDIVIDUAL. IT STOOD ON THE EDGE OF THE WASH ABOUT TWO FEET ABOVE HIM. AT FIRST HE THOUGHT IT WAS A CHILD, UNTIL THE FIGURE TURNED AND LOOKED DIRECTLY AT HIM. SEEING WHAT IT WAS, SAM BROUGHT HIS CAMERA UP AND QUICKLY SNAPPED OFF ONE PICTURE. BEFORE HE HAD TIME TO TAKE ANOTHER, THE FIGURE TURNED AND RAN QUICKLY UP THE BRUSH-COVERED HILL DIRECTLY TO ITS REAR.

Sam chased up the hill after the strange figure, but saw no trace of it. When he finally reached the top of the rise, he heard the strange swishing sound again, but nothing strange was visible in the sky.

Sam returned to the area and searched for footprints but found only a few scuff marks. He went back to his truck walking on legs that felt like "wet noodles." He developed the photograph at the local drug store, and then called Ron to tell him what happened.

Ron studied the photograph for more than an hour and is convinced that it depicts a genuine extraterrestrial. "Its eyes were extremely large and full of life," writes Ron, "not glass eyes set into some Halloween mask . . . Its skin was light gray and its eyes were quite large and bulged out slightly. Some thin character lines were visible on its forehead and around the corner of the eyes. The area above the eye, where the eyelid is, resembled the surface of an accordion. There was a slight shadow in the cheekbone area, and the mouth was quite thin and small . . . Its head was rather large for its body and was minus hair. The ear was situated much lower than ours, and was no more than a fleshly lump with an opening. The nose was almost nonexistent, but had small nostrils. Its chin was long and broad."

Ron noted other details. The figure was about four feet tall. It had four long slender fingers on its hand. The expression on its face was pleasant and nonthreatening. Also interesting was its tight-fitting garment. Says Ron: "Its texture looked at though it had thousands of minute wrinkles throughout the surface, and no buttons, clamps or zippers could be seen."

Ron was impressed by the photo and asked Sam if he could borrow it and make copies. Sam refused saying, "I'm afraid I've taken a picture of something I shouldn't have." He asked Ron what he should do.

Ron advised against contacting any authorities, but suggested that a UFO research organization might be helpful. Afraid of publicity or attention, Sam said only that he would think about it. He gave permission to Ron to talk about the case, as long as Sam remained anonymous.

While Ron contacted UFO investigators, Sam told his brother about the photo. Sam's brother also urged Sam to go public, saying that they could make money from the photograph. Unfortunately, Sam has so far declined to go public and the photograph has not been released.

Writes Ron, "I'd like to know how the general public, and the government will react to seeing this remarkable picture. I saw it, and the alien is real."[95]

Underground Base in Sedona?

On May 7, 1993, a group of about ten people were hiking in the Schnebly Hill area of Sedona around dusk when they saw two helicopters hovering next to a rock formation. A small crowd had gathered to watch when the rock face disappeared to reveal a cave. Instantly several lighted objects shot out of the cave, flew erratically, and were gone. The cave closed up and the helicopters hovered for a few minutes and then departed. Says one of the witnesses, who reported her sighting to NUFORC: "I still don't know exactly what we all saw, but it was definitely something that we had never before imagined or could deny."[96]

Multiple Landings

Throughout the late 1980s and early 1990s, the Pima County Sheriff's Department received an average of one or two calls every month reporting

UFOs. Several of these reports were investigated by Sergeant Ron Benson. "When I was out in the field checking these out," says Benson, "it seemed most of them dealt with landings on the western end of the Santa Catalina Mountains." Benson said that their reports usually increased during the summer months. Unfortunately, Benson has never located any of the landings sites or seen a UFO but says: "I'd sure like to."[97]

A Pterodactyl?

As bizarre as it might sound, there is a growing database involving people who have seen unbelievable creatures flying around in our skies. In this next case, a lady in Paradise Valley saw what she says was a flying reptile.

On the evening of May 10, 1993, Shelly (pseudonym) stood on the balcony of a friend's home overlooking the lights of Phoenix. There was no wind. Suddenly, movement from the corner of her eye drew her attention to something gliding overhead about 100 feet high. At first she could only see a silhouette of a strange shape. *A mylar balloon*, she thought, and wondering what kind it was, she fixed her gaze on it.

It moved slowly and steadily closer and was only about 200 feet away when she saw that the balloon was actually a living winged creature. Its skin looked leathery, like rawhide. What appeared to be bones lined the perimeter of its wings, and two chicken-like legs with three toes each dangled down from beneath its body.

Shelly became frightened that the creature would catch her gaze and she turned away. At that moment there was a "great suctioning sound" coming from the road in front of the house. Glancing toward the sound, Shelly saw a car suddenly appear on the street.

Shelly was confused and shocked because she could see down the street for miles in either direction, and no car had been visible before. It was as though it appeared out of nothing. The car continued driving and Shelly looked up toward the flying reptile, but it was gone. Scared and confused, she ran inside the home.

Writes Shelly, "I never thought about reporting this, but I feel I should . . . I know I saw a live being flying out on the horizon not far from me."[98]

Grand Canyon Aliens

Tom Dornan (pseudonym) worked as a line cook at the ritzy El Tovar hotel, a prime tourist spot for people who want to visit the Grand Canyon. Around 10:00 p.m. on November 19, 1993, Tom was off work and went to get something to eat from a vending machine when he saw a strange glow about fifty feet off into the woods. He got his buddy, Luke, (a pure-blooded Navajo) and they took off to investigate.

They tromped into the woods when—about twenty feet away—they saw several strange-looking figures about four or five feet tall. They appeared to be looking for something on the ground. Intrigued, they moved in for a closer look. Says Tom:

> AS WE GOT A LITTLE CLOSER, ONE OF THEM TURNED AROUND AND YOU COULD SEE ITS FACE. HONESTLY, IT DIDN'T LOOK LIKE MOST ALIENS YOU SEE ON TV OR SKETCHES. THEY LOOKED VERY HUMAN.

Tom says that the figure's head and eyes were larger than normal, and it was bald and wore a strange suit, but otherwise looked normal. Says Tom:

> THIS ALL HAPPENED SO FAST. AS SOON AS IT LOOKED OUR WAY, THE OTHER TWO WALKED OFF QUICKLY BEHIND THE TREES. THE ONE JUST STOOD THERE AND LOOKED AT US KIND OF LIKE AN ANIMAL, WAITING TO SEE WHO WOULD MOVE FIRST. IT THEN TURNED AROUND AND WALKED IN THE SAME DIRECTION AS THE OTHER TWO.

Both Tom and Luke stepped backwards and turned to run away. At that moment, the strange glow in the forest went dark and became silent. Both men smelled a strange "dry, sweet, burning" odor, but they never saw any UFO or object. They fled the forest, not stopping until they reached the parking lot.

The next day, he returned to the spot and saw four impressions and a large amount of strange reddish glass beads on the ground. The strange odor still hung in the air.

Tom and Luke shared their experience with a few people, but found that few people believed them. Finally, he reported his case to MUFON, writing, "I just wanted to share my story. If you believe me or not, it does not matter."[99]

Terror in Lake Havasu

"What I went through caused me to pack up my entire home, leave overnight, and move an entire state away," says Marianne Hector (pseudonym). Her ordeal began on April 24, 1994, around dusk. Her daughter, the only other witness, was three years old. They were outside their home in Lake Havasu when an eerie vacuum of silence descended over the area. They looked up and saw an immense object moving slowly over their house only a few hundred feet high. The object had four large glowing domes that appeared to be translucent; she could see "things milling around inside."

The object slowly moved away, leaving nothing but a strange electrical smell. Following the sighting she learned that the security guard at her place of employment reported seeing a UFO on the same night.

About two weeks later, she arrived home to see a strange "dark figure" running out of her house through the back kitchen. Other events occurred that Marianne refuses to talk about as they are too frightening. She continues to experience frightening paranormal incidents. She feels like she's being watched, wakes up in the middle of the night in fear, and other odd events. She has shared her experiences only with her family. "At first I tried to talk about it to others, but after much ridicule, I stopped and kept it to myself."

Still, Marianne was determined to share her encounter in hopes of receiving validation. As she says: "Now, for some reason, my senses are begging me to reach out . . . So, for my own piece of mind, I'll give this one last try . . . I just want to put this thing to bed."[100]

Snake-Like ETs

Jim has had strange alien experiences his whole life, but events came to a dramatic turn in 1995 while driving east along Interstate 10 late at night. He was about 100 miles into the state, out in the middle of a desert area filled with high mesas. Without warning he felt an "overwhelming influence" to pull over and look at one particular mesa. Unable to resist, he got out of his car and looked over at the mesa to see strange lights circling it.

He felt himself falling into an odd waking trance. Images of snake-like beings swum before him and he began to hear them communicating with him. They showed him that they had a large mothership hidden in the mesa and that they had been there for a very long time.

At some point Jim woke from his trance and left the area. Ten years after this experience, in 2006, Jim moved to Phoenix. He felt another overwhelming impulse to go visit the same mesa. Says Jim: "This turned into a several months camping trip."

He still felt compelled to stay and his patience was rewarded when one night the snake-like beings returned. Jim saw four glowing saucer-shaped objects that hovered nearby, moving closer and closer.

As before, he felt the snake-like ETs begin to communicate telepathically. They told him that they knew who he was and about his prior contacts with them. They told him that they wanted to show him something, and they began to guide him to another location. Says Jim: "Though they made hiss-like sounds I could not understand, I could understand most of what they said."

Jim hiked through the desert for most of the night following their guidance when finally he came upon a group of cows that had somehow escaped their pen and were wandering free.

Then one of the UFOs that had remained back at his camp zipped upward and immediately descended over the cow. A yellow-orange and blue glow came over the cow, which shook, mooed once and fell over. Says Jim:

OTHER ALIENS CAME UP TO IT . . . THEY USED STRANGE LIGHT DEVICES ON IT. SOMEHOW IT WAS CUT OPEN. I ASKED IF THEY WERE GOING TO EAT THE COW. THEY SAID THEY WERE RECOVERING SOMETHING THAT HAD BEEN GROWING IN THE COW, THAT THEY HAD IMPLANTED THERE SOMETIME BACK.

Jim asked what they were growing in the cows, but was unable to understand their answer, or perhaps, he thinks, they didn't want to tell him. He had the impression that it had something to do with "strange, new diseases to affect most humans in odd new ways." Says Jim:

I SUSPECT THEY TRIED (AND MOSTLY DID) TO KEEP THE FULL MATTER FROM ME . . . THAT WAS ONE OF MANY TIMES SINCE I WAS A SMALL CHILD THAT I HAVE HAD ENCOUNTERS. I HAVE SEEN MUCH MORE HORRIBLE THINGS FROM THESE ALIENS THAN KILLING AND CUTTING UP A COW.

Jim reported his encounter to MUFON, saying that what he had shared was only a small portion of what he had actually experienced.[101]

Tucson Bedroom Visitation

"In November of 1996, one of my roommates and I experienced an encounter," writes Elizabeth Wall of Tucson. "For a month, I would see these dancing lights just outside. I would be compelled to go, or look outside. Also I would feel like I was being watched. I would be watching TV and feel a presence, but when I turned around I didn't see anything."

The feeling became so pronounced that Elizabeth began to sleep with the bedroom lights on. One night she went to bed around 3:00 a.m. She woke to find the room filled with a whitish-bluish light. She tried to move and discovered that she was being held in place. Then, says Elizabeth: "I saw this tall hooded figure walk across the window in my room! I couldn't move and I was frightened."

Strangely, Elizabeth found herself becoming inexplicably calm. Moments later, she fell unconscious. Her next memory was waking up in the morning and wondering what had happened.

She told her roommate and discovered that he had the same experience on the same night. Says Elizabeth: "He woke up frightened and on the floor. The room was filled the whitish-bluish light and a tall hooded figure was hovering above him. He was scared out of his mind and was wondering what the heck is going on."

Thankfully that was the only encounter reported by the witnesses, though Elizabeth admits that as a child she had seen similar unexplained lights. "But I don't want to encounter what my roommate and I encountered again," she added.[102]

Landing in Globe

On July 15, 1998, Vilus Stalte (age 66) was hunting for geodes in the Tonto National Park outside Globe when he saw a metallic disk hovering low in the sky. The disk quietly descended and landed nearby. Next it emitted a beam of light, which struck a rock wall. Some moments later, the disk departed and Vilus went to examine the landing site. Once there, he found a circular impression about fifteen feet in diameter, though the craft itself appeared much larger. The rock wall also appeared to have scorch marks on it.

Vilus was amazed and it reminded him of an incident that occurred in 1942 when he was a young boy living in Latvia. He was outside when he saw a torpedo-like object about twenty-five feet above him. He ran towards it and it slowed down just enough for him to keep pace with it. He ran along with it for a short distance, then—running out of breath—he slowed to a walk, at which point the craft made a high-pitched noise and accelerated off into the distance.[103]

UFO Dreams

As investigated by MUFON field investigator Jim Kelly, on June 28, 1998, at around 10:00 p.m., a family of three was driving through North Scottsdale when the wife, "L," had a feeling to look up and immediately observed a large diamond-shaped object traveling over their car about 1,000 feet high.

They stopped and exited the car to watch. "L" reports that the object was convex underneath and had a green light on each corner of the diamond. They watched the object—which was totally silent—rotate and then move toward the McDowell Mountains. They chased it as it sped away, slowly rising in altitude the farther it went.

The husband, "D" (a former air force encryption specialist), agreed with his wife's observations but added that the convex bottom of the craft appeared to have intersecting lines from each diamond point moving toward the center. He said that all three of them felt like they had seen something "special."

But their encounter wasn't over yet. That evening, after returning home, both the father and his daughter dreamed that the UFO they had seen came to visit them, hovering over their house.[104]

UFO Exits Cave

On March 5, 1999, a gentleman was driving along Interstate 10 near Marana when he saw a fireball-like object shoot out of cave located on a mountain south of the freeway. Says the witness:

IT TURNED SOUTH AND FLEW OVER KITT PEAK OBSERVATORY. IT CAME BACK AND CIRCLED THE MOUNTAIN ABOUT FIFTY TIMES, AND THEN DISAPPEARED TO THE NORTH. APPROXIMATELY FIFTEEN MINUTES LATER IT REAPPEARED AGAIN, CIRCLING THE MOUNTAIN. I JUST SAT IN THE BACK OF MY PICKUP, PULLED OFF THE FREEWAY AND DRANK A FEW BEERS WHILE THIS THING KEPT BUZZING AROUND. FINALLY AFTER AN HOUR OR SO, IT SHOT STRAIGHT UP AND THEN FLEW BACK INTO THE CAVE. I NEVER SAW IT AGAIN.[105]

Strawberry Landing

On the evening of October 15, 2000, a civil engineer with six years in the air force, and his father-in-law (a general contractor) and brother-in-law, were hunting in Fossil Creek Canyon outside Strawberry when they came upon a strange craft landed on an inaccessible portion of a mountainside about a mile away. Says the engineer: "It was disk-shaped and on the ground. It had lights on top and a doorway that was open to the ground. [There were] windows and movement on the surrounding shrubbery and grass."

The witnesses also saw what appeared to be steps coming from the doorway. The object rested on "legs" that came out from underneath.

They were able to view the object through the scope on their deer rifle. This area is the location of the Childs Electrical Power Station, which was experiencing a wave of sightings. The father-in-law spoke with an employee at the power plant who said that this was a "regular occurrence." On one occasion the worker was driving near the power plant when a craft flew overhead, causing his car engine to fail and his watch to stop.[106]

A Flying Humanoid

After midnight on June 20, 2001, a high school student and his mother sat on the porch of their Tucson home watching the stars. The student was thinking about what it would be like to see a UFO and aliens when his mother pointed to something floating just above the trees. The student looked and saw a humanoid figure with dark skin. It was the alien he had just made a wish to see! Says the student:

THE ALIEN SEEMED LIKE IT KNEW WE WERE LOOKING AT IT AND STARTED FLOATING IN SMALL CIRCLES IN THE AIR. I FELT LIKE THE ALIEN HAD MADE EYE CONTACT WITH ME FROM THIS DISTANCE. AS SOON AS I BLINKED, THE CREATURE DISAPPEARED OUT OF THE SKY.

The student never saw any UFO. He reports that following the sighting, his life changed "in a lot of different ways." He insists that "this is a real event."[107]

Aliens in the Window

In 2001, Alice (pseudonym) and her husband, who had recently retired, were moving to a forty-acre lot east of Yucca, twenty-five miles deep in the desert where they had set up a mobile home. On the evening of September 2, Alice exited her home to see something very strange. "Up above me to the east," says Alice, "was what appeared to be a large window with two beings in it, facing each other as [if] in conversation. The area around it was totally dark. The person (?) on the right was either taller or standing and facing the one on the left, who was either shorter or seated."

Alice was trying to determine what exactly she was looking at when her husband came out of the house with a flashlight. Instantly, the window blinked out and was gone. She screamed at him to turn off the flashlight, but all trace of the strange beings was gone. Alice estimates that she stared at the weird beings for about thirty seconds. Says Alice: "But I know what I saw. Has anything like this been reported before?"[108]

An Alien in the Forest

On July 28, 2002, at around 3:10 a.m., a man was in a wooded area in Sedona looking at some odd white light making oval patterns in the sky. Shortly later, he saw a strange glowing figure with black eyes standing among the trees. The figure wore a black strip diagonally across its body. Says the witness: "Both of us stood there about twenty seconds. I feel crazy sending this in—but I still see a vivid picture of this 'person' every day."[109]

Quartzite Landing

"I am not nuts, and not a drunk or a druggie." So says the anonymous gentleman who (on October 4, 2002) was driving home on Interstate 10 traveling west from Phoenix to Quartzite. "I noticed this triangular shape of lights gently take off from the desert floor. It had big lights on each tip, forming a triangle. I pulled off the highway and it just took off over the highway, not making any noise . . . It went over me at about 100 mph, flew to my right, and went about a quarter-mile past me, made a hair-pin turn and flew back over me and landed again." The entire incident lasted about three minutes. The amazed witness reported his sighting to NUFORC two years later.[110]

"It Followed Us"

On March 5, 2003, at around 9:00 p.m., two witnesses were driving through Chino Valley along a dirt road when they came upon a black object sitting on the road (or hovering just above it). Says the witness:

> IT WAS AT LEAST AS BIG AS A SCHOOL BUS, BUT IT DIDN'T SEEM TO BE MADE OF ANYTHING SOLID. IT WAS LIKE A BLACK AND GRAY CLOUD THAT MOVED LIKE AN OCTOPUS. IT CAME AROUND TO THE SIDE OF OUR CAR AND PASSED OVER THE HOOD AND WINDSHIELD ABOUT TEN FEET OFF THE GROUND. IT MADE NO SOUND AT ALL. IT FOLLOWED US FOR ABOUT HALF MILE, AND WE WERE SPOTLIGHTED IN A BRIGHT, WHITE LIGHT THAT MUST HAVE BEEN ABOVE US. THEN IT WAS GONE.[111]

Landing Photographed, Almost

On August 14, 2003, a man and his wife were driving through Sedona taking pictures of the beautiful red rock mesas with their Kodak CX6330. They saw nothing unusual at the time, but upon downloading the images into their computer saw what appeared to be "a small bubble-type craft."

Several days later, the gentleman was talking to a construction worker who was working on his home when the worker saw the photo and asked where it was taken. When he explained to the worker that the photo was taken in Oak Creek in Sedona, the worker said that he and two of his fellow construction workers had a flat tire on that same road and also observed the object, which had actually landed on the mesa pictured in the photograph. He showed the photos to the other men and they all asked for copies, having been disbelieved and ridiculed by their family and friends.[112]

ET in the Thickets

As reported by the aunt of the witness, on July 10, 2004, one week after the Fourth of July holiday, her nephew and two of his friends were blowing up their leftover firecrackers along the local riverbank in Parker. They threw some firecrackers down when suddenly a strange figure jumped out of the thickets. The children said the creature had bright orange skin and large dark eyes. When it saw them it started to approach them. The kids quickly threw some more firecrackers at it, and it retreated back into the thickets.

Then a bright beam of light came down on the boys and they ran home. The light beam continued to shine down on them the entire way and was still over them when they reached the house of one of the friends. Says the aunt:

"Other sightings have been witnessed in this particular area." This was the first case she had heard of an alien on the ground.[113]

Something Not from This World

It was February 2005, and Eric Dosh had worked all day long at the Snow-Bowl Ski resort near Flagstaff. He returned home and, feeling tired, went to bed early, around 10:30 p.m. A few hours later, around 1:30 a.m., he woke up because he sensed someone had just entered his room. "All I really remember," says Eric, "is a person with a rather large head and eyes looking down on me in bed. I tried to move, but wasn't able to. There must have been some sort of force field holding me down."

Eric struggled against the paralysis, moving first his hands and then with great effort, moving his head up. Freaked out and angry, he flipped up his middle finger at the "being." Finally, it went away.

Says Eric: "I know it sounds funny, but this event scared me so bad, I couldn't sleep in my bed for weeks fearing that they would come back."

Eric told his father what happened, but his father laughed and said it must have been "just a dream." Says Eric:

HERE'S WHERE THE STORY TURNS TWISTED ... THREE TO FOUR WEEKS LATER, MY YOUNGER BROTHER, DEVIN, HAD THE EXACT SAME THING HAPPEN TO HIM IN HIS ROOM. I NOTICED HE WASN'T SLEEPING IN HIS ROOM FOR A WHILE, SO I ASKED HIM WHAT WAS GOING ON. HE TOLD ME THAT HE HAD AN ENCOUNTER WITH SOMETHING NOT FROM THIS WORLD IN HIS ROOM THE NIGHT BEFORE. HE THEN EXPLAINED TO ME EXACTLY TO DETAIL WHAT HAD HAPPENED TO ME A MONTH OR SO PRIOR TO HIM.[114]

A Tucson Visitation

One March day in 2007, a woman, her husband, and son were watching a spring training baseball game in Tucson. Immediately adjacent to the game, Davis-Monthan Air Force Base was having an air show. Looking up, the woman was surprised to see a metallic disk hovering overhead as if watching the air show. "I see you," she said and impulsively sent a thought to the disk. She immediately turned to her husband and son and pointed out the object. All three of them watched it for several minutes when it suddenly disappeared. Strangely, nobody else seemed to notice it.

They watched the rest of the game and returned home. That evening, says the woman, she was woken up by "a lime green light in my face." The light was rectangular and seemed to contain strange glowing symbols. She looked at her husband, who lay sleeping soundly next to her in bed.

"I then looked slightly to the left at the foot of my bed," says the woman, "and saw that there were three small people standing there."

Feeling unnerved, the woman looked away and wrapped her arms around her husband and fell asleep. She did not see the beings leave.

The next morning, she and her son went to the car and saw a strange handprint with three fingers and a thumb. At that moment they turned to the west and saw a "very, very bright white light."

Says the witness: "I put my arm around my son and led him back into the house." The son then told her that something had woken him up last night. The witness didn't ask her son what he had seen. But she did call her daughter who lived out-of-state to share the story. Her daughter said, "Mom, you aren't going to believe this, but there was a green light in my room for just a fraction of a second."

Several years later, the woman reported her experience to NUFORC, writing, "I do not drink or take drugs, and I'm not crazy. The story you've read is my account of the events that occurred to the best of my recollection."[115]

The Flying Man

When it comes to areas of high UFO activity in Arizona, Sedona and the surrounding areas are at the top of the list. UFOs and other paranormal events seem to occur there on a fairly regular basis.

One of the stranger accounts comes from a lady who lived with her boyfriend in his parents' house in Sedona. Their house overlooked Bell Rock, Courthouse Butte, Lee Mountain, and UFO rock, an area of known UFO activity.

It was a clear and beautiful day on July 12, 2009, and the witness sat in the dining room working on the computer. Movement from outside the window caught her eye. She ignored it at first, but when it continued she finally turned and looked through the slats in the blind. A white object, she saw, was flying back and forth. Says the witness: "I got up and went out to the patio and realized it was a humanoid figure without a powerpack of any sort. It flew from the far left of Lee Mountain and between Courthouse."

At that point, her boyfriend's mom also came out to see what the witness was doing and they watched the figure together. The figure moved with intention in a controlled horizontal path "without sways and dips."

The witness is certain that the figure was "very humanoid." The witnesses kept the experience to themselves, though one of them was inspired enough to report the encounter to MUFON. Says the witness: "I thought it was cool, because I am pretty open to the possibility of what there is for us to learn about other life forms within our Earth and outer-space."[116]

The UFO House

Around 9:45 p.m. one December evening in 2012, a lady and her husband stepped outside their home before bedtime to look at the stars. Instead, their attention was drawn to a field nearby their house. Says the witness:

> WE WERE ONLY OUT THERE ABOUT A MINUTE BEFORE WE NOTICED WHAT
> APPEARED TO US TO BE A SINGLE UNIT MOBILE HOME OR RECTANGULAR-
> SHAPED HOUSE IN THE FIELD ACROSS THE STREET. THIS FIELD IS TOTALLY
> FENCED IN AND THERE HAS BEEN NOTHING THERE FOR SEVERAL YEARS.

The couple was completely mystified because they hadn't heard or seen anything. It was as if the house had magically shown up. Says the witness:

> THERE APPEARED TO BE A DOOR WITH A WINDOW ON EACH SIDE. LIGHTS
> WERE ON, BUT THE HOUSE/OBJECT APPEARED TO BE EMPTY. WE SAT THERE
> DISCUSSING HOW ODD IT WAS THAT WE NEVER SAW IT BEING MOVED IN,
> OR HOW QUICKLY ELECTRICITY SEEMED TO BE HOOKED UP, BUT SHOOK IT
> OFF AND WENT TO BED.

The next morning, the couple got an incredible shock. The "house" was gone. There was no evidence that it had ever been there. The field was still totally fenced in. Says the witness:

> WE DON'T KNOW FOR SURE WHAT IT WAS, BUT IT WAS VERY, VERY ODD. TO
> THIS DAY EVERY TIME WE DRIVE BY WE ALWAYS LOOK AT THE FENCING TO SEE
> HOW SOMEONE COULD HAVE PULLED IN A TRAILER, AND THERE IS NO WAY.

Two years after the incident—still mystified—the couple reported their case to MUFON. (Case#60151)[117]

Another Pterodactyl?

On the evening of January 19, 2014, two ladies were returning from a weekend rock-climbing trip and were driving west along Interstate 40 near Kingman. It was shortly after sunset, near the intersection of Interstates 40 and 93 when the two ladies saw something unbelievable.

Says the witness: "My first impression was that it could have been a large bird of prey, but I know of no native North American birds that would have as much surface area as this did. It followed an upward diagonal trajectory, and appeared to be featherless and tailed."

It was only in view for a few seconds, and disbelieving her own eyes, she turned to her partner and asked, "Did you see that?"

Her friend responded, "You saw that too?"

Says the witness: "She also described a featherless, grey-skinned pterodactyl-like creature with a very long tail flying quickly upwards."

The witness reported her sighting to MUFON, stating that neither of them was under the influence of drugs or alcohol.[118]

Another Flying Humanoid

On May 21, 2014, at around 7:30 p.m., a man was having dinner with his wife and seventeen-year-old daughter. Looking outside, they saw "what we thought was a flying humanoid pass by our sliding glass door window. My daughter stated that out of the corner of her eye she saw a brown mass swoop past the window, but did not see any detail."

The daughter noticed only that the "mass" was big enough to completely cover the window. The father says that he saw the figure in more detail including "a pair of legs swooping down through the sprinklers heading in a westerly direction."

His wife, however, sat directly facing the sliding glass door, and she got the best view. Says the father:

[SHE SAW] A HUMAN FIGURE ALSO SWOOPING TOWARD THE GROUND AND HEADING IN A WEST DIRECTION. SHE SAID IT WAS DARK BROWN AND LOOKED AS IF THE PERSON WAS LYING FACING DOWN WITH THEIR ARMS TO THE SIDE.

The father ran outside to look for the flying humanoid, but it was gone.[119]

Chapter Five

Onboard Experiences

Onboard UFO experiences are perhaps the most controversial area of UFO research. It is one thing to see a UFO in the sky or on the ground, but it is quite another to be taken inside. And yet thousands of people believe they have been abducted by aliens, and there are strong indications that the experience is much more common that most people believe. According to a survey taken by the Roper Organization in 1991, one in fifty people show the markers common to alien abductions. Some of these markers include: a close-up UFO sighting, missing time, unexplained scars/marks, and more. If true, there are millions of people who have been inside UFOs.

Whatever the case, onboard cases cannot be ignored. In fact, they have the potential to impart more information than perhaps any other type of UFO experience. In these cases, people are able to actually interact with the ETs, sometimes even having long conversations.

The nearly fifty onboard cases that follow represent only a fraction of the actual number of cases.

"I Floated through the Ceiling"

One night in 1952, a little girl who lived with her parents in Tucson awoke to see a white beam of light shining down at a slanted angle through the ceiling. She gripped her doll as the beam of light struck her. Says the witness: "I floated up the bright white light through the ceiling." She doesn't remember anything after that, but states that the event has never left her memory, and that following that incident she had other encounters. She also pointed out that their home in Tucson was located along the perimeter of the original west fence of Davis-Monthan Air Force Base.[120]

"Although this happened many years ago, I am just now able to talk about it. I struggled for years as to whether this was an actual event or just some sort of hallucination." So writes a young man of an experience that occurred outside Phoenix. At the time, the man was a guitarist in a small band that was touring the country playing music. The year was 1968. They had finished their gig in Phoenix and were hanging out in their van around 3:00 a.m. smoking marijuana when one of them noticed a bright light approaching them from the distance. Assuming it was the cops, they stashed their drugs and waited. Says the witness: "Well, it didn't take long before we realized it was not a cop car, but something we could not explain."

Everybody in the group began to panic as they realized that they weren't hallucinating, and it wasn't the police. Instead, it was something they were not prepared for. Says the witness:

> I WASN'T THE ONLY ONE THAT SAW THIS THING. SOME OF US STARTED GIGGLING UNCONTROLLABLY. I WET MYSELF, AND OUR SOUND GUY FAINTED. NEXT THING I KNOW I AM IN A ROOM LAYING ON A TABLE LOOKING UP AT SOME VERY BRIGHT LIGHTS. NOT COOL . . . I WAS FREAKING OUT. THEN THINGS STARTED TO GET WEIRD.
>
> TWO SKINNY PALE DUDES WITH BIG EYES—I CAN'T TALK ABOUT WHAT ALL THEY DID. I THINK I BLOCKED IT OUT TO KEEP MY SANITY. HOWEVER, I HAD A SOUR STOMACH FOR A COUPLE OF WEEKS AFTERWARDS, DIFFICULTY URINATING, KIND OF A CRUEL PREVIEW OF HOW THINGS ARE FOR ME AT AGE SIXTY.
>
> I DON'T REMEMBER BEING RETURNED TO THE VAN, BUT WE ALL WOKE UP IN THE VAN NAKED, WHICH IN ITSELF WAS QUITE TRAUMATIC. SEVERAL HOURS HAD PASSED, BUT NONE OF US COULD CLEARLY RECALL WHAT HAPPENED. NONE OF US EVER TALKED ABOUT WHAT HAPPENED THAT NIGHT; IT WAS TOO WEIRD AND STRANGE, EVEN FOR THE '60S. I KNOW THIS ALL SOUNDS CRAZY, BUT IT REALLY DID HAPPEN.

In desperation, the witness reported his experience to NUFORC, writing, "What can I do to get some help? I still have night terrors, flashbacks, and more from this incident. I found your site using Google. I have nowhere else to turn. Thank you for listening."[121]

The Contacts of Paul Solem

Throughout the 1960s, numerous figures such as George Adamski, Truman Betherum, Daniel Fry, and others claimed to have made contact with friendly human-like extraterrestrials. Lesser-known among these contactees is Paul Solem.

In June of 1948, Solem, his wife, and brother-in-law observed three unexplained glowing objects over his ranch in Howe, Idaho. Solem says that he heard a mental message saying, "We are from another planet. You shall hear from us again."

Four years later in the fall of 1952, Solem saw another UFO over his ranch and followed it until it landed. There he encountered a man with long blond hair wearing a white uniform who told him that he was from Venus and that future disasters would soon strike the Earth.

Eighteen years later, on August 7, 1970, Solem appeared in Prescott, Arizona, where he attempted to prove the reality of his contacts by calling down a UFO in the presence of witnesses, including Joe Kraus, editor of the Prescott *Courier.*

Solem stood outside for about fifteen minutes mentally calling out to the ETs and then said, "They're here. I can't see them yet, but they're here."

Moments later one object appeared. Says Kraus: "It rose in the sky, stopped, hovered, wavered to one side, and then continued across the sky, repeating the maneuvers." The object stayed in view the entire time Solem spoke, but as soon as he stopped, it disappeared.

Numerous other witnesses in the area also reported UFOs. Baptist minister Reverend John Foster saw "an erratic pulsing light." Others also reported what was apparently the same object, which they said zigzagged overhead. Among the witnesses was Chuck Roberts, the photographer for the *Courier* who was able to take a photo of the object.

Another witness was Irene Wood, who described the object as "a huge, brilliant mass of light." She watched it move overhead, turn to the east, stop, and split into two sections. One remained hovering while the other went downward and disappeared behind the hills. Wood returned to her home and watched another red glowing object disgorge six smaller objects."

The cluster of sightings seemed to confirm that Solem was truly in contact with UFOs. Two nights later, on August 9, 1970, more than a hundred people gathered to watch Solem call down UFOs, which promptly appeared for the stunned witnesses.

The next day, on August 10, 1970, he called down UFOs again, this time in the presence of 108-year-old Chief Dan Katchongva, Hopi elder and chief of the Sun Clan.

Katchongva observed the object as did several other witnesses. Among them was Nonnie Skidmore: "The craft came in a rolling motion like a moon and was about 500 to 800 feet off the ground."

Apache Indian Alvis Smith and Pima Indian Joe Manuel also stepped forward claiming to have seen the object.

Following this, Solem tried to call down UFOs the following year, but nothing materialized and like many other contactees, Solem's story faded away into history.[122]

The Abductions of Brian Allan Scott

Born on October 12, 1943, in Philadelphia, Pennsylvania, Brian Allan Scott had several strange experiences that would hint at even stranger events to come. At age sixteen, for example, he was walking outside when a small orange ball of light descended from the sky and hovered right next to him, only to dart instantly back upward. The mysterious ball of light returned several times, on one occasion even going inside the house.

But Scott's alien experiences didn't begin in earnest until he moved to Arizona. The first occurred on March 14, 1971, outside Apache Junction. Scott was twenty-eight years old and had gone out into the wilderness of the Superstition Mountains to go target shooting with his friend, Nick Corbin. Scott was standing outside the car when he saw a large glowing oval-shaped object hovering overhead. Immediately the object moved toward him.

Scott wanted to run to the car but instead found himself rising into the air. He looked up and saw a door open in the bottom of the craft. He was pulled up inside it and set down inside a corridor. The interior was warm, musty, and brightly lit with a strange foggy light.

Then Scott saw his friend Nick being pulled through the door and deposited beside him. Both men felt numb and unable to speak. Two seven-and-a-half-foot-tall gray-skinned figures came through another doorway and began to undress the men. Corbin became frightened, and tried to resist. He passed out and was taken out of Scott's view.

Scott felt a little fear but was unable to resist as the creature led him to another room where there was another figure. The second figure was manipulating a strange alien instrument which emitted a beam of light, striking Scott's body. The light numbed Scott and gave him a headache.

Next an even taller creature entered the room and placed its hand on Scott's head, and then proceeded to communicate. The alien said its name was Voltar, and it showed Scott images of its home planet, which had been destroyed by a mutated virus.

Scott and his friend Nick were then put back in the corridor where they had first arrived and then floated down gently to the ground. The object darted away and Scott and Nick returned to their car. It was now past 11:00 p.m.; they had been gone for two hours.

At this point, Scott could consciously remember everything that happened. But as they got in the car and drove away, his memory instantly faded. By the time he arrived home, he recalled only that he had seen a strange craft in the sky and was somehow missing two hours of time.

Two years later on March 22, 1973, Scott returned to the site of the missing time event where he saw a small humanoid entity. He fled the scene.

Following this, he experienced a series of abductions, on October 25, 1973, November 21, 1975, and December 22, 1975, during which he was missing for a full twenty-seven hours.

By this time, Scott realized he needed help. His case was researched in depth by APRO, CUFOS, and MUFON. He went under regressive hypnosis and was able to recall what had happened during his first abduction.

Scott also began to fall into trances during which he would make strange drawings or channel alleged alien entities. At the same time, numerous small balls of light were often seen around Scott, a fact verified by his ex-wife and several investigators. He also began to exhibit the ability of bending metal. It usually happened when he lapsed into a trance. There were other strange phenomena surrounding Scott including water drops materializing over his head, or the materialization of an ancient Greek gold coin whose authenticity was later confirmed by numismatists.

Researcher Bill Hamilton personally interviewed Scott and saw him perform spoon-bending. He also sat in on channeling sessions. Scott's voice was recorded during channeling and electronic analysis showed that it was different from Scott's voice. The information given during these sessions typically involved very deep subjects such as binary and trinary computer mathematics, genetics and cloning, orbital mechanics and astronomy, electromagnetics, quantum physics, and more.[123]

Roberta's Encounters

One evening in 1973, Roberta T. was on the patio of her home in Phoenix when she saw a star-like object drop from the sky. In seconds it revealed itself to be a large spherical object, and it now hovered behind some trees near her home. An opening appeared in the side, like a "garage door opening," said Roberta. The opening was brightly lit and, to Roberta's surprise, a human-like figure appeared.

Roberta shouted out, at which point the figure turned, leaned out of the opening, and looked directly at her. According to Roberta, he was tall, wore a tight fitting garment, and had a large head.

A second UFO appeared, making a humming noise. She saw it approach and then it disappeared. She turned back to the other object, and it too was gone. At this point her conscious memory stops, and she recalls waking up on the patio in a different position.

She later underwent hypnosis, and the full story emerged. The tall creature had approached her on the patio, told her not to be afraid, and that she was going to be "taken somewhere." She was floated up into the sky. At the same time, she saw a dog that had been barking constantly also being floated upward. She suddenly found herself in a dark "enclosed" place. She felt (but couldn't see) an uncomfortable instrument of some kind being placed on her head. She heard figures talking to each other in a strange language. That was all she recalled. By the time she woke up on her patio, at least four hours had passed.[124]

The Chesser Encounter

One evening in October 1973, Ernest Chesser was camping with his family near Mesa when he was contacted by Nordic-type ETs. He was taken onboard their craft and given a physical examination. Gray-type ETs were also present, but seemed to cooperate with the Nordics. Chesser then allegedly communicated with a female Nordic and had sexual relations with her.[125]

The Abduction of John Williams

On December 4, 1975, John Williams says that two human-looking ETs visited his leather shop. He was physically examined and then later had sex with the female alien, who told him that they needed to replenish their genes by cross-breeding.[126]

The Abduction of Frank Ramsey

One day in April 1976, Frank Ramsey was visiting a ranch near Loy Butte in Sedona. After taking pictures of the sunset, he was walking around in the dark when the ground around him lit up like daylight. Says Ramsey: "I looked above me and there was a bright white sphere, probably thirty to forty feet off the ground."

Ramsey ducked out of the beam and quickly scrambled for his camera. At that moment, the object blinked out and reappeared miles away. Then it returned, only to blink away again. It moved back and forth several times, causing Ramsey to make a dash back to the ranch. He was almost there when he saw a figure standing on the hillside waving a light at him. Thinking it was his friends, he turned on his flashlight and moved toward the figure.

At that point, he saw his friends driving up on the road to the ranch. Puzzled, he turned back to the figure, which was now about a hundred feet away. He saw now that the figure stood next to a bright white sphere. A door to the sphere was open and inside he could see a muted light. The figure itself also appeared to glow.

Realizing then that he was viewing the landed object, he turned to run away but found himself immobile. There was a strange shift and the object and figure was gone and Ramsey found himself standing, with his camera, in a completely different location. He knew the ranch well, but it took him awhile to realize that he was now at least a mile and a half from where he had seen the figure.

It took him a couple of hours to make his way back. Meanwhile, he had flashes of recall. Says Ramsey: "I have a memory of being inside that sphere. I remember looking out of a porthole-type window and I remember seeing stars outside of it."

In the weeks and months following the incident, Ramsey also recalled the appearance of the ETs, which he described as short, with large hairless heads, large almond-shaped eyes, and no visible ears.[127]

The Abduction of Travis Walton

On November 5, 1975, a group of seven young men, all woodcutters, worked in the Apache-Sitgreaves National Forest in the Mongollon Rim area, not far from the town of Snowflake. They had spent most of the day thinning trees and, around 7:00 p.m., began the long drive home. At 7:15, all their lives changed forever when they came upon a large glowing object that hovered alongside the dirt road.

At first they saw only a light shining through the trees. But as they crested a small hill, the object was to their right, less than a hundred feet away, and well below tree level. Mike Rogers, who was driving, stopped the truck.

The seven men stared in wonder at a cleanly structured craft with glowing panels of light. Almost immediately, Travis Walton, who sat in the front seat next to the door, quickly exited the vehicle and began to walk toward the saucer. In a few moments, he stood almost directly beneath it. The other men screamed for him to get back in the truck.

Travis turned to retreat when suddenly the saucer made a high-pitched sound and began to rise. He instantly felt a powerful jolt and fell unconscious.

Back in the truck, the men couldn't believe their eyes. As Travis stood up, a blazing beam of white light shot from the craft and struck him on the chest, sending him flying backwards to the ground.

Some of the men were now hysterical and panicking, and they screamed at Rogers to start the truck and get out of there. After a few seconds, Rogers complied. Fearing for their lives, the men took off down the road and left Travis lying beneath the UFO.

A few minutes later, Rogers pulled the truck over and the men began to talk excitedly about what had just happened. All of them were terrified and a few were weeping. None were sure if Travis was alive or dead. They knew that they had to return and look for Travis, but all of them were frightened to go back.

As they tried to process the situation, movement back at the sighting location caught Rogers' eye. Turning his head, he caught a brief glimpse of the object as it rose up from the trees and darted away at super high speed. He shouted out, but none of the other men saw it.

Meanwhile, back in Snowflake, residents were reporting some unusual electromagnetic disturbances. MUFON field investigator Willard D. Nelson later interviewed a witness who—near the time of Walton's encounter—became annoyed by problems with the television. Says the lady:

I REMEMBER IT BECAUSE IT MADE ME MAD. I WAS TRYING TO WATCH THE SIX O'CLOCK NEWS AND THE PICTURE WENT OUT FOR ABOUT TWENTY MINUTES, RIGHT AFTER 6:15. AT FIRST WE THOUGHT THE POWER HAD GONE OFF, BUT WE CHECKED THAT. A LADY IN HEBER LATER TOLD ME THAT SHE LOST THE PICTURE TOO, AND THEY HAD A DIFFERENT POWER COMPANY, SO IT WASN'T A POWER OUTAGE.

When the Walton story broke into the news, both witnesses realized their television disturbances had occurred on the same night. Nelson discovered that the timing fit perfectly. And learning that law enforcement agencies are required by the FCC to maintain records of communication interruptions, he contacted three local sheriff's departments and police stations. Unfortunately, five years had passed and the records had been destroyed.

Meanwhile, back at the abduction site, the six remaining woodcutters turned the truck around and returned together to the sighting location. Both Walton and the UFO were gone. It appeared that the UFO had taken their co-worker. After searching for Walton and calling his name, they knew that they had to go to the police and tell them what happened. Walton was missing and had apparently been taken by the UFO.

They told their stories to deputies Ellison and Flake, Sheriff Gillespie, and under-sheriff Coplan. The police insisted on returning to the site with the men. Some were afraid to go. The police insisted that some of the men had to return, so Allen Dalis, Kenneth Peterson, and Mike Rogers agreed, while Dwayne Smith, Steve Pierce, and John Goulette stayed behind.

Back at the site, they searched again for any sign of Walton, but couldn't find any. William Spaulding of Ground Saucer Watch says that the magnetic readings at the site were several times higher than normal. Other than that, there was no evidence of anything unusual.

The authorities were baffled. The men were clearly sincere and obviously emotionally upset. But had Walton truly been abducted? Could this be a hoax? Maybe the men had accidentally killed Walton, or maybe murdered him? Sheriff Gillespie knew he was in for one of the strangest investigations of his career.

Walton's family was immediately notified of his disappearance. While the family gathered together and tried to deal with the shocking news, a massive manhunt began the next day as dozens of people combed the site looking for Walton.

As the search was in progress, the woodcutters were asked to take lie detector tests. The men agreed, and each of them easily passed except for one who was too emotionally upset by Walton's disappearance to take an accurate test. Cy Gilson, who performed the original polygraph tests on all the witnesses, said: "I think they did see something they believed was a UFO. I gotta say they passed the test."

Around this time the media heard about the strange case of the missing woodcutter and the small town of Snowflake was besieged. Reporters, UFO organizations, and curiosity-seekers descended on the town and scrambled to speak with the witnesses and Walton's family.

While the search for Walton continued, the police continued to investigate. They were unable to find any evidence of hoaxing or foul-play whatsoever. In fact, a few of the authorities had seen UFOs themselves in the past, as had other people in the area. None of them felt that the men were lying. Sheriff Chuck Ellison said: "One of the men was weeping. If they were lying, they were damned good actors."

It appeared then that the men were telling the truth. Walton had been abducted inside a UFO. For all anyone knew, he was never coming back. The Walton family, however, still held out hope. None were ready to accept the possibility that Travis might be dead.

Meanwhile, the last thing Travis Walton remembered was seeing the object above him and then being knocked unconscious. He woke up lying on his back, while a rectangular light shone from above. He was in intense pain, disoriented, and struggling for consciousness. As he opened his eyes, he saw white faces above him and felt the figures fussing with his clothes.

His memory came rushing back: He had been under the UFO. He must have gotten hurt and now he was in a hospital. He tried to focus and saw a strange device on his chest.

Then he looked up and got a terrible shock. The people that he first thought were doctors were actually alien-looking figures. There were three of them, each about five feet tall, with large over-sized bald heads, and "luminous brown eyes the size of quarters." Each wore a featureless orange jumpsuit.

Walton panicked, jumped up from the table, and pushed the closest figure away from him. He looked around for a weapon and saw several small items on a metal bench attached to one of the walls. He picked up a clear glass-like tube and swung it at the figures, each of who quickly exited the room.

A few moments later, Walton exited the room and turned the other direction. He walked down a curving metal-gray corridor and came upon another room to his right. A smallish chair with weird controls and screens on the armrests stood in the center. Walton walked in and to his surprise, the walls became transparent and he saw a vast field of stars. He moved over to the chair and pressed one of the levers. When the stars began to move, he quickly let go and decided not to mess with it. Instead, he searched the room for a door, hoping he could open it and escape from the craft.

Within moments he saw a male human-looking figure appear at the doorway. He was tall, muscular, good-looking with golden-hazel eyes, and brown hair. He wore a tight-fitting blue suit and a transparent helmet over his entire head.

Walton assumed the man was from Earth and bombarded him with questions. The strange man ignored Walton's questions and instead grabbed his arm and led him out of the room, down the corridor, into a smaller elevator-like room, and then outside of the craft. Still holding Walton, they walked into what appeared to be a massive UFO hangar holding two or three other craft. Walton realized with wonder that although he had escaped the alien craft, he was now inside a giant mothership.

The man led Walton across the hangar to another room where there were two men and a woman who had the same general appearance as the first man—each wearing the same blue suits, minus the helmets. None spoke but instead they maneuvered Walton onto a table in the center of the room and placed some type of mask over his face.

Walton blacked out. When he woke up, he saw that he was lying alongside a highway. Above him a smaller craft was quickly lifting away. He stood up and recognized the area. He was more than twenty miles away from where he had been originally abducted. He ran down the highway to where he knew there was a group of three phone booths. Finally, he arrived at his destination and called his stunned family, telling them where he was, and could they please come and get him?

On the night of Walton's reappearance, a lady was driving through the area and saw something startling. As she says:

I WAS TRAVELING BACK FROM LAS VEGAS WITH TWO FRIENDS AROUND MIDNIGHT, TWELVE MILES FROM WINSLOW, HEADING EAST. A TRUCK DRIVER AHEAD WAS STOPPED ON THE HIGHWAY, AND THERE WAS A BLUISH GLOW EVERYWHERE IN THE DESERT. AT THAT TIME, I STOPPED AND A HUGE BLUE FIREBALL WAS DESCENDING ACROSS THE HIGHWAY, ABOUT ONE MILE AHEAD OF MY CAR.

The object moved downward at a slow controlled speed and went behind a desert mesa. Then everything went black, though there was no evidence of any crash or explosion. Wondering if they had seen a UFO, they drove on to Albuquerque only to learn a week later that Travis Walton had reappeared on the same night of their sighting and in the same general location. Says the witness: "Did I see the ship that dropped him off?"

While Walton's disappearance had sent shock waves throughout the community and beyond, it was nothing compared to his miraculous return. Walton's reappearance hit Snowflake like an atom bomb.

At first the Walton family told nobody of his return, not even the police.

Walton was in no condition to talk to anyone. He had just learned that he had been missing for five days, and the memory of his frightening encounter was still causing him intense emotional distress. Fearing publicity, they rushed him out of town to visit a doctor in Tucson. Only then did they call the police.

Soon the story was leaked that Walton had been returned. Both the police and the Walton family found themselves the center of attention. Calls came from every major city in the United States and some from other countries.

After being examined, Walton was found to be in good health, though he had lost ten pounds. He then told his story to the police. Walton was asked to take a lie detector test, which he agreed to and passed. Psychiatrist Gene Rosenbaum examined Walton one day after the event. Says Rosenbaum:

THIS YOUNG MAN IS NOT LYING. THERE IS NO COLLUSION INVOLVED, NO ATTEMPT TO HOAX. AND THERE IS NO EVIDENCE OF DRUGS IN THIS ISSUE . . . HE REALLY BELIEVES THESE THINGS.

Meanwhile, two UFO groups, APRO and Ground Saucer Watch, vied to handle the Walton case. Walton chose APRO and was interviewed by James Harder, PhD, and Jim Lorenzen. Both Lorenzen and Harder were convinced of the authenticity of Walton's case.

Articles appeared in newspapers across the world, some skeptical and others supportive. Walton soon learned that very few of them accurately portrayed his encounter, and some of them were almost completely fabricated.

Their phone continued to ring off the hook with requests for interviews, movie offers, other UFO witnesses wanting to share their stories, and even callers accusing him of hoaxing or issuing bizarre threats.

Within a year, journalist Bill Barry wrote a full-length book on the encounter. Walton, still getting requests for interviews, seeing his story being misrepresented and watching others profit on it, also decided to write a book.

Later the film and new book, *Fire in the Sky*, told Walton's story again. Walton had gone ten years without a phone to avoid publicity and had just installed one the day before when film producer Tracy Torme called about telling Walton's story. The movie was well received and accurately portrayed Walton's story except for one crucial part: the segment during which Walton was taken onboard the craft was entirely fictionalized.

Walton's case continues to attract interest today, and Walton is a frequent guest at UFO conferences and on radio programs. His life since the encounter has never been the same and has left a lasting legacy. Says Walton: "It will always be there. It changed everything . . . All in all, I've lost badly from this thing."

While the case was viciously attacked by UFO debunker Phil Klass and others, nobody was able to produce any evidence pointing towards a hoax. Furthermore, none of the percipients have ever backed down or changed their story, even when offered substantial sums of money.

Walton was later hypnotized to see if he could recall the missing five days, but the hypnotists encountered an extremely strong memory block and worried about Walton's health; they gave up. As a final note, researchers have discovered that—as has been seen in other UFO cases—trees and plants at the landing site are growing at many times their normal rate.

Years later, Walton has had no further encounters, nor has his family. Why was he abducted that evening in 1978? Says Walton: "So far as I know, I was just in the wrong place at the wrong time, and too curious for my own good."[128]

Contact in Camp Verde

Sometime in 1978, Derrick Olson (pseudonym) was surprised to see an article in the *Verde Independent newspaper* about a sighting over the local Childs Hydroelectric plant, run by the APS (Arizona Public Service.) It supplies electricity for the city of Phoenix. According to the article, two employees of the plant observed the object and reported it to the local press.

About a month later, Olson was driving in the area of the plant when he stopped to help a lady change a flat tire on her truck. By coincidence, she turned out to be the wife of one of the engineers who worked and lived at the plant. As Olson writes:

WHILE HELPING HER I ASKED WHERE SHE WAS GOING AND SHE SAID THAT SHE LIVED AT CHILDS. I THEN ASKED HER IF SHE KNEW THE EMPLOYEES THAT SAW THE CRAFT HOVER ABOVE THE PLANT. SHE SAID THAT SHE WAS ONE OF THEM AND THAT THEY NOT ONLY SAW IT, THEY MET THE ALIENS PERSONALLY. IT'S HARD TO DISCOUNT SOMEONE LIKE THIS, IN MY MIND, UNLESS THEY WANTED TO CREATE ATTENTION AND LOSE JOBS. NOT LIKELY. THEIR REPORT WAS THAT THE CRAFT HOVERED ABOVE THE PLANT AND SUCKED ENERGY FROM IT, CAUSING THE POWER DIALS TO DROP AND CREATE A VERY NOTICEABLE CHANGE IN ELECTRIC TRANSMISSION, SOMETHING THEY WOULD HAVE TO REPORT TO APS OF COURSE.

"I am not sure of the time and duration," says Olson, "but the lady told me that they did not want to cause too much trouble or get too much attention, so they did not tell the news that in addition to this experience, they not only saw them but met them as well. I did not want to pry and forgot to ask what they dressed like or how they communicated. I did ask what the aliens were like, and she replied, 'They were just like humans only they were very nice, very peaceful,' or something to that effect."

After replacing the tire, Olson drove away and never saw the lady again. But he was unable to get the story out of his mind. Years later he tried unsuccessfully to locate a copy of the original article. He still feels that an investigation into this incident might locate further witnesses. In support of this incident are several reports of UFO sightings and even a UFO landing in Childs.[129]

Family Experiences Missing Time

On the evening of August 20, 1979, at around 9:00 p.m., a mother and her two daughters were cooling off in the above-ground pool in the backyard of their Phoenix home. At some point, they heard a "light buzzing sound."

Says one of the daughters:

[WE] TURNED AROUND TO SEE A CRAFT WITH ORANGE-ISH COLORED LIGHTS, HOVERING LESS THAN TWENTY YARDS FROM US. THAT IS ALL ANY OF THE THREE OF US REMEMBER. AND IN FACT WE DIDN'T TALK ABOUT IT FOR ALMOST TEN YEARS, LIKE IT HAD BEEN TEMPORARILY ERASED FROM OUR MEMORIES, UNTIL ONE NIGHT WHEN SOMEONE BROUGHT UP UFOS AND THE THREE OF US SPOKE UP ABOUT OUR EXPERIENCE. HOW COULD SOMEONE PUT SOMETHING LIKE THAT INTO THE BACK OF THEIR BRAINS? AFTER TALKING ABOUT IT FOR AWHILE, NONE OF US RECALLED THE CRAFT LEAVING AND WE BELIEVE THAT WE MAY HAVE LOST SOME TIME.

Shocked by how she had completely forgotten the incident, the witness decided to report it to NUFORC.[130]

Missing Time in Mesa

One evening Chandra was with her family in their home in Mesa when her brother came rushing home in a frightened state and told everyone to go outside and look at something in the sky. Says Chandra: "My whole family—mother, grandparents, stepfather, and one of my brother's friends—all went outside to see what he [her brother] was so upset about. We observed this object coming closer to us. It was no joke—about the size of a football field."

The entire object glowed. It flew very low at a slow pace and was "extremely large." The circumference of the object was lined with window or metal panels. As it passed overhead, it made "a low kind of warm, humming sound."

When it reached the end of the block, it swayed slightly and then accelerated at high speed to the northeast and was gone in a split second.

The next day she told her teacher who became very excited and told her that he had seen the same object.

Years later, in June 1979, Chandra (now sixteen years old) was at a friend's house watching the television show, *The Waltons*. As always, she left at 8:50, ten minutes before the show ended, and began the short drive to her home. Her parents were strict and Chandra's curfew was 9:00 p.m. sharp. She had never missed it before, and tonight was no different, or so she thought.

She pulled into the driveway around 9:00, and then something strange happened. "I was surrounded by the most intense blue-white light. My car kind of rumbled. It's hard to explain. At the time I thought I had been hit by lightning. I could feel the energy."

As quickly as it had started, the light winked out and Chandra—now confused and frightened—exited the car and rushed inside. Says Chandra: "I was greeted by two very upset parents. I was an hour late. I completely forgot what had just happened. Even when trying to defend myself I had no excuse and was very confused. All I know is I left at 8:50 and walked in at 10:00 p.m."

Chandra called her friend upset and crying, asking her how come she was so late. Her friend said that Chandra had left on time and had no idea what Chandra was talking about. About three years later, Chandra remembered the strange light that had illuminated the car. She recalls the same thing happening two other times in her life.[131]

Abduction in the White Tank Mountains

On June 28, 1980, two ladies named Lu and Carol, and Carol's daughter, Laura, (and their two dogs) went driving through the White Tank Mountains hoping to see some UFOs which had been sighted recently in the area. They drove along a long dirt road, and parked where it dead-ended at the foot of the mountains.

It was now late at night. Shortly after they arrived, Lu noticed strange lights not far from them near the mountains. Carol felt a strange tiredness sweep over. Shortly after seeing the lights, all three ladies inexplicably lost consciousness.

All three woke up when they heard a voice saying, "Oh, there is a car." Looking up, they saw what appeared to be a hearse drive by. They became frightened when they could hear no sound coming from the car; nor was it kicking up any dust.

They tried to start the car but the engine wouldn't work. They tried again and this time it worked. They sped away. A few hours later when the sun came up, they wondered what exactly had happened and they decided to return to the scene. They found nothing unusual, but learned that the car horn no longer worked.

Certain that something strange had happened, Carol decided to go under hypnosis. While under trance, Carol recalled falling asleep in the car, only to awaken moments later because there were three small figures dressed in diving suits and helmets standing next to their car.

Carol found herself exiting the car with her friends and following the figures over to a large silver dome-shaped object that was landed not far away. A fourth being stood on a rim that protruded from the circumference of the landed object. He held a flashlight-like instrument which he pointed at Carol, beaming her with light. Only then was she taken into the craft, followed by the others.

Carol counted five of the small helmeted figures inside what appeared to be a control room filled with buttons and screens and colored lights. She was floated off to another room where a tall being with a veil before its face undressed her and put her on table where he proceeded to examine her. She felt an electrical pulse shocking her and the man explained that he was adjusting her energy centers. He then told her not to eat meat as it was disrupting her energy patterns. He told her that she hasn't been fulfilling her mission to tell the people of Earth the truth about the coming of the aliens.

Carol next found herself being dressed and taken out of the craft and back to her vehicle. As soon as they were put back in their car, the ETs vanished and they all lost their memory of the onboard experience.[132]

The Contacts of Russell

On August 25, 1980, Russell X. was heading west on Bell Road in Paradise Valley when he saw an orange ball of light approach from the southwest. As it got close, he realized the light was actually a domed craft with three hemispherical domes on the bottom surface. Russell was surprised when he then found himself inside the craft. He stood next to a small humanoid being who was operating the craft using a strange metallic plate that he controlled with his mind. At one point, the ET darkened the room and showed Russell a star-chart with lines between various stars designating travel routes taken by the ETs.[133]

UFO Researcher Visited by Aliens

On May 8, 1981, UFO researcher Bill Hamilton III was dozing in bed in his Phoenix home when he saw three alien-looking figures standing at the foot of his bed. Says Hamilton: "These three little figures were marshmallow white and wore helmets with visors."

To Hamilton's surprise, the center figure removed his helmet and stared at Hamilton intently. Hamilton asked who he was. The figure said his name was Yamatrix and that he had come from Casa Grande.

Casa Grande was a city south of Phoenix. Confused, Hamilton rephrased his question, asking the figure where he came from. The figure replied, "The Pleiades."

Hamilton could feel a powerful force coming from the figure. The figure told him that this was due to evolved brain functions. At that point, all three figures vanished and Hamilton jumped to his feet. The entire room was filled with the scent of ozone. Otherwise, there was no other evidence that aliens had just been in his bedroom.

The next day, Hamilton learned that his friend Christy had been out walking her dog around the same time when she saw an unidentified light high in the sky fly up from the south and hover over Phoenix. Further confirmation came a week later when another friend who lived in Casa Grande said that on the same night of Hamilton's encounter, he had seen a strange light inside his trailer. Going to investigate, the light disappeared, and all that was left was a very strong odor of ozone.[134]

They Came from the Sky

In May of 1981, Nancy was in her home in Sedona when she felt a low powerful vibration. Rushing outside, she was stunned to see a gigantic fish-shaped object floating above her house. It was larger than an aircraft carrier, a dull metallic color and had a glowing dome on top. Stunned, she watched it pass slowly over her house.

One year later, in April of 1982, she went camping with her daughter and granddaughter in Fey Canyon, Sedona. That night they saw a strange lighted disk hovering in the sky.

Later, in their tent, they were visited by a "small entity" that grabbed Nancy's arm and took her and the others from the tent. She doesn't remember what happened next, only that the creature spoke inside her head, telling her that they were rearranging her molecular structure for the purpose of facilitating communication and travel.

Nancy believes that not only was she abducted, but that her daughter and granddaughter were also abducted. Three months later, on July 4, 1982, Nancy had another sighting. As a result of these experiences, she recalled that this wasn't the first time she had seen something strange. Memory flooded back and she recalled that at age six, she had seen seven figures come down from the sky and talk to her. She still remembered what they said, that she had a purpose in life and that she was not a bad girl.[135]

A Fleet of Objects

On November 13, 1981, two friends were living on an isolated ranch seventy miles east of Parker. The ranch was located in an empty valley about fifteen miles wide and eight miles long. It was around dusk, and the two witnesses stood at the top of a small levy that afforded them a perfect view of the entire valley. Off in the distance they saw an orb of light, apparently about two feet in diameter.

At first they didn't pay it much attention. Then it began to move erratically. It darted straight up about 5,000 feet, stopped suddenly, then darted straight back down. It flew across the valley in less than a second, and continued to dart around for the next fifteen minutes.

At that point, a group of dozens of similar orbs appeared in the north end of the valley. By the time darkness fell, there were so many orbs darting around that they were unable to count them.

One of the friends was an aviation enthusiast. He had been to numerous air shows and taken twenty hours of flight training. What he was now observing was unlike anything he had ever seen. It appeared as if the objects were surveying and mapping the entire valley.

For the next hour, they watched the UFO display. At one point they noticed that all the animal sounds had stopped. "You could not hear anything," says one of the witnesses. "The silence was deadening. No frogs, coyotes, nothing—not normal for a night in Arizona."

Around this time, something strange happened. The witnesses lost their memory, losing hours of time. Says the witness: "The next thing I remember is looking to the north end of the valley. I grabbed my friend's arm and said, 'Look!'"

A giant ship several times larger than a modern aircraft carrier was moving to the east side of the valley. It stopped and hovered about 2,000 feet high. "At this time," says the witness, "in a matter of a split second, all of the small orbs came to a complete halt. Then, in less than the blink of an eye, they attached themselves to the mother ship. We looked at each other in awe then looked back at the ship. While we watched, this large craft shot straight up and out of the atmosphere in a split second. We looked at each other in disbelief."

The witnesses returned to their home in a daze. It took them a while to process the entire event. One of them later reported the encounter to MUFON, writing, "I would not trade this experience for anything."[136]

Missing Time in the AZ Desert

In June of 1982, the Milner family (pseudonym) packed up all their things and began the move to their new home in New Mexico. While the parents traveled in one car, their son, Rob Milner, decided to follow them on his motorcycle.

It was late at night, and they were driving through the Arizona desert when Rob became distracted by something in the sky. About sixty feet above him was a large circular craft covered with bright white lights. To his shock it began to perform a series of maneuvers, circling above him as he drove down the highway. Impressed, Rob pulled off the highway, parked his bike, and looked up.

The object continued to circle directly above him. He could now hear "a very soft humming/swishing sound" as it passed overhead. Says Rob: "On about its fifth or sixth pass, it hovered for two or three seconds; then in the blink of an eye it was gone . . . I got back on the road to catch up."

Excited to tell them what he saw, he accelerated upwards of 100 mph. He quickly reached the next town where he found his parents finishing dinner. Both of them wanted to know what happened and why he was so late. That's when Rob realized he was missing time.

"An hour and a half had gone by," explains Rob. "To me it felt like I had spent no more than five minutes stopped by the side of the road observing the craft."[137]

Missing Time in Phoenix

One evening in 1984, Cory Stanton (pseudonym) was in his Phoenix home on Lupine and 36th Street when he and his stepsister noticed what appeared to be three unusually bright stars hovering above the McDowell Mountains east of Scottsdale Airport.

It quickly became apparent that the objects weren't stars because they appeared to be "teetering or swaying." Cory and his sister also ruled out planes or helicopters because they could hear no sound. The objects were high in the sky in a triangular formation.

"They hovered above us silently for about two minutes," explains Cory. "Then one of them shot off to the south like a bullet and it was gone. These were the fastest things I have ever seen to this day. The other two hovered a while longer and then one zipped off into the east. The one that remained hovered for about thirty seconds and then it went straight up until we could no longer see it. We were overwhelmed at what we witnessed."

Later that evening they watched the news and heard reports from other people. Cory found himself transformed by the sighting. "It's like they connect with you somehow," he says. "My life forever changed after that night. I began to have feelings of insight or intuition as I call it."

Not long after the sighting, Cory went to a party in the desert with some friends. Realizing it was getting late, he decided to leave, but found that he was the only one of his friends who wanted to go, and none of them would give him a ride back. It was only a few miles and would take about thirty minutes to walk. He had been walking for about fifteen minutes and was halfway to town when he saw "an intense blue flashing strobe" overhead.

Says Cory: "I don't remember anything after that or losing any time, but that thirty-minute walk took hours longer than it should have." Cory found himself just outside of town two hours later than it should have been. He has no memory of what happened. As he says: "That was a very scary night."

Following his missing time, Cory began to suffer from migraines. Stranger than that, however, were the intuitive episodes. "It's all very strange and confusing," says Cory. "I have predicted things like putting on my seat belt ten seconds before my wife and I were involved in an accident. I had a feeling something was about to happen and put on the seat belt real fast and the next thing I know we were involved in a pretty serious accident. I was with a friend at a late-night movie asked him for some strange reason to look up at the lights and at that exact moment the entire parking lot lights (about fifty) all shut off at that second. Even I was freaked out by this; I don't know why I asked him to look at them—I just did."

Other episodes followed. One evening while at the movie theater he had a feeling something was wrong at home. They rushed home to find a candle had burned down and set a shelf on fire. Says Cory: "It might seem trivial, but something as simple as driving someplace, feeling when to leave with my intuition, and I experience no traffic and make it through every green light. Does anyone else experience these types of things? I was able to start putting computers together without any knowledge of them. I automatically knew how they worked and I instantly knew how to build them. There are many more things I have experienced, but it would take all day to write them down, and I feel very strange writing about this. It feels better to finally get this off my chest."[138]

A Three-Day Long Abduction

On July 21, 1985, ranch hand Scott Wilkins (pseudonym) worked at the K-4 cattle ranch in Yavapai County, located seventy-four miles outside Prescott.

It was around 9:00 p.m., and Scott was working in the maintenance barn when he was called outside by three other ranch hands who stood with their families looking upward. Scott turned and saw a strange object moving at a "snail's pace" toward the main house on the east edge of the ranch. The object, says Scott, was "over 100 yards long, triangle shaped, with three huge bright blue lights on the bottom and smaller porthole-like lights all the way around the object."

The craft moved until it was directly over the main house where it came to a standstill. All the animals on the ranch became silent. Scott saw that the horses bunched up together against the fence, as far from the object as they could get, and the dogs—normally very loud—were retreating to the barn and hiding behind the hay bales. He ran to his house and got his wife and daughter outside to observe the UFO. At the same time, he and the other ranch hands grabbed their rifles and pistols in case they should need to protect themselves. Some of them brought cameras and began to take photos.

The next thing everyone on the ranch knew, they were all back in their homes, waking up the next morning. The owner of the ranch paid out the prior day's wages as he normally did, and they began the new day as usual.

Scott and the other employees began the long drive out to town to cash their checks at the local market. When he arrived at the store, he got a huge shock. Says Scott:

IT WAS THREE DAYS LATER . . . THE STORE EMPLOYEES HAD EXPECTED US TWO DAYS PRIOR. THEY SHOWED US THAT DAY'S NEWSPAPER. WE JUST

STARED AT EACH OTHER IN DISBELIEF. BUT WE WEREN'T ALONE. WALNUT CREEK STATION HAS FOUR RANCH HEADQUARTERS . . . AND ONE FOREST SERVICE FIREFIGHTERS FACILITY THERE . . . THE STORE EMPLOYEE AND NIGHT MANAGER TOLD US WE WERE PART OF A STREAM OF PEOPLE WHO WORKED IN WALNUT CREEK WHO SHOWED UP ON THE WRONG DAY TO BUY OUR MONTHLY STOCK OF FOOD. AND THE LOCAL FEED STORE REPORTED THE SAME STRANGE EVENT AS DUSTY "OLE" COWBOYS AND THEIR FAMILIES CAME TO BUY TACK, CLOTHES, BOOTS, SHIRTS, BARBWIRE, ETC.

According to Scott, the strange event caused shock waves through the entire community. Several of the wives moved off the ranch and back into town. Others nailed their windows shut and placed deadlocks on their doors. Some even bought new guns and guard dogs. Some refused to ever go on the ranch again.

Several of the ranch hands found strange marks on the backs of their children or next to their belly buttons. Other ranch hands and their wives found marks on or near their knees.

Around the same time of the incident, the ranch had experienced several strange cattle mutilations. According to Scott, they involved "mainly pregnant cows, the calf laying there still in the birthing sac, but the mom cut to pieces— their rear end just gone—eyes, tongue, guts—just gone, and hardly any blood."

There were other strange after-effects. "What was really strange," says Scott, "we all seemed to just forget about it, never discussing it." It wasn't until the Phoenix Lights occurred more than ten years later that Scott even thought about the event.

Scott also reports that the object has returned, often around July 21. He later had the opportunity to examine some of the photos taken of the UFO hovering over the main ranch house. The photos from the new digital cameras didn't come out. The one camera that worked was an old Instamatic. The photo showed only a big blur shaped like a triangle.[139]

An Underground Abduction

In 1987, Kaye Kizziar's life was turned upside down. A retired Motorola Electronics technician, Kizziar was in her bedroom with her husband, who had just fallen asleep. It was around 11:00 p.m. Says Kizziar: "A beam of light came into the bedroom and this being stepped out. He put his hand out and took me to these magnificent caverns beneath Fish Creek."

Kizziar was amazed by her experiences and was determined to talk about them. But she also feared that people would disbelieve her. Compromising, she decided to write a semi-fictional book inspired by her experiences called, *Eyes of the Superstitions*. Kizziar received letters from reader saying that they also had similar experiences, which inspired her to write more books. While it is unclear how much of these books are true and how much is fiction, Kizziar maintains that her contacts are real.[140]

Beamed at Fort Huachuca

On June 1, 1987, a young lady, Tracy, (pseudonym) decided to take her girlfriend to an "all nighter" dance at Fort Huachuca. The dance ended at 3:00 a.m. Hoping to avoid the rush for the exits, they decided to leave a half-hour before closing, at 2:30.

Tracy describes what happened next:

IT WAS A VERY LONELY DRIVE BACK, AS FAR AS TRAFFIC WAS CONCERNED. ABOUT TEN-FIFTEEN MINUTES OR SO INTO OUR DRIVE, WE CAME ACROSS A VERY BRIGHT LIGHT. AT FIRST WE THOUGHT THERE WAS AN ACCIDENT AND THAT IT WAS A HELICOPTER, BUT THE LIGHT KEPT GETTING BRIGHTER AND BRIGHTER. MY GIRLFRIEND WAS DRIVING AND I YELLED AT HER TO PULL OVER BECAUSE WHATEVER IT WAS, WE WERE GOING TO HIT IT. THE LIGHT WAS SO BRIGHT THAT WE EACH HAD OUR HANDS IN FRONT OF OUR FACE TO BE ABLE TO SEE THE ROAD. I BELIEVE WE WERE BOTH KIND OF SCARED BECAUSE WE DID NOT HEAR ANY MOTORS OR ANY OTHER NOISE.

This is when Tracy noticed a very unusual quality about the light. Says Tracy:

WHEN I LOOKED OVER TO MY GIRLFRIEND, I NOTICED THAT I COULD SEE EVERY SHAPE OF EVERY BONE IN HER HAND, AS IF THOUGH THE LIGHT WAS X-RAYING HER HAND. THEN I LOOKED AT MINE AND TOLD HER TO LOOK AT OUR HANDS, BECAUSE THE LIGHT WAS ALMOST SHINING RIGHT THROUGH THEM. THE LIGHT DID NOT EMIT HEAT, NOR SOUND, WHICH WAS EVEN SCARIER. AT THAT POINT WE DID NOT KNOW WHAT IT WAS.

The two ladies became concerned when the light continued to move closer. "Just as she was going to pull over," says Tracy, "the light disappeared as quickly as it had appeared. My girlfriend looked at me and said, 'Girl, I ain't never telling nobody about this and you better not tell anyone either! They're gonna think we're crazy!'"

Tracy agreed. But their ordeal wasn't over yet. Says Tracy:

FOR SOME ODD REASON, WE DID NOT GET BACK HOME TO TUCSON, UNTIL ABOUT 5:15 [A.M.] OR SO, AND WE JUST LOOKED AT EACH OTHER AND SAID: "WHY THE HELL DID IT TAKE US SO LONG TO GET BACK HOME?"[141]

One evening in August of 1987, Dave W. (a former nursing assistant for the US Army, a security guard for a juvenile detention center, and a construction worker) was walking outside his Morgan Ranch home with his neighbor and friend, Dottie, and her ten-year-old daughter, Missy.

They were talking about the day's events when Dottie said, "Dave! What's that?"

Dave turned and looked and couldn't believe his eyes. "I don't know," he said.

"To our left, about ten feet away and eight feet off the ground," explains Dave, "were three spheres, each about five feet across and forming a triangle. They were amber red."

The three of them stared at the floating spheres in shock when something strange happened. "The next thing I knew," says Dave, "we had turned and were side by side, the three of us, facing them. But I don't remember changing positions."

They continued to stare at the strange objects. Dave felt as if he was completely mesmerized. Then he found himself losing consciousness. Unaware how much time had passed, Dave found himself awake:

SUDDENLY I REGAINED CONSCIOUSNESS AND I WAS STILL STANDING AND STARING, AND THE GIRLS WERE RIGHT WHERE THEY HAD BEEN. WE STARED A MOMENT AND THEN SUDDENLY THE OBJECTS BEGAN TO MOVE AWAY FROM US AT GREAT SPEED. THEY MOVED IN A STRAIGHT LINE AND REMAINED THE SAME DISTANCE FROM THE GROUND, DUCKING INTO VALLEYS AND OVER RIDGES, UNTIL THEY DISAPPEARED BEHIND GRANITE MOUNTAIN INTO THE GRANITE MOUNTAIN WILDERNESS.

As if nothing unusual happened, they continued walking home, none of them talking about what had just transpired. They entered Dave's home and sat for several moments in front of the fireplace, still not speaking. Then Dottie appeared to break from her trance and said, "We have to be getting home."

Dottie left with her daughter. Dave believes that they began their walk about 4:00 p.m. After Dottie left, it was 8:00 p.m. They were missing a minimum of three hours. Says Dave: "To this day I have no recollection of what occurred during that time."

From that day forward, Dottie and her daughter have refused to talk about the incident. Dave, however, still wonders about that night and is interested in locating a dependable hypnotist. As he says: "I would like to find out what happened during the several lost hours."[142]

In late August of 1987, Colin Morrison (pseudonym) was standing in the front yard of his home in Jakes Corner. Standing next to him were his grandparents, son, and a friend. It was just around sunset when everyone's attention was drawn to a white light moving on the hillside across the street. Colin assumed at first it was a dune buggy, except for the fact that instead of two headlights, there was just one, and it was "extremely bright."

The object continued around the hillside, then without warning, launched into the air. It moved slowly and soundlessly toward the witnesses. Everyone was mystified, and they watched the light (which Colin likened to a floodlight) for the next twenty minutes. Finally, Colin and his friend decided to drive to another location to see the light from a different angle.

As they drove down the street, Colin was surprised to see a small red light fly up from the ground and into the object. He then saw other lights moving around the main one.

At that point, their attention was drawn to a second closer object on the other side of the road. Says Colin: "The object was very close to the road. It had an extremely bright white light shining out of an opening. We couldn't see the object's shape, but it was very big . . . we decided to drive up to it. As we neared it, perhaps forty to fifty feet away, the car engine died."

At the same moment, the opening on the craft started to close shut. When it winked closed, the car engine started. Now frightened, Colin and his friend raced home only to find that the first object was now directly over his home. His grandparents were watching it with binoculars. Still unable to identify it, his grandmother went inside and called Luke AFB, who told her that they had not received any calls.

Colin couldn't believe what happened next. "I realize this is strange," he says, "but it's true. Everyone seemed to act like: *So what? There's a UFO over the house.* My grandparents and son went inside to bed. My friend and I decided to go to sleep on the front lawn, as if that was perfectly normal. We just fell asleep on the ground."

At some point, Colin woke up to see a bright blue light flooding the yard. He then discovered that he was unable to move. What happened next was even more bizarre. Says Colin: "Small people approached us and said they were going to check our feet, and that they would not approach my grandparents. They did some physical exams. My friend was completely unconscious, but I was awake and speaking to them in some manner . . . The people did not move their mouths when they spoke.

"At one point," continues Colin, "they told me a being was there—I understood it to be a type of scientist. The creature or 'thing' was like nothing I can describe. It somewhat resembled a giant praying mantis. It was fish-like or bug-like, and was absolutely the most horrible thing I've ever seen. I became terrified and was fighting them. It was my impression that this creature did not have any compassion for humans. It did not speak to me, but had a very cold presence. The next thing I know, my friend and I woke up in the morning still lying on the front lawn."

He asked everyone what happened, and while everybody remembered seeing the UFO, they were acting strangely blasé about it. Says Colin: "I was the only one that seemed to think something incredible had occurred."

Colin told his friend about the strange little people and that they seemed interested in feet. Colin's friend revealed that he did have something unusual about his feet: webbed toes. Colin was surprised as he wasn't aware of that fact. Colin also revealed that he had a slightly unusual anatomical anomaly: his toes were double jointed.

Colin told his son about the "episode," and his son said that the beings also spoke to him. Says Colin: "I've often wondered about what happened that night, and although it sounds incredible, what I've related is true. After the event I had an interest in science and have since earned a masters in astronomy. As long as I live, I will never forget the sight of that object driving up the side of the hill and going into the air."[143]

Visitations in Phoenix

All her life, Susan (pseudonym) has been plagued by unusual nighttime experiences. When she was very young, she would often be woken up by glowing beings inside her bedroom. They reminded her of glow-sticks she had seen. At the time she wondered if they were angels—or maybe just dreams.

Then one day, in March 1988, when she was thirteen years old, Susan had a terrifying sighting involving missing time. "My mother and I were going to the store to get some chips I think," says Susan. "We got into the car and I saw this light in the sky. It seemed to be changing colors and coming closer. Its distance was hard to figure, maybe a few thousand feet or so. It was still in the sky to the west. For some reason I became extremely fearful; freaked out is another word for it. I remember an extremely bright light hitting the car and looking over at my mom who was going to sleep. That is when I really began to freak."

At this point Susan blacked out. Her next memory was waking up in bed the next day. Says Susan: "It took me a few months or so before I would sleep in my room again."[144]

"I Was Terrified"

In the late 1980s, Bill Lewis was attending a series of seminars in Phoenix. One evening, while returning from the seminar to his home in Payson, he felt an irresistible compulsion to drive out of town.

Unable to stop the car, Lewis soon found himself about fifty miles north of Phoenix on Highway 87. Then he heard a voice tell him to stop the car.

As if in a trance, he found himself pulling over and exiting the vehicle. He walked away from the road up into a small desolate valley. At this point, he became afraid. "All of a sudden I got this incredible sense of fear," says Lewis. "I felt threatened. The hair stood up on the back of my neck and I felt a chill go up my spine. I was terrified."

He saw a light over his shoulder. He whirled around and, looking down into the valley, saw that it was filled with light. Says Lewis: "It was almost like a tangible light, like the light had substance. The whole valley was lit up with this incredibly brilliant white light."

Lewis found that he was paralyzed. Unable to move, he could only stand and watch, feeling a mixture of terror and exhilaration. The next thing he knew, he was driving home to his wife and kids in Payson. Arriving home, he discovered that he was missing more than three hours of time.[145]

From the Mouths of Babes

Rayna's first conscious encounter occurred in Colorado in 1981 when she saw a group of four of five gray-type ETs standing outside her rural home. The encounter frightened her badly, but strangely she forgot about it entirely. It wasn't until August 10, 1989, when she had another encounter that she consciously realized ETs were a part of her life.

At the time she was living in Sedona. A few months earlier, she and her friends were sitting outside at Red Rocks Crossing when they observed six or seven orange glowing objects dart upwards in a V-formation. As if to accentuate their strangeness, one of the objects departed the formation, performed a few incredible maneuvers, and darted away in a different direction.

Rayna didn't think much of the incident other than the fact that the objects were beautiful. Then a few months later, on August 10, 1989, she was taking a nap when she woke up to hear a "loud cracking sound." A strange tingling sensation enveloped her body and she realized she was paralyzed. That's when she saw a "small being" standing by the head of her bed.

"Go away!" she screamed. "Don't take me away! Go away!" Rayna was unable to resist. All she could do was observe the figure. "It was a whitish-gray color and seemed to be wearing some sort of form-fitting jumpsuit. It had a large head and large, dark eyes. The feeling from it was rather impersonal and businesslike."

Rayna heard the being talking to somebody and sensed that it was describing her physical condition. Moments later it disappeared and Rayna's paralysis broke. However, she was now nauseated, her muscles were very sore, and there was a series of small red dots in a C-shape on her neck. The marks, which hadn't been there before the incident, never healed.

Following that incident, memories began to flood in of her earlier encounter in Colorado. At the same time, new incidents occurred. One evening she and a friend decided to drive up to the top of a canyon near her home. They had just started the drive when they found themselves at their destination with no memory of how they got there. The drive, which took thirty minutes, was gone from their minds. Frightened, Rayna and her friend drove home.

In 1991, Rayna found herself woken up around 2:30 a.m. by a bright light shining in the window. She began to get up and check on her daughter. Instead, she unaccountably fell asleep. A few hours later, both she and her husband were woken up by a "low hum that got louder and higher and faded away."

Further confirmation came when their neighbor mentioned seeing "a small bright light" float past her window on the same night.

Following that night, Rayna's two-year-old daughter began to exhibit unusual behavior. She was terrified of any lights or reflections that she couldn't connect to its source. Any unusual or unexplained sounds were enough to make her anxious. She started placing her dolls under lamps, telling her mother, "I'm healing them."

Rayna questioned her daughter who said that "something really scared her." She told her mother that "some little white guys" came into her bedroom through the window and took her into "their mommy's house" which was floating "over the street" next to their own house. She said they stuck a pen inside her nose and pinched her toe. Rayna looked down and saw a mark on her daughter's toe. Her daughter looked up and asked if her mother would go with her next time.

Rayna comforted her daughter as best as she could, then went to the other room where she broke down and cried. For so many years she had tried to ignore the possibility that she was being visited by aliens. But now that her daughter was involved, she could no longer deny the truth. She located hypnotist and UFO researcher Richard Boylan, PhD, who placed her in a support group and assisted her with understanding and coping with her experiences.

One evening, in July 1992, Rayna was preparing a bottle to feed her new baby. It was about 3:00 a.m. when she heard a sound like a "fast-forward recording of someone talking in a musical tone." She was too tired and anxious to investigate and returned to bed. Two days later, she was cleaning the house and discovered a couple of "strange-looking" handprints on the top of stereo. Says Rayna: "There were two very long fingers on each hand, with large bulb-like shaping in the tips." Rayna photographed the prints, leaving them there as a reminder that something unusual was happening in their home.

One month later, in August, Rayna had just dropped off a few friends at their home when she saw a large craft hovering only a few hundred feet in the air, just above the treetops. "It was about the size of four or five houses with a row of large blinking lights across the bottom. The top part was strangely ark, like a shadow [with] a definite outline that was similar to an inverted pie tin."

Rayna has spoken publicly about her experiences and says that the encounters continue. She sometimes experiences telepathic communications with the ETs, and at other times, it's as though they download her mind with a complete communication that she has to unravel in a linear fashion to understand. She has learned to deal with her encounters in a positive manner. As she says: "This has been—and continues to be—an ongoing process for me. The ET contact has changed me, and I am thankful for that . . . At some point it will be time for all of us to move beyond our initial fascination with their presence and the appearance of their ships to discovering the reason for—and the meaning of—their being here."[146]

Missing Time in Cottonwood

In the fall of 1989, a resident of Cottonwood was alone in her house when she became distracted by a mysterious buzzing noise. Thinking it was one of her appliances, she searched the house until she realized that the sound was coming from outside. Peeking out the window, through the venetian blinds, she saw several groups of bright red lights hovering low above her house. At some point, the objects left and the woman realized she was missing about one hour of time.

Sometime in 1989, a Florida couple was visiting the Sedona area. One evening the wife awoke around 2:00 a.m. to see a small orange-colored orb of light hovering in their room.

"They're here," the husband said. The wife woke up the next morning to find that she had a nosebleed in both her nostrils. Convinced that something strange had happened, she later sought hypnosis.

Under hypnosis, she recalled finding herself in a room that was brilliantly lit by blue-white lights. She saw several figures with large eyes staring down at her. She felt some kind of strange collar around her neck restraining her. Alarmed by her memories, she immediately ceased hypnosis.[147]

A Flying Saucer Ride

While onboard UFO accounts are sometimes involuntary abductions, this is not always the case. As uncovered by Tom Dongo, the following incident took place near Cave Creek in Sedona in the late 1980s. Gary (pseudonym) was a very old man and in extremely poor health. One day he was driving through the Arizona desert when his car engine sputtered and died, forcing him to quickly park alongside the road.

He exited the car and opened the hood to examine the engine. A "blond man" walked out of the desert toward him. The man spoke, saying that he was not from Earth and would return in four months to take Gary up into his ship. Despite the strange statement, Gary was most impressed by the man's kindness, gentleness, and wisdom. The man then turned and walked back out into the desert. When Gary tried to start his car, it functioned normally.

Four months later, the man showed up and gave Gary the promised ride. Gary told only a few people the story, then passed away shortly later. Dongo obtained the story from Gary's daughter.[148]

Abduction in Gila Bend

As reported by UFO researcher Tina Choate of the International UFO Research Center in Scottsdale, a woman and her husband were driving in the Gila Bend area (date not given) when they saw a large craft with a ring of blue lights around the circumference. Convinced that they were seeing something unusual, they pulled off the road to observe.

Their next memory was waking up to find themselves twenty miles farther along the road. Later, the woman, who was a nurse, decided to go under regressive hypnosis to recover her memories of the missing time. Under hypnosis she recalled that both she and her husband were taken onboard the craft. The ETs (not described) told the nurse that they had abducted her because she had a basic understanding of the human body, and they wanted her to interface with them and learn about biochemistry and healing applications.[149]

Contact in Southern Arizona

Sheri claims to have had ET contact periodically throughout her life. However, on February 20, 1991, she experienced a particularly dramatic encounter. At around 2:00 a.m. she woke up in her southern Arizona home and felt the familiar urge to go outside. Not far away was a large cylinder-shaped object about 100 feet long and twenty feet thick. A steady blue light glowed from the rear while the front was illuminated by a pulsating pink light.

She was taken onboard where she met three different types of ETs, including "humanoids" (which she had encountered previously), grays (who were busy operating the ship), and a large reptilian type that she had never seen. The reptilian, said Sheri, had scales instead of skin and bright gold eyes. The ship itself appeared to be larger on the inside than it appeared from the exterior. The front section was the navigational area while the back part of the craft was filled with machinery.

While onboard the craft, Sheri was given strange round silver pills by the ETs, which she was told would "rejuvenate" her body. She consumed the pills as instructed. A sample of the medicine was later examined by UFO researcher Gem Cox. "The medicine appeared to be metallic, about the size and shape of a BB," said Cox. "The spheres seemed to heat up when held in my hand." Cox took a photograph and asked Sheri if she could get more of the medicine for a scientific analysis.

Sheri said she was given a strange mineral sample by the ETs, who told her that it was an "alloy of metallic hydrogen," which they used in the construction of the skin of their spacecraft. The ETs also showed her the formula they used to produce the alloy.

When Sherri returned home, she discovered that she had been gone for five hours, which surprised her because she could only recall spending a short time aboard the craft.

Also supporting Sherri's case are photographs taken by her friend, Dorothy, showing UFOs in the area where Sherri's contacts were taking place. Writes Cox, "Sheri's story is very interesting itself, when reinforced with all of Dorothy's photos of UFOs in the area, as well as the physical evidence—the medicine and the mineral sample—her case becomes very exciting and worthy of some follow-up efforts."

Fearing publicity, Sherri has insisted upon total anonymity. As of yet, there has been no analysis of the medicine or mineral sample revealed to the public.[150]

Abducted in Dewey

Around midnight on September 28, 1991, Leslie Ballard (pseudonym) woke from a sound sleep to hear something moving in her home. She sat up in bed and looked through the open doorway and down the hallway, which was now lit up with a strange, almost opaque, blue-white light. She immediately looked at her baby (who was only a few days old) and saw that she slept soundly in her crib next to the bed.

When she looked back to the hallway, she saw a short child-like figure. It was fat and "blobby" and looked brown in color. It was followed seconds later by a small gray humanoid figure. Leslie jumped out of bed to observe them more closely when she saw another taller, thin insectoid figure with blue-gray skin step through the wall and into the hallway facing her bedroom. "This thing was thin and huge," reports Leslie. "It was acting dainty-like; it put its hand out towards me and for some reason, I walked to it. I wasn't scared at all."

Leslie felt like the ET was female. It was about six or seven feet tall and moved with a calm grace. It had large wrap-around liquid eyes, with visible eyelashes on the bottom and a slit for a mouth. Leslie also noticed that the skin on its face was pock-marked with either large pores or blemishes. She found herself grabbing the ET's hand, which had only four fingers. She turned around and looked back in her bedroom. The "gray little one" turned to look at her. Leslie saw that her husband and baby were still both soundly asleep.

She turned and looked back at the tall figure. Leslie couldn't believe what happened. "We stepped through the wall and into their craft."

The interior of the craft was a creamy pearl-white. Fascinated, Leslie reached out and touched the translucent-looking walls, which caused her hand and fingers to glow. The seats on the craft were molded into the wall. She could see outside the craft, which appeared to be moving at super-high speeds.

She saw a strange "bulb-light thing" in the center of the craft. It hummed loudly, causing the air around it to vibrate. Says Leslie: "I went to put my right hand on it and the short, fat brown being grabbed my wrist. His hand felt like sandpaper."

The gray motioned the short being to let go of her hand. The tall blue-gray being then pointed outside and Leslie saw that it was now daylight and the craft was hovering in place. The craft dipped down and Leslie was surprised to see water.

The three beings turned to look at Leslie. Then the gray turned to Leslie and sent her a telepathic message, saying, "We do exist where we can't be seen."

The short figure manipulated the "bulb" and suddenly the craft dropped and plunged into the water. Leslie continued to look outside at what appeared to be the ocean depths. Bubbles floated upward and she saw spears of sunlight coming down into the water. Says Leslie: "I saw a beautiful coral reef. You could see some fish swimming around, some plants. I remember a huge yellow fish with a blue stripe next to the wall of the craft."

Next the craft moved upward and out of the water. It began moving at super-high speeds and it became dark again outside and Leslie found herself being led out of the ship and back into her hallway. It was now fifteen minutes after midnight. Leslie obediently crawled into bed and turned around just in time to watch the tall being disappear through the wall.

Leslie found herself transformed by the experience. "From that day on," she says, "I have had a new perspective about life elsewhere and where they may be hiding out." Leslie is also considering regressive hypnosis to explore the incident further.[151]

Missing Time in Snowflake

The following report comes from a young woman who experienced a strange event with her mother. At around 9:00 p.m. on August 28, 1992, they were outside the barn on their property. A light appeared on the southwest horizon and began to race quickly towards them. The daughter assumed that it was a plane coming in for a crash landing and she screamed for her mother to run behind the barn.

Her mother, however, remained still and continued to watch the approaching object. Just when the daughter was sure the object was going to crash, it came to an abrupt stop about twenty feet away, hovering very low to the ground.

The two of them looked at each other and said, "It's a UFO!" The object glowed brightly, but didn't illuminate the area around it. Fascinated, they both walked towards it. Says the daughter: "Just as we got close it began to slowly ascend, forming a cloud in front of it."

The object moved higher and higher until it moved out of sight. Says the daughter: "Mother and I were amazed that we had a close encounter, and we are still amazed. One thing troubles us though: we remember the light coming and then leaving, but we don't remember what we did after it left."

Looking back, the witnesses don't know why they didn't call the police to report what happened. "Before this UFO sighting," says the daughter, "I didn't believe in UFOs, but I'm a true believer now."[152]

Touched by a Gray

In February of 1997, Louise (not her real name) and her husband moved into the new mobile home in Chandler. One month later, she woke up one evening to find her room filled with light. "I saw three small thin aliens," said Louise, "the exact kind we call the grays. One was next to my husband's head; one was at the foot of the bed. And when I went to sit up in bed, I turned to my side and there was one right next to me...the gray took his long skinny index finger and touched me light on the forehead, right between the eyes."

Louise had just enough time to notice that the alien had only three fingers and a thumb when she fell unconscious. She woke up the next morning and instantly remembered what had happened. Adrenaline pulsed through her as she pulled herself out of bed. She discovered that she was extremely thirsty and weak, and her body was sore all over. She felt as if she had just been drugged and come out of surgery. She dragged herself to the kitchen and was drinking a glass of water when she saw her six-month-old kitten outside. She gasped in shock, because the kitten had been in her bedroom. It had never been outside before, and all the doors were locked; there was no possible way it could be outside. She went outside to rescue her cat and with another shock, saw that her hair scrunchie—which she had worn to bed—was now lying on the outside porch.

The next day Louise called her mother and told her about the incident. Her mother revealed that Louise's grandparents had once been followed by a UFO as they drove to Las Vegas. The object had struck them with a beam of light. The next thing they knew, it was morning. When they arrived at their destination, their family was frantic because the grandparents were six hours late. The police were out searching for them thinking that they were in an accident. Later, the grandmother recalled being inside a small room examined by four gray-type ETs.[153]

Abducted in Phoenix

Around 10:30 p.m. on October 1, 2001, Cory (pseudonym) woke up and found himself compelled to venture outside his Phoenix home. He was walking up his street when he saw three strange flying objects: two triangular-shaped and a smaller circular craft, each of which was rotating. He turned around and was surprised to see his friend walking toward him in a trance. Says Cory: "I attempted to talk to him, but he did not respond. Then I can't remember anything for about three hours."

Cory's next memory is waking up in bed at 1:00 a.m. He felt that there were "aliens or something in my room" and that "they were making it hard for me to move." After fighting the paralysis, he fell asleep. The next morning he woke up feeling fine, but still wonders about what happened during the missing three hours.[154]

Missing Time in Globe

On March 17, 2002, a couple was driving from Mesa to Safford. They were about twenty miles east of Globe when the wife (who was driving) saw an "odd light" in the rearview mirror. It was too low to be an aircraft, but too high to be a car. The husband was in the passenger seat. "I took a look behind the van," he says, "and observed this egg-shaped light."

The light appeared to be about a mile behind them and forty feet above the road. Says the husband:

> WE WATCHED IT BEHIND US FOR WHAT SEEMED LIKE A COUPLE OF MINUTES. I CANNOT REPORT WHAT HAPPENED NEXT. THE TRIP SEEMED TO SIMPLY RESUME, AND NEITHER OF US SPOKE ABOUT THE OBJECT AGAIN. UPON OUR RETURN HOME WE NOTICED THE CLOCK—WE WERE ABOUT AN HOUR AND FIFTEEN MINUTES LATER THAN WE SHOULD HAVE BEEN.

The couple had made this trip many times and knew how long it took. Unable to figure what happened to the missing time, they went to bed. But they never forgot what happened. "We're reporting this now," says the husband, "because we'd like to simply forget that night; but you can't forget something you can't remember? What we do know is that since that evening, when we pass that exact area late on a Sunday night, conversation ends and we both get quiet. It's an odd feeling to sense something happened, but the harder you try to remember, the more something inside insists you don't."[155]

Trucker Abducted on Highway 40

On the evening of June 18, 2003, a trucker was driving at 70 mph west on Highway 40 heading toward Kingman (near a large power-station) when to the north, alongside the highway, he saw "this thing moving over the hills." It first caught his attention because it moved so slowly. He wondered if it might be a new type of military craft. As he watched, it crossed the road in front of his truck. At this point his memory starts to get "fuzzy." Says the trucker: "All I know is that the truck lost rpms and speed [and] there is a time lapse of about thirty minutes I can't account for."

Following the missing time, the trucker has had trouble sleeping, and has "this feeling that I am to find something and return it, but I can't remember what." The word "barron" keeps coming to his mind. The trucker was so affected by the encounter that he sought the help of a therapist. Together they tried hypnosis, but he was unable to reach a deep enough trance.[156]

Missing Time in Tucson

On July 4, 2004, a man suffering from renal cancer was unable to sleep. At 3:30 a.m., he decided to take his golf cart around the local golf course. He was climbing a small hill in the golf cart when he saw a yellow-blue-red light. A strange feeling came over him, and moving closer, he saw that the light was coming from a landed craft. Says the witness: "As I hit the top of the hill, everything stopped—like time stopped. I told myself, *this is a dream*." At this point, he saw "things" walking around and examining the wild pigs that roam the golf course at night. The next thing he remembers is: "I woke up on the ground and my golf cart was parked where I had seen the craft. I don't remember anything else."[157]

A Family Abduction

"This is not a joke," says the witness. "I do hereby swear and promise on the Holy Bible in the presence of our Lord as our Witness that this is the truth and the whole truth as best remembered, so help us God."

Sonia (pseudonym) was a single mother from Cashion with four children ranging in age from nine to fifteen years old. One evening in August 2004, about an hour before midnight, she and her four children walked to the neighborhood park, which was a short two-minute walk. At the park, she looked to the north over Interstate 10 and saw a large round bright light. It sat there for about five minutes, then began to descend and move toward the witnesses. Says Sonia: "My son and I made a fuss over this light and became concerned as it started getting closer to us."

In less than two minutes, it was right over their heads. It appeared to be a "pitch black triangle with dull soft lighting coming from the two back corners of the craft." A soft red light glowed from the center, and "strange markings" decorated the bottom of the craft. It was about the height of the street lights and made a soft humming sound. Says Sonia: "I cannot explain the length of time that we stared at this scary thing in the sky. Time seemed to pass forward and we didn't realize what had happened to us."

The next thing Sonia knew, she and her son were screaming and running frantically from the park. The three younger children were confused. They hadn't seen anything unusual and had no idea that their mother and fifteen-year-old brother were running away. Realizing she had left her three youngest children at the park, Sonia turned around and ran back. The craft was still there. She gathered the kids and they went home, at which point the craft moved south toward Phoenix, then vanished. When they arrived home, it was 1:20 a.m. Sonia and her four children were missing two hours and forty minutes of time.[158]

Giant Craft Over Mesa

On November 8, 2007, around 8:30 p.m., George (pseudonym) sat in the backyard of his Mesa home, while his wife sat ten feet away inside the house working on a Sudoku puzzle. Looking up, George's attention was drawn to a row of ten lights in a row about 100 feet long rising up from behind his neighbor's house. They were very bright and directly facing George's home. His first thought was that his neighbor was putting up a giant row of lights. But then the lights rose slightly higher and began to move slowly toward him. He now realized that the row of lights was actually some sort of airborne object.

In about two minutes, the object was over him. It had a flat black surface with a red light in the center about six feet in diameter. The craft completely covered the entire backyard and part of his house. It now stopped moving and a loud noise blared from the craft. It was only thirty feet overhead. George covered his ears, thinking to himself that the entire neighborhood must be hearing the noise, which he likened to "a high wind and a high-pitched engine sound."

Looking over at his wife, he was surprised to see that she sat there calmly working on her puzzle. He jumped up and told her to come outside. She told him that she was busy. He yelled at her to come outside immediately, and asked her if she could hear the loud noise.

Strangely, she heard nothing. Suddenly the noise stopped, and George realized that the noise must have been inside his head. For the next ten minutes, they watched the craft together at which point it moved away.

George, who worked as a production planner providing weapon systems to the army and the Marines, is convinced that he and his wife observed a genuine UFO.

In the months following the incident, George began to suffer from a variety of strange symptoms including "severe left ear infections and scabs that totally covered my left ear and back of my neck and, at times, the left side of my face; eye problems with swollen red eyes [and] skin."

Three years after the encounter, George began to suffer memory problems and was then diagnosed with a rare brain tumor called Glioblastoma Multiforme, which is fatal in most cases. Surgeons were able to remove the tumor, and George was one of the lucky few to survive.[159]

Kingman Abduction

On May 11, 2009, Lisa (pseudonym) was shocked to see a UFO being chased by a jet over her home in Kingman. Following the incident, she had a minor headache and became "extremely tired." Around midnight, she decided to go to bed. It was then she found herself experiencing what she thought was a particularly vivid and realistic dream in which she was taken onboard the craft she had just seen. Says Lisa: "I can't remember all too well, but I went onto the craft. It was bright. I spoke to them. All I remember is they were green and tall. I don't remember what else happened—only that we were traveling somewhere."

Lisa woke up hearing a loud noise. She was surprised to find herself in "a completely different spot and position on my bed. I felt as if I was being watched by something."

The next morning, Lisa got another shock. Not only did she have a raging sinus headache, there were several cuts on her body. Most were surface cuts, but a few appeared to be deep. She told her boyfriend what happened and learned that he also had been abducted. Says Lisa: "Apparently my boyfriend has had the same experience. I don't know what to make of it."[160]

Contact in Tonopah

On the evening of July 21, 2009, Henry, his friend James, and each of their girlfriends (Heather and Jamie) drove to an area outside of Tonopah, not far from the Palo Verde nuclear power plant, in hopes of seeing a UFO. They had gone UFO hunting in this area before and had seen strange things in the sky. They knew that some of the local residents had seen UFOs there on a regular basis and some said that they were chased by UFOs while driving their cars. Says Henry: "This is a hotspot." It was about ten miles away from Luke AFB out in the desert.

They were driving down a dirt road "in the middle of nowhere" when they saw a flashing light. They drove closer and were able to approach within 250 yards of the light, which now appeared to be a craft of some kind. At this point, emotions were running high. Says Henry: "All of us were scared, but at the same time curious. My friend's girlfriend was crying and telling us to turn around."

Henry and James, however, were transfixed by the sight. "It was the size of three football fields," says Henry. "It was triangular in shape [with] windows around it. It was about three stories tall and thirty feet off the ground. We flashed our lights and it flashed back in the same sequence of flashes. My friend James and I got out and walked closer. The closer we got, the better we could make out what was standing in the windows."

To their shock, they saw two different types of alien figures, including short figures with large heads, and other figures around eight feet tall. As they watched, some of the windows (which had been darkened) lit up to reveal more alien figures. James was videotaping the entire event. Says Henry: "I was terrified, but excited at the same time. We walked closer, but had to stop because the heat coming from the craft was so intense.

"The craft hovered, and then landed. A large panel at the bottom of the craft opened, and then two aliens proceeded to walk out. This absolutely terrified us more, but we couldn't move or talk. I remember trying to scream, and say run; we couldn't move or talk. Heather and Jamie were in the car honking the horn, screaming to come back, but we couldn't respond or move. The aliens walked up to within twenty feet of us. One of them was very thin and tall—about eight to nine feet; the other was about three to four feet. We stood there in amazement and shock."

Still unable to move or speak, Henry and James had no choice but to wait for what would happen next. Says Henry: "Then a calmness came over us. They were speaking to us telepathically. They were saying not to be scared, they weren't going to harm us . . . this conversation went on between the four of us for fifteen minutes. They said they were here to help us, so that we would not destroy our planet—and that there was a horrible event coming soon, that it had to be stopped. James asked if it was something like 9/11. They commented, 'No, bigger,' and it would be coming from the Middle East."

As he stood there, Henry recalled having been visited by these same ETs earlier in his life, as a child. One of the ETs then confirmed this and told Henry that they contacted him when he was six years old.

The conversation continued. The ETs said they had been expecting them, and that they wanted Henry and James to warn people about what would happen if humans didn't start taking care of their planet. Says Henry: "Visions of disaster entered our heads, as if to show us what was to come if we didn't warn people. The taller alien walked closer and held my hand, and I was no longer scared; neither was James. He said we would see him again soon and to warn people about saving our planet, to both James and I."

Then the conversation ended. The ETs turned around and entered the craft, which departed in a split second. Henry and James (who had recorded the entire event) both fell to the ground in shock. They immediately got to their feet and went back to the car. Their girlfriends were no longer crying, but just hugged them.

They tried to start the car, but the engine wouldn't turn over. They sat there for about a minute when finally the car worked. They started to drive away when suddenly there was a bright spotlight on their car, and three military helicopters appeared overhead. Seconds later, there were five military jeeps following them. The girls started crying, while Henry told James to hide the camera.

Henry continued to drive away until somebody in one of the jeeps began to speak over a loudspeaker ordering them to pull over or they would be forced to shoot. Says Henry: "We pulled over and military soldiers surrounded the car. Two men dressed in black opened the door and asked us to get out."

While other men searched the car, one man began to question the witnesses, asking them why they were in that area, what had they seen, how long they had been there, if they had any contact with the alien craft. They wanted to know the size and shape of the craft and if they had communicated with it. Henry and the others played dumb. "We answered no to everything," says Henry.

The men searching the car found the camera and after reviewing it, confiscated the camera and told the witnesses that they were not to speak of the incident. Then one of the officials separated Henry from the others and questioned him in the back of one of their vehicles. The man wanted to know if Henry had any prior experiences with the ETs. Henry denied this, and the military officials dropped him off at a restaurant in Tonopah near Interstate 10. Henry called James from there.

One month after the incident, Henry reported his encounter to NUFORC, writing, "It was a crazy night, but I had to report this . . . our evidence is gone, but this really happened. We questioned people who lived in the area . . . and they all saw the craft and the military soon after, so we aren't crazy, and there are four of us who witnessed this along with the people who live in the area who saw the craft. We talked to fifteen people who lived in the area, and all but one saw the craft."[161]

A Boy's Encounter

Gerald was a child when he had his first encounter. One evening he went outside because his dog was barking incessantly. He was about to bring her inside when she suddenly became quiet. Looking up, Gerald saw a dark shape passing very low overhead. At this point he experienced a period of missing time. "I don't know what happened," says Gerald. "I woke up in my room." Gerald also noticed that his cell phone was broken. He told only one person what happened.

His second encounter occurred early one summer morning around dawn. He was in the kitchen getting a glass of milk when he looked outside and saw a very strange figure. "Its face was bony," says Gerald, "very skinny, sucked in to the bone. It had no eyes, no nose. It had holes on the side of its head, like a reptile's ears."

The figure, says Gerald, looked human and had pale skin with a slight greenish-blue hue. It was tall and hunched over. It had four arms and two small legs. It had a large prominent spine that was visible through its translucent flesh and something like gills where a person's ribs would be.

Gerald was understandably shocked. As he says: "I dropped my glass of milk, and he (or it) turned to look at me. It stared for what felt like hours. I know exactly what it feels like. I could almost feel the creature through the glass [window.] I blacked out. I woke up later, around twelve."

In July 2011, Gerald was in Page with a friend. The friend (who is Navajo) invited Gerald to meet his family on the reservation. That night, the two of them went hiking. It was then that Gerald had a third dramatic encounter. Both Gerald and his friend observed a bright light appear over the valley. Says Gerald: "It grew brighter and brighter, and then it kind of coned into a small area—like a stage light—but really bright."

The cone grew smaller and the boys could feel an intense heat emanating from the light. There was a loud buzzing sound, followed by a humming, then a loud ring. The cone of light seemed to strike the earth like lightning, causing the boys to flee the scene. When they returned to the site later, they found a thirty-foot-wide circle of glassified sand.[162]

Phoenix Abduction

Two friends were talking about UFOs one evening when one of them revealed that he was pretty sure he had been abducted. On the evening of October 30, 2011, the young man was sitting on his couch watching television when he started to doze. Says the witness:

> BAM, I WOKE UP, AND MY BODY'S SHAKING LIKE I'M HAVING A SEIZURE. I COULDN'T FEEL ANYTHING. I COULDN'T MAKE A SOUND. I LOOK UP THROUGH MY KITCHEN AND I SEE TWO VERY TALL (EIGHT TO NINE FEET) AND VERY THIN ENTITIES STANDING STRAIGHT UP AT MY BACK SLIDING-GLASS DOOR. A BRIGHT LIGHT [SHINED DOWN] OVER THEM AS THEY JUST STOOD AND STARED. THE LIGHT STARTED TO GET BRIGHTER. THEN ALL I REMEMBER IS WAKING UP ON MY COUCH.

The witness's friend questioned him, asking if it might have been a dream. The witness shook his head and said that "there was no way" and that "it was, very, very real."[163]

Abducted at Cave Creek

On July 20, 2013, a small group of people were camping about forty-five miles north of Phoenix in the Black Mountains near Cave Creek. It was late at night and everyone was in their tents. They were drawn outside because of a strange static-electric feeling. Looking up they were shocked to see several "swirling lights" moving overhead. The group of them were all shocked and moved closer together, staring at the lights.

Without warning, the lights merged together into one light, which now became a solid object. It descended into a clearing about seventy-five feet away. The group moved closer and saw "three beings walk out and slowly look over their craft as if something was wrong with it. They looked man-like, but walked in an exaggerated upright way and very stiffly. It was at this moment that we were noticed, and we all walked toward the being against our wishes. It felt like we were on a treadmill being drawn toward the craft. The next forty-five minutes were very hurtful and make me sick to even think about . . . we were all violated in different ways."[164]

Abducted in Broad Daylight

Alex Barry (pseudonym) has had alien experiences his entire life. His first experience occurred at age five when he received two "scoop marks" on his right arm. Throughout his life he has had other visitations, including several nighttime abductions.

Once, however, he was abducted during broad daylight. It was 1:30 p.m. on May 22, 2014. Alex was mowing the lawn of his Phoenix home when he felt a strange "energetic change in the atmosphere." His vision began to become affected, making it difficult for him to see the block wall directly in front of him. The energy around him increased and he wondered if perhaps he was having a stroke.

He recognized the feeling. He was being abducted again! He panicked and tried to turn the mower around. At that moment he saw a "being" standing four feet in front of him. It appeared to be semi-transparent and was holding something in its hands. In fight or flight mode, Alex tried to run the being over with the lawnmower, but discovered that he was paralyzed and helpless. The creature raised the object, which emitted a bright flash. Alex immediately fell unconscious to the ground.

He woke up an undetermined amount of time later feeling himself being dropped downward. He fought for consciousness and was finally able to open his eyes. He found himself in his bed, fully dressed in the clothes he had been wearing. The clock now said 5:30 p.m. He was missing four hours of time.

He felt a pain on his shoulder and saw that he had a large bruise. Going outside, he saw that the lawn was still only half-mowed. The lawnmower was now in the middle of the porch and there were grass clippings spread out everywhere. "I never leave things this way," says Alex.

Following the incident he felt "woozy and perplexed" and couldn't remember what had just happened. He went to bed a few hours later but was too upset to sleep. Finally he dozed off, but woke up around 4:30 a.m. in a panic as the memory of what happened that afternoon flooded back into his mind.

The aliens, he realized, had abducted him in broad daylight, right in front of his home. "This has scared me to death," says Alex. "There is something more benign about night abductions. Being taken away in the middle of the day, and obviously against my will, is new to me. I want to know if this has happened to anyone else."[165]

Chapter Six

UFO Crashes

UFO crashes represent perhaps the most extensive type of encounter. Unlike sightings, landings, and onboard experiences, a UFO crash never actually ends. The UFO craft remains on Earth, though in virtually every single case, the debris and bodies are quickly retrieved by what appear to be military officials. Ironically, the cases with the most evidence of all also have the least amount of evidence. In other words, most of the UFO crash/retrieval stories rely almost entirely on eyewitness testimony, and the alleged alien hardware is available only to the privileged few.

Interestingly, UFO researchers were slow to even accept the possibility of UFO crashes. The UFO phenomenon raged for more than twenty-five years before there was any serious attention paid to their crashes. The only exception was Frank Scully, whose best-selling and ground-breaking book, *Behind the Flying Saucers*, revealed the Aztec UFO crash in New Mexico and others—including a crash in Arizona. The book was attacked viciously by debunkers, and Scully was made to look as though he was the victim of a hoax. Today, however, many UFO researchers recognize the validity of UFO crashes and, as a result, more cases are being revealed.

A myth about UFO crashes is that they are rare. When people think of UFO crashes, they think of the UFO crash at Roswell. Others might bring up the UFO crash at Aztec, the crash at Kecksburg, Pennsylvania, or even Arizona's own UFO crash in Paradise Valley. Overall, they believe there are only a handful of such cases. The truth may be very different. Researchers are now uncovering literally hundreds of such cases across the United States and the world. What was first thought to be impossible, and then very rare, is now trending towards becoming common.

Arizona has its own share of these types of cases beginning at the modern age of UFOs in 1947 and continuing to the present day.

Early one morning in October 1947, Selman Graves (age twenty-two), and his brother-in-law, Bob Malody (age sixteen), decided to go rabbit hunting and explore some of the many abandoned mines. They drove to their friend Walt Salyer's ranch house; Salyer was supposed to go with them.

Strangely, Salyer was nowhere to be found, so Graves and Malody retreated to the basement of the ranch house to wait for their friend. Salyer arrived twenty minutes later and seemed strangely agitated. Whenever Graves or Malody got anywhere near the large freezer in his basement, Salyer seemed to become "especially nervous."

Salyer told his friends that they couldn't go hunting on the west part of his ranch because the air force was there and had restricted the area. He said that the air force might be spooked by any gunfire. When Salyer didn't elaborate, Graves and Malody set off alone on horseback, believing that Salyer would join them later.

Next, they climbed to the top of a large hill, which afforded a perfect view of the surrounding area. To the west of Salyer's house, they saw something incredible. "What we saw," said Graves, "can best be described as a large aluminum dome-shaped thing sitting upright in the desert." He estimated it was about thirty-six feet in diameter and about one mile away.

Graves and Malody wondered if the object might be some kind of observatory dome, but there were other strange things going on. Two military vehicles were parked next to the object, and five men were milling around next to it. None appeared to be dressed in military uniform.

Graves wasn't sure what to think of the incident. After going hunting, they returned to Salyer's home. At this point Graves' memory becomes confused. "There were men running around in the basement asking us questions about what we saw," said Graves. "I'm not sure what I told them, but I do remember telling myself not to forget. Not to forget." Graves now believes he was brainwashed and made to forget.

Two years later, something peculiar happened: Graves saw a man with a bulldozer right at the same area where he'd seen the object. "I couldn't figure out what he was doing," said Graves. "First off, he was rather well-groomed for that kind of work, and he seemed to be digging ditches helter-skelter."

Intrigued, Graves approached the man on his break and asked him why he was digging random ditches in this area. Says Graves: "He laughed and admitted that he had been ordered to just mess up the ground."

Years later, in 1962, Graves drove to Salyer's ranch "on a whim," to ask what he remembered about the 1947 incident. Salyer was not happy.

Says Graves: "He immediately got angry. He said, 'Nothing like that happened, and furthermore, you have never been here at my ranch before.'"

The television program *Unsolved Mysteries* heard about the case and decided to do an investigation. Unfortunately, Salyer had died years earlier. They were however, able to obtain some confirmation of the event. Reporter Don Devereaux of the *Scottsdale Progress* newspaper found a resident who had spoken with Salyer about the UFO event.

Writes Devereaux: "He was supposedly talking about the incident, including the bodies in the freezer. The people in the bar thought it was funny and were razzing him about it."

Strangely, Malody has no memory of the incident at all. But he does believe that Graves is telling the truth. As he says: "I don't doubt it." Graves remains convinced that both he and his brother-in-law were victims of some sort of "mind-bending hypnosis" by military officials to make them forget what they had seen.

UFO researcher Sean Casteel, who published an article about the case in *UFO Universe* magazine, writes:

So there you have it. Arizona produces one mystery after another, some rooted in the ever-changing present while others seep up from the dark well of the almost forgotten. If there are answers, they continue to elude us—at least for now.[166]

UFO Crash at Globe

In early 1948, Wayne Henthorn (a former navy seaman) and his brother Glen were driving the back roads outside Globe searching for real estate to purchase. As they traveled down a remote dirt road, they came upon a military road block guarded by police. They were told to turn around and immediately leave the area. The brothers turned around, but not before they both caught a quick glimpse of a large disk-shaped object being loaded onto a trailer used for hauling large and heavy equipment. The object had a large transparent dome, three tripod legs, and looked as if it had been damaged in a crash. They were told to say nothing about what they had seen. Neither of the brothers recognized the object as anything familiar, and it wasn't until later that they realized what they had seen: the recovery of a crashed flying saucer.

The Henthorn brothers can be forgiven for their ignorance. At that time, flying saucers were brand new, though in a few months time, a giant super-wave would leave little doubt that something strange was flying in our skies. Researchers now know that many UFOs crashed in the late 1940s and early 1950s; however, at the time, these events were covered up almost completely.[167]

UFO Crash at Paradise Valley

Frank Scully's explosive book *Behind the Flying Saucers* was the first UFO book published, and also the first to claim that crashed UFOs had been retrieved and studied by the United States military. The book was a bestseller, and Scully almost single-handedly popularized the idea of flying saucers. Later, he was told by Commander Ruppelt (of Project Blue Book) that his book caused the air force more problems than any other because it was so close to the mark.

Scully's book was viciously attacked by the government, and later, even within the UFO field, most researchers gave the book little credence. Scully, it was believed, was the victim of a hoax. However, some researchers eventually took a second look at the case and reversed their opinions. Timothy Good, Linda Moulton Howe, Robert Wood, and other leading researchers now believe the book contains valid information. The book featured chiefly the Aztec UFO crash, outside Farmington, New Mexico. However, Scully also mentioned that other crashes had taken place. His book was the first mention of the May 21, 1953, UFO crash in Paradise Valley, Arizona.

Scully's sources told him that they were actually in Phoenix when the crash occurred. As Paradise Valley is just north of Phoenix, they arrived at the site shortly after it occurred. On the scene, they found a smallish craft thirty-six feet in diameter and two deceased extraterrestrials.

Writes Scully:

ONE OF THE LITTLE MEN WAS HALF OUT OF THE ESCAPE DOOR OR "HATCH," AS THE DOCTOR CALLED IT. THE LITTLE MAN WAS DEAD. THE OTHER LITTLE FELLOW (THERE BEING ONLY A CREW OF TWO ON THIS SHIP) WAS SITTING IN HIS SEAT AT THE CONTROL BOARD. HE WAS ALSO DEAD.

The book, while a bestseller, was debunked with what some researchers believe to be a concerted campaign by military intelligence. The debunking campaign was successful to the point that even UFO researchers believed Scully had been hoaxed and that accounts of flying saucers were pure myth. It was only after Roswell was uncovered in the early 1970s that researchers began to reexamine the Aztec case, and along with it, the Paradise Valley case.

The next hint of the case was perhaps revealed to MUFON researcher Richard Hall back in 1964. Hall spoke with a man (soon to be a commander in Vietnam) who said that, in 1953, a UFO crashed in Arizona. Four bodies were recovered, and the craft was described as thirty feet in diameter and undamaged. "I could not imagine a less likely hoaxer," says Hall.

The third big break on the case came from highly respected researcher Raymond Fowler, perhaps best known for his research into the Betty Andreasson abduction case. Other than Scully, Fowler was the first to speak with a firsthand witness to the crash-site.

Initially known as "Fritz Werner," his real name is now known to be Arthur G. Stancil. He is one of the early whistle-blowers saying that our military had in its possession a crashed UFO. Stancil was an engineer manager at the Air Material

Command at Wright Patterson AFB in Ohio, which has been named by multiple witnesses and researchers as the clearinghouse for UFO hardware. While employed there, Stancil worked closely with Dr. Eric Henry Wang, who was head of the Department of Special Studies.

At the time of the crash Stancil was studying blast effects at Frenchmen's Flats in Nevada when Wang diverted him to a special project. Wang explained to Stancil that a UFO had just crashed nearby, and Wang had been placed in charge of its recovery. He ordered Stancil to go to the site with a group of about forty other scientists to assist in the recovery. Stancil's job was to calculate the velocity and trajectory of the disk based on the structure of the UFO, how deeply it had burrowed into the ground, and the entire blast pattern.

He was taken to the site on a bus with blacked-out windows. He was told to concentrate only on his assigned duties and not look around. Upon arrival, Stancil saw a thirty-foot oval object constructed of "an unfamiliar metal which resembled brushed aluminum." The disk was undamaged and had penetrated only twenty inches into the sand. He saw a hatch about three and a half feet high. There was no apparent landing gear.

After making his measurements and studying the crash site, Stancil concluded that the craft had struck the ground at an estimated 1,200 mph. He also concluded that the craft was not human-made. "The object was not built by anything, obviously, that we know about on Earth," said Stancil. "It was more like a tear-drop-shaped cigar . . . like a streamlined cigar."

Next to the craft there was a tent being guarded by military police. Said Stancil: "I managed to glance inside at one point, and saw the dead body of a four-foot human-like creature in a silver metallic suit. The skin on its face was dark brown."

Stancil says that each of the other scientists was escorted one-by-one to perform their specialty, and then was returned to the bus. Afterward, an air force colonel made them sign the Official Secrets Act and made them all swear under oath to never reveal what they had seen.

Despite the oath, Stancil spoke with another scientist who said that he looked inside the object and saw two small swivel seats and a strange-looking instrument panel. After being interviewed by Raymond Fowler, Stancil signed an affidavit attesting to the truth of the event.

Another possible source comes from crash/retrieval researcher Leonard Stringfield. Reportedly, the witness was taken in April (May?) 1953 to a desert area to examine the crash of a flying saucer. The witness described the object thirty feet in diameter. It had no apparent damage. He was not allowed to enter the ship, but he did see a hatchway about four feet tall and two feet wide. His job was to analyze the metal. He spent the next two days on the site. After his tests, he concluded that the object was not constructed on Earth.

In 1977, after Stringfield gave a lecture talking about the Kingman UFO crash, a National Guard employee approached him and said that back in 1953 he was stationed at Wright-Patterson AFB in Ohio. He was there when a group of crates arrived from a UFO crash site in Arizona. The crates, he learned, contained three humanoid bodies. They were four foot tall with large heads and brownish skin. Each body was packed in dry ice to preserve it. One of the bodies was apparently female.

Some of the crates also contained debris, which the officer said had Sanskrit-like symbols etched into it. The witness refused to make a written statement. He did ask his superiors if he could leave a written statement to be opened upon his death. His superiors emphatically denied the request.

Further confirmation of the crash comes from Judy Woolcott, whose husband claims to have been among the first at the crash site. Woolcott told his wife that he was on duty at the air control tower at Kingman when he and the other personnel began to track an unknown object. They watched as the object quickly lost altitude and disappeared from their scopes. Moments later there was a huge flash of light in the distance outside the city.

Woolcott and a group of other men piled into their jeeps and drove to where the object had impacted the ground. They searched the area, finally coming upon a large object that was partially imbedded into the sandy soil. He saw no bodies, nor did he see any damage to the craft. They were about to examine it more closely when more military officials arrived and ordered them off the site.

Woolcott and the others were taken back to the base and told that nothing had happened, they had seen nothing, and they were not to speak about it. However, he did hear other witnesses say that they had seen bodies.

Ten years after the incident, while serving in Vietnam, Woolcott wrote all this in a letter to his wife. One week later, he was killed in action.

Researcher Linda Moulton Howe received confirmation of the Kingman crash in a roundabout way. On April 9, 1983, Howe met with Richard Doty of the AFOSI at Kirtland AFB. While there, she was shown a document titled in all caps:

BRIEFING PAPER FOR THE PRESIDENT OF THE UNITED STATES OF AMERICA ABOUT

THE SUBJECT OF UNIDENTIFIED AERIAL CRAFT (UACS)

Howe began to read the document and saw that it listed several UFO crash retrieval incidents, including Roswell, New Mexico; Aztec, New Mexico; Kingman, Arizona; and others.

More information about the Kingman crash comes from Bill Uhouse, who says that the disk was in effect given to the US military by the ETs. "This ET craft was a controlled craft," says Uhouse, "that the aliens wanted to present to our government. It landed about fifteen miles from what used to be an army airbase, which is now a defunct army base."

The first soldiers to enter the craft reportedly became nauseous and disoriented to the point that they by the time they exited the craft, they had little memory of what they had seen.

The disk, says Uhouse, was transported to Area 51. "It made loud humming noises the whole time," explains Uhouse. "The military didn't know what to do. They weren't sure if it was going to explode or what, so they left it sitting out in the open, on the tarmac for nine months."

More recently, researcher Len Kasten has uncovered a source that says the Paradise Valley craft actually contained live aliens who survived the crash and ended up working closely with the US military. The Paradise Valley UFO became the model used to reverse-engineer other UFOs, and the ETs allegedly assisted in helping the military scientists to understand and use the craft.

Robert Carr, an expert in nonverbal communication who was apparently one of the scientists "in the know" when it came to crashed saucers has gone on record talking about the subject long before most researchers. Normally tight-lipped on the subject, Carr did grant an interview to researcher Gray Barker, during which he revealed some facts about the Paradise Valley UFO crash.

"The other wreck," says Carr, "was found that summer in the desert in Arizona by visual observation. This one was burned and it had been out there in the desert for too long. There were organic materials left, but the predators and the heat of the desert had pretty well taken care of the occupants. But they scooped it up and took it along."[168]

Crash at Fort Huachuca

Another UFO crash in Arizona that has received almost no publicity occurred in the early 1950s south of Fort Huachuca. In 1981, while giving a UFO lecture at Fort Huachuca, researcher Wendelle Stevens was approached by a retired deputy county sheriff who said that he was a firsthand witness.

The sheriff was on patrol on the south edge of town when he saw a large number of vehicles and a crowd of people alongside the road. The sheriff stopped and saw that the military police were trying to move people back. They told him that a UFO had crashed back in the ravine off the road, and they needed his help to keep people away. He assisted setting up barricades and watched as military men wearing navy-blue coveralls arrived with heavy lifting equipment and floodlights. The sheriff was cleared from the area before he got to see anything else. The entire operation went on all night, and the next day, all the equipment was removed from the area, which was scrubbed clean of evidence.

Stevens later found another witness, Michael H. Landwehr, who was working as a dispatcher on the base at the time of the crash. Landwehr didn't see anything, but he heard about the crash when it occurred and said that the whole base was buzzing about it.

Further confirmation of the Huachuca UFO crash comes from researcher Lou Farish, who received a letter in 1985 from a lady whose husband worked at the Airfield at Huachuca. Before he died, he told his wife that in early 1950, he was on duty when they picked up a blip on radar moving at high speed. No known aircraft were in the area, so the base was put on alert. They watched the blip as it descended to the ground and disappeared.

Thinking a plane had crashed, they immediately sent out a team to investigate and rescue. Upon arrival, however, they found a saucer-shaped craft sticking out of a dune at a 45-degree angle. There were no windows, doors or markings. Seeing that the craft was not a plane, the military police immediately began to clear the area. The lady's husband got a good look at the craft and insists it was not a plane.

They were all shuttled back to the base. Shortly later, a major arrived and forced each of them to sign a statement that they heard and saw nothing, and that nothing had occurred that night. In the weeks and months following the incident, the officer learned that the disk was transported to Nevada to an underground area for study, but officials were unable to gain entry into the craft. All attempts to dent, scratch, burn, drill, or cut the craft were met with failure, and the disk remained sealed.[169]

Secret Canyon UFO Crash

As reported to NUFORC, on August 4, 1994, a resident of Sedona was stargazing with her husband when she noticed what appeared to be a very bright star in the northwest sky. She pointed it out to her husband. Minutes later, they saw a "white laser beam" come from the east and strike the object, which they realized then was not a star. Says the witness: "We could see the object flare at first, and then about twenty seconds later it exploded, causing a firework type of effect [with] sparks floating down. There was no sound and we just sat there shocked at what we had just seen."

Two hours later, their friends in West Sedona called to tell them that there was a fire burning west of Highway 89-A in Secret Canyon. The next morning they went to the local coffee house and heard people talking about the fire. Says the witness: "One couple stated that about an hour before the fire was reported, they saw a small flaming object fall into Secret Canyon, and they thought that was the cause of the fire. That would have been about the time that we witnessed the explosion in the sky."

According to the witness, the fire was so remote that it was allowed to burn out. For the next ten days the fire burned, and firefighters only began to fight it once it began to come close to the resorts in Oak Creek Canyon. The canyon itself was closed for three months, during which time residents saw trucks traveling in and out of the area.

The witness also reported that she heard stories of hikers (including two police officers) exploring the area, but being turned back by military-type men in black uniforms with M-16 rifles. According to the witness: "There is a lot that has—and still does—go on in this area revolving around UFOs and alien life forms. People just don't talk openly about it anymore."[170]

The Show Low UFO Crash

One evening around 10:00 p.m. on June 4, 1996, a lady was in her home in the small town of Concho in rural Apache County, about twenty-three miles east of Show Low. She was entertaining three guests when one of them jumped up, shouted an expletive, and said, "Did you see that?" He excitedly explained that he had just seen a UFO on fire streak downward across the sky, apparently crashing. Another guest said that she saw the object too and confirmed the details.

All four witnesses ran outside and drove off in a jeep toward where they had seen the object go down. After crossing Highway 61, they came upon an elderly couple who had parked along the highway and were staring off into the field. They stopped, and the couple asked if they had seen the UFO crash. They explained that they were driving west down Highway 61 when they saw it crash, and they pointed to the area where they saw it go down.

For the next hour, the witnesses continued to the site via an old cattle trail until they came upon a deep canyon. They couldn't go any farther. At the bottom of the canyon, to their amazement, was the crashed UFO. Says the witness: "It was an oblong egg shape. The color was strange—it was the color of a Caucasian's skin with a fading tan, and it faintly glowed."

The object appeared to have two pillars, side by side, as though framing a doorway. It was about fifty feet across. There was a pickup near the object and a helicopter had landed nearby. They watched for awhile, but after there was no activity, they decided to return home. The witness reports that she had seen UFOs before, but had always been alone. This was her first sighting with other witnesses.[171]

Crash Over Seligman

On January 5, 2004, three friends were driving home from Las Vegas. They were near Seligman when the driver pointed out the two "really bright stars." It was about forty-five minutes before sunset, and when the "stars" began to move, the witnesses realized that they were seeing something else.

A few minutes later, one of the lights turned into a cigar shape and became bright red in color. At that point it appeared to explode. As they watched, it fell to the ground. At the same time, the second white object also turned bright red, then darted several miles within seconds, stopped and turned different colors, then lifted into the sky, only to drop down again and dart in the reverse direction, then take off upward again.

It performed these darting maneuvers until it reached the end of the mountain range along Interstate 40, where it was joined by five or six identical-looking objects, each one of varying intensity. All of the objects continued to zigzag back and forth performing rapid accelerations, stopping, moving up and down and side to side.

Then one-by-one, each object moved off behind the mountains or just disappeared. The witnesses were interviewed by Peter Davenport of the UFO Reporting Center who said that they sounded "sincere and quite credible."[172]

Aliens Hidden by the Military

More evidence of crashed UFOs in Arizona comes from researcher Dr. Berthold E. Schwarz, who had the opportunity to interview a highly decorated military intelligence officer about a remarkable UFO experience in the Arizona desert. The officer insisted upon remaining anonymous. He told Schwarz that, around 1975, he was working in military intelligence in Arizona when he told a coworker and friend that he had seen UFOs while overseas. His friend responded by saying: "Well, would you like to see some aliens?"

Seeing that his friend was not joking, the officer agreed. The officer and his friend proceeded to drive to an unnamed base in Arizona. They entered an underground area, and walked to a vaulted room.

Says the officer: "When we got in, I observed five humanoid figures. I'll give you a description as best I can. Remember I doubted what I saw. They were very, very white. There were no ears, no nostrils—there were only openings—a very small mouth, and the eyes were large. There was no facial hair, no head hair, no pubic hair. They were nude. I think the tallest one could have been about three-and-a-half feet, maybe a little bit taller."

Each of the bodies was in its own tank. The officer saw that they each had small even teeth. His friend explained that the aliens were vegetarians and were estimated to be at least 200 years old. Some of the bodies had suture marks where they had been autopsied.

His friend also showed him various pieces of alien machinery and hardware. He was even allowed to enter inside a crashed UFO, which he described at about twenty feet across with a slight dome in the center. Inside, the walls were dull brown and soft to the touch. There were no rivets or screws or weld-marks. Everything was utterly smooth. There was a tiny chair in front of a computer or television screen, with knobs, switches, and lights off to the side. There were also little compartments hidden in the walls that held containers of food. A very narrow aisle separated the various chambers.

The officer was not happy to see the aliens and the UFO, and as soon as he realized what they were, he became very frightened. As he says: "I wanted out. I was scared. I wanted my security, and what protection did I have if I were caught. I had no right to be there . . . I wanted to have a clean record."

The officer was right to be fearful. Not long after his secret rendezvous to see the alien craft, his family members and friends and neighbors were visited by intelligence officers asking all kinds of questions about his background.[173]

Chapter Seven

Contemporary Cases: 2000-2015

If there is one thing that all researchers agree upon, it's that the UFOs are not going to leave. As the following current cases show, UFOs are here to stay.

Sunflower UFO

On the evening of April 10, 2000, two siblings (a brother and sister) were driving into Sunflower when the valley below them lit up with a strange red light.

"Oh, my God! A fire!" said the sister.

The brother wasn't so sure. As they descended into the valley, they approached the lighted area that was "bright as day."

Finally, they passed a grove of trees and saw the source of the light. Hovering about thirty feet above a two-story home, and about 500 feet off the road was an enormous metallic craft, dwarfing the house in size. It was about twenty stories tall with a row of bright white lights blazing from each of the twenty stories.

A bright red light shone down on the house below and was shining out from every window.

Says the brother: "I stopped the truck and turned out my lights and just looked in amazement. My sister panicked.

"Let's go!" she said.

The brother wanted to stay and watch, but finally drove off. The ship never moved the entire time it was in view. Says the brother: "This was, and is, a mother ship."[174]

Bubba

Throughout July and August 2000, a mysterious red light appeared over and over again over the Gilbert area. NUFORC received more than fifty reports from witnesses, each of them describing a bright red light that would hover at a high altitude, sometimes remaining for a few minutes, sometimes for much longer. The object appeared with such regularity that witnesses nicknamed it Bubba. UFO researcher Tom King was able to capture video footage of the object. Whatever it was remains a mystery.[175]

UFO Causes Dust-Devils

On November 21, 2000, a father and his daughter were driving westbound through Kingman when they came upon an enormous 1,000-foot-tall dust-devil off to the left. The daughter (who was driving) exited the freeway to get a better look. They parked in front of a field and watched the huge dust-devil dance around the field about 500 feet away.

Then they saw something else. Directly above the dust-devil was a "highly reflective saucer-disk shape." A few minutes later they watched another disk-shaped object approach the first. The two objects remained about fifty feet apart as they swayed slightly back and forth. After about eight minutes, the objects disappeared, and the dust-devils collapsed and were gone.[176]

UFO Escorted by Military

One of the most common skeptical explanations of UFOs is that they are really secret military craft. While most investigators disagree with this, there is evidence that at least some UFOs may be flown by Earthlings. In late November and early December, a wave of black triangle sightings swept over parts of Arizona. In a few of the cases it appeared that the military was not only aware of the craft, but was escorting it.

On November 28, 2000, Jason Ingraham observed a dark triangular object with deep red lights blinking on and off on each corner. The object moved in a straight line, then leaned to the left and rotated in a clockwise motion before disappearing behind some distant trees. Says Jason: "The movements were so smooth and wavering that it seemed unreal."

Jason also says: "There were six normal airplanes in the sky along with the very different flying triangle." While it's not clear whether the planes could see the triangle, another case a few days later was less ambiguous.

At 6:45 p.m., on December 1, 2000, a witness in Avondale observed a large triangular-shaped object covered with lights moving toward South Mountain. Says the witness: "There seemed to be helicopters flying alongside the flying triangle that looked like they were protecting it."

A half-hour later, at 7:18 p.m., Rob Meyers of Rimrock looked out the window of his living room and saw a group of lights hovering about 1,000 feet overhead. He called over his friend, Dara, who looked at the lights and shouted out, "That's a UFO!"

Rob and Dara dashed outside and saw that the lights were actually a huge "ship." Nearby, they saw another ship. The first craft shined a beam of light down and started to move toward them. It stopped and then the other ship blinked once and disappeared.

When the first craft remained, Rob dashed inside and telephoned a neighbor, asking him to go outside and look at the UFO. The friend went outside and also saw the craft.[177]

Light Display Over Casa Grande

As reported by MUFON investigator Ken Kerber, on May 29, 2001 at 8:20 p.m., an unidentified object hovered over the Casa Grande area. The main witness, Leonard Chavez, was driving south on Chiu-Chiu Road when he saw a pair of lights appear about fifty feet above him and to the right. The lights were about six to ten feet in diameter, bright but muted, as though shining through semi-opaque glass. As he watched, the two lights blinked out but were replaced by two more lights next to the first two. Then these blinked off and two more appeared. Finally, all eight lights flashed simultaneously.

Chavez now realized he was seeing a large triangular-shaped object, dull black in color with no visible markings. The lights continued to blink on and off in sequence. Chavez could see that the lights were inset into panels. The object was totally silent and hovered in place.

Realizing he was seeing an actual UFO, Chavez quickly drove a short distance to his home, picked up two members of his family, and drove back to the location of the UFO. The object was gone, but after driving around, they spotted it again about a mile to the south. They chased the object as it moved south over the mountains and disappeared into the distance. Another car behind Chavez also saw the object, but these witnesses have not been located.

After interviewing the witnesses, MUFON field investigator Ken Kerber said they were "of sound minds, and honest in their recollections without exaggeration."[178]

UFOs Over Luke AFB

At 8:45 p.m. on October 19, 2001, a gentleman went outside of the store where he worked in Phoenix to have a smoke. Movement overhead caught his eye.

The witness describes what happened next:

> I LOOKED UP TO SEE A GROUP OF THREE RED/ORANGE, SOMEWHAT BRIGHT YET FUZZY-LOOKING LIGHTS FLYING AT WHAT SEEMED TO BE A COUPLE OF HUNDRED FEET ABOVE MY HEAD, BUT COMPLETELY SILENT. IT TRAVELED AT A VERY FAST SPEED FROM EAST TO WEST ACROSS THE SKY TOWARDS LUKE AIR FORCE BASE. THIS TOOK A TOTAL OF ABOUT SIX TO EIGHT SECONDS. JUST AS IT WAS PASSING OVER THE TOP OF THE ROOF THE HOUSE, MY RECEPTIONIST LOOKED OUT THE DOOR AND SAID, "WHAT'S THAT?"

As the witness explained what he had just seen, they both saw another boomerang-shaped "cloudy" object move across the sky at "an extremely fast speed."[179]

UFO Hovers Over Gold Mine

There are dozens of cases on record in which UFOs have been seen hovering over various mines. A stunning example occurred on December 28, 2001, over a gold mine in the desert outside Tucson.

"I am a regular guy," says the witness. "I am a four-year veteran of the army . . . I have an associate's degree in structural engineering and an advanced degree in heavy equipment operation. My name is Barry."

Barry was running the night shift, using a track hoe to feed an incinerator. His co-worker was a retired special forces major. A winter storm was moving in and there was a cloud ceiling at about 9,500 feet.

Looking up, he was shocked to see an "immense craft" hovering over a nearby mountain, directly above a gold mine. Using the highway to gauge the size, Barry estimated that the craft was more than a mile long. It had a row of sequential running lights that illuminated the cloud cover above it. Says Barry:

> MY ESTEEMED COLLEAGUE GOT A DEATHLY WHITE SHEEN TO HIS FACE AND WOULD NOT COME OUT OF HIS PERSONAL JEEP; HE WAS SCARED AND HE WAS BABBLING LIKE A CHILD. ME, I TURNED THE TRACK HOE TO FACE IT AND KEPT FLICKING MY DAY-LIGHTERS IN THE HOPE THEY COULD COME AND SEE WHO WAS BEHIND THOSE LIGHTS . . . I FELT AT EASE—NO PANIC. YOU SEE, I FELT AS THESE WERE MY FRIENDS, LIKE WE HAD MET BEFORE.

The object disappeared and reappeared two more times in slightly different locations, but "never too far from this gold mine it was hovering over."

The next night, two military attack Cobra helicopters hovered over Barry's jobsite and just sat there in the sky until Barry finally turned on the floodlights. At that point, the helicopters circled the jobsite several times and then took off "directly towards that gold mine."

Two weeks later, Barry's coworker quit, and made it clear that he never wanted to talk about what happened. Barry, however, says that he has had encounters in the past. Less than a year after the sighting, he reported it to NUFORC.[180]

Quartzite Orbs

A remarkable UFO was seen by several witnesses on March 20, 2002, over the town of Quartzite. Around 11:30 p.m., they saw a very bright light low in the sky moving horizontally and then suddenly upward. Behind the light, they could just barely make out "a dark, rounded shape." Then the object vanished. This was followed by a wave of sightings. Says the witness: "There was a great deal of light movement activity in the sky for over an hour. Lights moving vertically, zigzagging, steady lights, rapidly blinking lights, disappearing lights—but they were not nearly as big as the first one we saw."[181]

Darting Spheres

On April 6, 2003, a witness was outside his home in Phoenix when he saw a "round object" very high in the sky. What caught his eye was the way it maneuvered at various speeds, stopping and then changing directions at a 90-degree angle. It rose up and down, moved slowly and then quickly, and then stopped again. The object had no visible lights but brightly reflected the afternoon sunlight. At one point, a commercial aircraft passed beneath the object, indicating that the object was extremely high, and therefore probably quite large.

Fifteen minutes into the sighting, the witness saw another similar object approach from a stop. Like the first one it made a "sharp 90-degree turn and headed east."[182]

UFO Hovers Over Runway

On September 29, 2003, about fifteen minutes after midnight, a security officer at the San Carlos Apache Reservation was sent outside to confirm that the airport runway was free of any debris. To his shock, the officer saw three lights over the middle part of the runway, each about 100 feet off the ground in a triangular formation about as wide as a football field.

Says the witness: "While approaching the runway, the lights started to fade out. I then called over the radio, and other residential securities who were in the area confirmed the lights. The entire sighting lasted only about forty-five seconds, but it was long enough for the security officer to become convinced that he had seen something very unusual.[183]

The 2004 Sightings

The year of 2004 produced several interesting and well-verified sightings. Activity began early in the year. At 7:30 p.m. on January 16, 2004, a police detective from Southern California was camping in the desert outside Quartzite when he saw a bright orange-white light appear in the southeast sky. Numerous other campers were also in the area.

The light zoomed towards the campers, then appeared to stop. Says the detective: "As we watched, another light shot from the bottom of the main object— like a shooting star—straight toward the ground at high speed until it dissipated to nothing."

The detective grabbed his video camera and was able to capture several moments of footage as the object moved away. Says the witness: "I have never seen anything before like this. We had several witnesses present."

There are many cases on record in which UFOs have been drawn to bright lights on the ground. An unusual example occurred at 9:00 a.m. on January 30, 2004, outside the town of Saint Johns. The witness was burning wood debris in a small bonfire outside his home when a UFO appeared. Says the witness:

> I SAW, ABOUT 100 YARDS AWAY, A PERFECT SPHERE ABOUT FIVE OR SIX FEET ACROSS, HOVERING SEVENTY-FIVE YARDS OFF THE GROUND, AND IT WAS MOVING VERY SLOW. IT APPEARED TO BE OBSERVING FROM A DISTANCE.

The witness decided to investigate.

> I WALKED TOWARD THE SPHERE AND IT CHANGED DIRECTION, AND AS I COMPENSATED, IT CHANGED DIRECTION AGAIN. HERE IS THE IMPORTANT POINT: I DON'T THINK I WAS SUPPOSED TO SEE THE SPHERE BECAUSE IT WAS ALMOST CLOAKED WITH THE BACKGROUND. THE CLOSEST I COULD COME TO DESCRIBING THIS WAS THAT IT REFRACTED THE LIGHT ALMOST AS IF YOU WERE LOOKING AT A MIRRORED BALL IN WATER.

The witness thinks that the object realized it was being observed because it then made several slow evasive maneuvers and then, dropping low to the ground, became fully cloaked. The entire sighting lasted about five minutes. The witness was so impressed by his sighting that he contacted radio stations and UFO organizations.

Less than two months later, on April 9, 2004, a couple driving home to Bullhead City saw a bright light "ten times larger than Venus" ahead of their vehicle facing north. It wasn't Venus, which they could see off to the west. The bright light they now saw was attached to a vertical wing-like structure. The object was moving in pivoting circles, sometimes slowing down or speeding up. Says the witness: "I'm a trained observer, and work security for the federal government. I've never seen a UFO before. This object was seen by many others."

A few weeks later, on April 28, 2004, a man driving east on Highway 60 outside Superior saw a low flying object near Gold Canyon on the north side of the road. What first appeared to be fireworks, he now saw were "evenly spaced rotating lights." The object moved off.

About fifteen minutes later, he saw the object again to the south. "This time it was lower in the night sky," says the witness, "and I got scared . . . It was certainly a craft of some sort." The area is known for being used by the military for F-16 fighter training flights, and the witness wondered if perhaps the government was testing a new aircraft. But unable to identify the craft, the witness realized that he may have seen a UFO, and a few months later reported his sighting to NUFORC.

There are numerous cases in which UFOs have caused power outages. There are also many cases in which UFOs hover over nuclear power plants. This next encounter provides an example of both.

On June 22, 2004, an unexplained surge left nearly 65,000 Arizonans across the state without power. The surge shut down all three units at the Palo Verde Nuclear Power Plant.

According to CBS 5 news in Phoenix, at the time of the sighting numerous people in the Palo Verde area observed and even videotaped strange lights that were hovering above the nearby nuclear power plant.

Astronomer Steve Kates (locally known as "Dr. Sky") examined the video footage of the object and believes it is legitimate.

One month later, on July 24, 2004, a Phoenix witness reported seeing numerous orbs over the downtown area. Says the witness: "They were multicolored with reds, white, orange, and blue, and there was a distortion around the objects like they were under water in the sky." The objects moved slowly in a meandering way for the next thirty-five minutes until moving off into the haze. Says the witness: "These are the weirdest objects I have ever seen. They were side by side the whole time as if shadowing each other."

UFOs come in all shapes and sizes. In this next case, two people observed a massive triangular-shaped object while driving on Highway 60 in downtown Phoenix. It was September 28, 2004, at 8:15 p.m., when they saw the triangle. About fifty red glowing lights pulsed along the arms of the V while a single bright light shone from each tip. Says the witness: "There was no noise; it was silent. It appeared to be hovering or moving at a real slow pace. There were two airplanes flying around the craft, appearing to inspect the huge UFO. The planes looked like ants compared to the huge craft."

The witnesses noticed that other people on the highway were also looking at the object, including the police officer driving alongside them. One of the witnesses filmed the object with her cell phone, but says that although the triangle is visible, it is very blurry. The witness was amazed by the sighting and called it as feeling "unreal."[184]

UFO Photographed at Catholic Church Rock

On April 6, 2005, one man was in the right place at the right time to capture a remarkable photograph. Says the witness: "My family and I were on vacation in Tempe, Arizona, and decided to go to Sedona for the day. While at the Catholic Church built in the rock in Sedona, I saw a flash in the sky, a reflection from the sun. I grabbed my camera and started taking pictures. I was only able to get one shot. I waited until now because this was my third sighting."[185]

Radiated by a UFO

As reported to the National UFO Reporting Center, a former deputy sheriff says that on April 17, 2005, at 11:30 p.m., he saw three cigar-shaped craft move over his home in Phoenix. Each craft had blue and yellow lights on the sides. They next started performing bizarre maneuvers, moving up and down and side-to-side, still staying in perfect formation. Finally, they came to a complete stop and hovered about a quarter-mile away, then moved away with a great burst of speed.

Within five minutes of their departure, the witness suffered "a very bad headache." He says he also felt "somewhat disoriented." A few hours later, he became nauseous and began vomiting. His wife discovered "several dry-skin red circular markings on my back."[186]

Cemetery UFOs Photographed

Researchers have noticed that there are an unusually large number of UFO sightings over cemeteries. Proof of this is the photo captured by a witness on May 14, 2005, over Mesa City Cemetery. The witness was visiting his deceased parents. As he left the cemetery, he decided to take a picture of the area. He noticed nothing in the sky at the time, however upon reviewing the photos was surprised to see two strange disk-like objects apparently hovering at a low altitude over the cemetery.[187]

UFO-Car Encounter in Gila Bend

Trevor (not his real name) never believed in UFOs until an incident that occurred on June 28, 2005. He was driving with his girlfriend along Interstate 8 near Gila Bend just after midnight when they saw a strange bright light ahead of them on the road. As they approached it, the light became even brighter, and they saw that it was about 250 feet off the side of the road. Their radio began emitting weird harmonic sounds. When they turned it off, they heard the same sound emanating from the craft.

They pulled over to observe the light and saw that it was disk-shaped. Several other cars also pulled off the highway, some of them taking pictures. A weird smoke or fog surrounded the craft. About six orange lights flashed in a seemingly random pattern around the object.

Trevor tried to start the car to leave, but the engine wouldn't turn on. The car parked ahead of him was also having the same problem. Finally, both cars started and they took off with a pack of cars. Immediately the object moved with the cars, pacing them for the next five minutes before disappearing. Says Trevor: "This sighting was a shocking experience and I don't care what anyone says. I've seen it with my own two eyes, and I was there."[188]

UFO Studies Jet Contrail

On the afternoon of April 30, 2006, a retired paramedic was out in the Sonora Desert about forty miles away from Phoenix Sky Harbor Airport when he saw a jetliner with a large double contrail passing overhead. He knew this was a busy flight path for aircraft and didn't think much of it until he glanced up and saw something strange. "A black object had appeared between the jetliner's contrail," explains the witness, "and looked to be following it."

The witness had his Kodak Z740 in his hand. He quickly zoomed in on the object and snapped a photo of it. The object continued to follow the jet for about thirty seconds, then "disappeared."[189]

Beamed by a UFO

In an undated encounter (circa 2006?), Victoria (a nurse) and her friend decided to go camping in the wilderness of Aravaipa Canyon between Tucson and Gila. Night had fallen when a large circular object with multicolored lights around the circumference flew into view and began to descend toward them. Without warning, a bright beam of white light shot out from the saucer, moved back and forth and came to rest on the two campers. At that moment, it turned off and the object sped away. Victoria was so impressed by her experience that she later spoke before MUFON groups to share the details of her encounter.[190]

UFO Circles Leupp

Siblings Sean and Deanna Dover had seen UFOs before, but this time was different. On January 24, 2007, Sean and Deanna were driving home to Leupp when they saw a bright object hovering ahead of them over the highway. It appeared to be a triangular shape with several lights on it. As they watched, the object disappeared and reappeared a few times.

By the time they arrived in Leupp, the object was flying over the local church and public school.

The siblings rushed home and got their parents. The entire family watched with night-vision goggles as the object began to circle the town. Before long, it was approached by two military jets.

Meanwhile, other witnesses in Leupp watched the spectacle. Denise Fredericks (a teacher) had just arrived home when her husband told her that their friends had just phoned them to say that there was a UFO over Leupp. Looking up, they watched the object approach. "It was flying straight," said Fredericks, "then it turned. It went toward Bird Springs and then turned toward Tolani Lake, and then came back this way." Fredericks also saw that the object was being chased by jets.

More witnesses gathered as the object circled overhead no less than fifteen times. Finally, the lights on the craft went dark and it darted southwest toward Winslow.

Those who saw the object were most impressed by the object's low altitude and lack of fear. Says Deanna: "I've never seen anything that detailed before . . . it was so close."

Four days later, on January 28, 2007, Victoria Liljenquist was with her friend, Robert, driving along Highway 60 in Apache Junction when a strange cloud caught her attention. She had a strange feeling that a UFO was going to come out of the cloud. She pulled out her camera and began taking pictures. They didn't see anything, but when she looked at the pictures she was astonished. "I know this may sound strange," says Liljenquist, "but it was like the UFO was just waiting to jump into the shot when I could photograph with a clear view . . . I share this because I was feeling so strongly the presence of something showing up, and it did. Many of you reading these reports may have feelings like this . . . I believe there is a telepathic communication that takes place when I film, and I know many other investigators and even novice photographers experience this."[191]

Brazen UFOs

In late 2007, a series of low-level sightings showed that, in some instances, UFOs have no fear of being seen. On October 28, 2007, a man was outside his home in Mesa when he saw a "dark mass" moving overhead just over the rooftops. It had no visible wings or tail structure, but it did have a bright light in front of it. It was silent until it approached within a hundred feet of the witness who said, "I could have hit the underside of it with a baseball if I had one in my hand at the time." The object moved away over the rooftops and toward the Superstition Mountains.

The downtown Capital Mall in Phoenix has a webcam that faces northeast. At 7:15 on November 23, 2007, the webcam caught an image of what appears to be a glowing craft hovering very low directly over a nearby building for almost fifteen minutes The next day the object was back, this time hovering for seventy-five minutes.[192]

Videotaping UFOs

On August 5, 2008, a videographer and his friend were videotaping an approaching lightning storm over Tucson. He had often filmed similar storms hoping to capture interesting images of lightning. On this occasion, as he examined the film, he found something strange: a ball of light that emerged from a cloud and zigzagged off into the distance. He examined the footage further and saw three disk-shaped objects flying together. Another piece of the footage shows a glowing object about 100 yards away, which darts up from behind a pine tree, flips over, and descends behind a vehicle across the street. Another section shows an object moving through the clouds and another moving low along the horizon. He tracked other objects zigzagging or moving in circular patterns, none of which he or his friend saw while they were videotaping the storm. After reviewing his footage, he became convinced that he had videotaped a number of UFOs, and he reported his case to NUFORC.

Another interesting case occurred to a gentleman who wishes to remain anonymous. He had worked for the navy and the SAIC for many years and had finally obtained a secret clearance. Then, one evening around 9:00 p.m. on November 1, 2008, the gentlemen was driving along Interstate 40 about twenty miles east of Kingman when he had an experience that changed his life:

> I SAW A LARGE LOW-FLYING CRAFT OVER MY CAR … I WAS DRIVING WEST AND IT WAS HEADING NORTHWEST. IT WAS THE BIGGEST THING I'VE EVER SEEN FLYING AND I WORKED ON THE C-17 AND THE MD-11. (THEY ARE BIG PLANES.) THIS THING HAS SPARKS AND ELECTRICITY ARCING AND CRAWLING ON THE BOTTOM. THAT'S WHAT I SAW FIRST; THEN I SAW THE ENGINES: SIX BUILDING-SIZED ION PLASMA ENGINES—THREE ACROSS THE TOP AND THREE ON THE BOTTOM. EACH WAS ABOUT TWENTY FEET TALL AND FIFTY FEET WIDE. THERE WAS A BLUE WHITE PURPLE GLOW AND HAZE OUT BEHIND IT BY THIRTY TO 100 FEET… THIS THING LOOKED LIKE THE OPENING SCENE IN STAR WARS. I COULD NOT MAKE OUT THE SHAPE OR OUTLINE, BUT THE ARCING DID LIGHT UP THE BOTTOM AND I'VE NEVER SEEN ANYTHING LIKE IT. IT LOOKED LIKE A GIANT CIRCUIT BOARD DESIGN FROM WHAT I CAN RECALL.

The craft appeared to be about 500 to 1,000 feet above his car. He had a video camera, but by the time he pulled it out, the craft was just a light on the horizon. He filmed what he could, and after reviewing the tape, he noticed something very peculiar. "I also didn't mention some weirdness about the video because I'm not sure about the speed setting. According to the time code on the video, I traveled one mile in thirty-two seconds! My car was packed to the roof with my stuff, going up a grade, in an old Pathfinder. No freaking way I was going 120 mph, not even 75."

The witness speculates that the "anti-gravity" engines on the craft may have caused the weird time discrepancy. He is not convinced that the craft was necessarily ET in origin. As he says: "What I saw was not impossible for NASA to build and that's why I think it was ours and we have a secret space program going with star ships."

In 2011, the witness finally decided to report his sighting in an official capacity. He wrote an email to a popular leading UFO researcher and pressed send. Immediately his computer crashed. He went to his navy laptop, re-wrote the email and pressed send. The navy computer promptly crashed. Says the witness: "That really frightened me."

After having his computers fixed, he reported his sighting and continued to experience a series of computer breakdowns. During this time, he was working on secret projects for the navy, and he wondered if they were trying to prevent him from telling his story. He received confirmation of his suspicions when somebody broke into his home. Writes the witness, "I am 200 percent sure that people were in my condo while I was at work, after I had contacted [the UFO researchers]." Nothing was taken.

In September 2011, after reporting his sighting, experiencing the computer crashes, and the home invasion, the witness reports that he was fired. While he was told the reason was financial, he wonders if his going public with his UFO story was a factor. Says the witness: "Please don't use my name. I don't know if I'll ever apply for another government job again."[193]

Disk Over Lake Havasu

A new video allegedly portraying a daylight disk over Lake Havasu is attracting the attention of UFO researchers. Taken on July 31, 2009, the video shows a shiny metallic domed disk cavorting over the lake, glinting in the sun. The case was reported to MUFON, which published a photograph of it in their monthly *MUFON UFO Journal*.[194]

Congress UFOs

As reported to MUFON (Case #27685), a retired air force officer was driving after midnight on May 19, 2010, when he had a terrifying encounter with a UFO. He was a few miles west of Congress when he pulled off to relieve himself. That's when he saw a strange red light, which he first thought was a helicopter. The red light was sending down a powerful beam of white light, as though searching for something. The officer was puzzled as the area was completely desolate.

The witness returned to his car, at which point the red light began to circle around him getting closer and closer. It had no strobes and made no noise, which also puzzled the officer.

The object quickly moved toward him and he realized that the object was not a helicopter. He saw now that it was a small ball of light, and it was hovering about twenty feet away and ten feet off the ground. It then moved around his vehicle, stopping about six feet in front of the windshield.

Says the witness:

I NOTICED THAT ALTHOUGH THE RED LIGHT EMITTED FROM THIS THING WAS VERY BRIGHT TO MY EYES, IT WASN'T CASTING SHADOWS AND DID NOT REFLECT FROM THE SURROUNDING BUSHES OR FROM THE POLISHED SURFACE OF MY HOOD . . . THE LIGHT SEEMED TO BE LUMINOUS RATHER THAN PROJECTED, AND WAS NOT RADIATING ANY HEAT THAT I COULD FEEL.

The surface of the object appeared fluidic and undulating, making it very hard to focus on. When it began to move closer, the officer became fearful. "I slammed the gearshift into drive and floored it. I wanted to put as much distance between that thing and me as fast as possible. I warily glanced in the rear-view mirror and was horrified to realize that it was pursing me down the road at 90 mph."

At this point, the officer tried using his cell phone, but couldn't get service. He raced forward down the highway and soon reached Congress, where he pulled over and watched the orb dart back and forth across the sky. It remained for two or three hours before finally moving away.

The officer then noticed that his eyesight had been strangely affected by the object. "I could not focus on any bright light source," he explained. "Whatever I tried looking at seemed to move away into the periphery."[195]

UFO Photographed

On June 16, 2010, a man and his wife were driving from Las Vegas to their home in Arizona. It was daytime, and they were in Arizona when they stopped to take some photographs of some interesting rock formations. Says the husband: "While I was snapping a photo, this object crossed my field of vision. It moved so fast that my camera was only able to capture a blurred object. You can clearly see it on the far left side of the photo. I heard no sound when the object flew by."[196]

Jets Chase UFOs

As reported to MUFON, on August 16, 2010, a family in Lake Havasu City was watching television when the son looked out the window to see a large boomerang-shaped object being pursued by eight jets. The parents and the son stopped watching television to observe the show going on outside their home. They next saw a "bright red light" ahead of the jets. The light stopped and abruptly changed direction. The jets all turned and tried to follow. Together they raced off into the distance.

Thirty seconds later, a "triangle-shaped object with a deep red light in the center" flew overhead, followed minutes later by the jets. To their surprise, the red light was also back, this time trailing the jets. For the next forty-five minutes, the triangle-shaped object and the red light darted back and forth across the sky while the jets vainly attempted to catch up. The witnesses are convinced that the maneuvers performed by the UFOs were "not possible with currently known technologies."[197]

Tucson Mini-Flap

It all began on September 23, 2010 when two employees of KGUN News Channel 9 observed something in the daylight sky over Tucson that they couldn't explain. While most people have no recourse when they see a UFO, these witnesses were professional newsmen. They decided to publicize their encounter.

Says reporter Forrest Carr: "It was tiny, it was bright blue, it was way high up, and it spent part of Tuesday afternoon hovering over the skies of Tucson. What was it?"

The witnesses described the object as a "brilliant blue dot" nearly stationary in the sky. One of the witnesses, KGUN Channel 9 photojournalist Jim Pfalzer set up his camera on a tripod, put the zoom on full and videotaped the object as it moved slowly to the east.

KGUN contacted the National Weather Service and the FAA, both who denied any knowledge of the object. KGUN posted the footage on their website, and it soon became their most popular news item. Writes reporter Cherlyn Gardner Strong of the *Tucson Citizen*:

> WHATEVER IT WAS, ONE THING'S FOR SURE: NOTHING CAPTURES PEOPLE'S IMAGINATION, OR CURIOSITY, LIKE THE APPEARANCE OF MYSTERIOUS OBJECTS IN THE SKY. AS OF FRIDAY EVENING, FOUR DAYS AFTER ITS ORIGINAL POST, THIS STORY WAS STILL THE FOURTH MOST POPULAR REPORT ON KGUN9.COM, AND THE BRIEF VIDEO SHOWING THE OBJECT IN THE SKY WAS STILL THE SITE'S TOP VIDEO.

Unfortunately, KGUN never received any confirmation of the sighting. Writes Strong, "Some mysteries just aren't meant to be solved."

But events weren't over yet. Two weeks later on September 22, 2010, the KOLD News Channel 13 newsroom received a deluge of more than a dozen calls from Tucson residents reporting their sighting of a large flying triangle. Calls came from the entire western side of the city. Most witnesses described a group of three to five lights in a triangular formation. While some felt the lights were planes, most witnesses disagreed.

One caller, Armando, says: "It's not a plane. Five lights stood still; then two lights disappeared and came back to a perfect straight line. Then it disappeared."

Another witness, Crystal, was with her children when they all observed the object. "I was freaked out at first, too; all my kids gasped. It had us talking about aliens the rest of the way home."

Some witnesses reported odd electrical effects. One said that as the object passed by her home, it knocked her satellite television system offline. Another said that the traffic lights and street lights all flickered as it moved over an intersection.

KOLD news jumped on the story as it was happening and immediately phoned Davis-Monthan Air Force Base. A representative from the base denied having any aircraft in the sky that matched the description given by the witnesses. Meanwhile, KOLD News Channel 13's Facebook page buzzed with activity as witnesses posted their various encounters. Some were skeptical, but most believed they had seen a genuine UFO.[198]

More Giant Triangles

On March 17, 2011, a couple was driving in northern Glendale around 7:30 p.m. when the boyfriend saw "a triangle-shaped craft, flying at fairly low altitude, much lower than I have seen planes normally fly. It had two bright, white lights positioned at each end of the back end and what looked like a red flashing light between them near the bottom of the craft."

It was moving quickly heading right over their car. Realizing it was unusual, the boyfriend alerted his girlfriend in time to watch the object move away. The object made no sound, and had a dim glow beneath it and lights on the back.

The witnesses reported their sighting to MUFON who assigned an investigator. The next day, on March 18, 2011, also at 7:30 [[p.m.?]], another witness in Pima County observed the same (or similar) object move overhead.

The witness described the object as large, triangular-shaped, with a strange fluttering reflection surrounding it. It moved very quickly in a straight line overhead. Says the witness: "The object made zero sound—not a hum, not a buzz, nothing. This, along with the speed at which it was moving, was the most disturbing part of this whole event to me."

The witness is convinced he saw something unusual. As he says: "I live right outside Davis-Monthan AFB. I was enlisted in the AZ National Guard for six years, and I grew up on the south side of Tucson where the Tucson International Airport is located, so I knew what a plane and fighter jet looked like."

MUFON field investigators assigned to the case were unable to identify the object and called the report "puzzling."

Ten months later, on January 11, 2012, the giant triangle was back, this time over Casa Grande. The witness—a truck driver—reported to MUFON that he was heading east on Interstate 8 when he saw what he thought was a plane moving so slowly it seemed to hover. "As I kept driving," says the witness, "I ended up almost right underneath the object . . . it had three lights that made a triangle shape on the bottom. I kept driving as I lost sight of the object, so I don't know how long it stayed there."[199]

Two UFO Car Chases

There are many cases in the UFO literature describing UFOs that harass cars driving down lonely highways at night. These next two cases, which occurred less than two weeks apart, provide particularly dramatic examples.

In early June 2011, a couple was returning to their home in Golden Valley in Kingman. The wife was driving when the husband pointed out the window at a glowing fireball-like object that was pacing their car only a few feet above the ground and off to the side of the road. Frightened, the woman accelerated and tried to catch up to the line of cars ahead of her. To her dismay, the cars moved too fast, while at the same time, the ball of light moved about fifteen feet in front of their car, still keeping pace. The object now appeared to be about three feet across with a greenish tinge.

It then moved to the side and continued to pace their car for at least two more minutes. Says the witness: "It seemed to have intelligence. It stayed about 65 mph and about twenty feet from the passenger window.

Finally, the object moved away and left them alone. MUFON researcher Sandra Anthony investigated the case but could find no cause for the sighting. She did note that one of the witnesses complained of a headache on the day following the encounter.

On June 24, 2011, at 1:30 a.m., "Jane," (as designated by MUFON investigators) was driving between Flagstaff and Leupp along Route 15 when she noticed a red light flying about 800 feet high off in the distance on the left side of the road. Jane thought the object might be a helicopter, but rolling down her window, she couldn't hear any sound.

Without warning the object swooped down until it was about fifty yards away and hovering only about four feet above the ground, lighting up the desert terrain in an eerie red light. It immediately began pacing her car. Fearful but curious, she continued driving at 65 mph eastward toward the Navajo Reservation.

At one point, the road turned and she lost sight of the object. As she completed the turn, a white sphere of light about eight inches in diameter appeared next to her car a few feet away and about three feet above the ground.

The object was still pacing her car. Jane attempted to photograph it with her cell phone, but strangely the light wouldn't register in the viewfinder. She also found it strange that as the light came closer, her fear left and she felt an odd calming sensation.

The object remained next to her car for about another quarter mile. After about five minutes total, the strange orb darted forward, made a 90-degree turn, and shot straight upward and to the east.

Jane pulled into her driveway at 1:30 a.m. To her shock, something very unusual was in the headlights: a giant rabbit.

Jane insists that the creature was "no normal rabbit." It was as tall as the hood of her car, and she estimated that its girth was twenty inches. It had large black eyes and remained totally unmoving. Beginning to panic, Jane turned off the car and moved slowly into her house.

She called the police the next day, who referred her to MUFON. The MUFON "Star Team" was quickly deployed. MUFON researchers Dominic Mancini, Vickie LeBlanc, and Charles Modlin worked together with Navajo Ranger Jonathan Dover to investigate the encounter.

The witness was interviewed in depth and the area was studied by the researchers. MUFON conducted a study on the car's oil filter, which appeared to have an unusually large amount of sodium nitrate. Overall, the researchers felt that the case was unexplained. As Frank Coffman (MUFON Star Team correspondent) writes:

THE FIELD INVESTIGATORS FOUND THIS WITNESS TO BE HIGHLY CREDIBLE AND SINCERE, WITH SEEMINGLY NO MEDICAL CONDITIONS OR MEDICATIONS THAT MIGHT INFLUENCE HALLUCINATORY EVENTS.[200]

Kingman UFOs

On the evening of August 4, 2011, Michael Baca (age twenty) was driving with his cousin in Kingman when they both observed a group of about a dozen lights moving in a "methodical" pathway creating oval and rectangular formations in the sky. Puzzled and intrigued Baca and his cousin followed the lights in their car. It led them out to the desert where Baca came upon a group of other Kingman residents also watching the lights.

Baca grabbed his iPhone and captured some video and multiple still images of the strange lights. He sent the photographs to Rob Chilcoat of the Kingman Army Airfield museum for his analysis. Said Chilcoat: "These weren't stars and they weren't aircraft. When I saw the pictures, the first thing I thought of was the Phoenix Lights."

A few days following the incident, the photos were published in the *Daily Miner* causing numerous comments, including one from a pilot claiming responsibility for the lights.[201]

Chandler UFOs

On the evening of January 20, 2012, a man was driving his two kids to their mother's house in Chandler when they saw three orange globes of light hovering about 500 feet high. Says the witness: "I knew immediately it was a technology that officials claim doesn't exist. We drove back and forth doing several u-turns while I told the kids, 'I told you UFOs were real.'"

Seeing how low they were the daughter said, "Oh, Dad! They're right there! I'm scared."

The witness pulled a final U-turn to observe the object one more time. That's when something strange happened. "On our last pass," says the father, "I had an image of seeing myself from their perspective in my mind and I blurted out: 'It's a father with his two kids.'"

At that exact moment, the object floated up at an angle then darted quickly away.[202]

Killed by a UFO

Jan Harzan is the executive director of MUFON. In a monthly *MUFON E-Journal* column, "What Hath God Wrought?" he published the preliminary details of a particularly disturbing encounter. A former air force mechanic was working at an unnamed air force base in Arizona (presumably Luke or Davis-Monthan—date not given) when a UFO appeared overhead. Two F104 jet fighters were scrambled to intercept the unknown object. One of the jet fighters was able to lock his weapons on the UFO. Immediately, the UFO fired a beam of light at the fighter jet, causing it to melt and drop from the sky, killing both the pilots. Writes Harzan:

THE MELTED REMAINS OF THE AIRCRAFT WERE RECOVERED AND HAULED BACK TO THE BASE ON THE BACK OF A FLAT-BED TRAILER. THERE WAS AT LEAST ONE OTHER WITNESS TO THE EVENT WHO HEARD THE SAME STORY AND SAW THE MELTED JET AFTER IT HAD BEEN RETURNED TO THE BASE.[203]

"It Saw Us"

On April 2, 2013, two friends, both Native Americans and residents of Fort Defiance Navajo Nation, were walking home when they saw a red glow descending from the sky. They realized quickly it wasn't a plane, helicopter, or shooting star. The object moved closer and began to zigzag above them. Says the witness:

I'M PRETTY SURE IT SAW US—JUST THE FEELING THAT WE FELT. I FELT PRESSURE BEHIND MY HEAD AND HE FELT PRESSURE IN HIS BACK ... I'M VERY HAPPY TO HAVE SEEN SOMETHING LIKE THIS IN MY LIFE.[204]

UFO Photographed

On Christmas night in 2013, a family in Maricopa were eating Christmas dinner when they were drawn outside around 7:30 p.m. to see an "orange light" in the sky. All the members of the family observed the object float toward them for about five minutes at an altitude of only 1,500 feet. After it passed, it made a right turn, then faded, and disappeared.

Moments later, a second identical-looking object appeared and followed the same pathway as the first. This time, they captured a photo. Says the witness:

THEY CROSSED DIRECTLY OVER THE AIR FORCE SPACE DEBRIS SURVEILLANCE STATION AT GILA RIVER INDIAN RESERVATION A FEW MILES OUTSIDE OUR TOWN ON HIGHWAY 347 ... WE HAVE SEEN THESE TYPES OF LIGHTS OVER THE AK-CHIN INDIAN RESERVATION.[205]

UFOs on the Radio

On January 19, 2014, a gentleman was driving his car through Prescott when he saw a bluish-colored "spear-like" object flying overhead. It paused, then jetted off in another direction. The entire time the object was in view, says the witness: "My radio malfunctioned and began to sound off loud clanging, screeching, a consistent hum with knocking, and the sound of metal pans began rubbed together." The moment the object was gone, the radio returned to normal.[206]

Sky Harbor UFO

On the evening of February 1, 2015, a graphics designer observed a strange reddish-colored craft with one white light move over his home in Tempe, a city in the Phoenix Metroplex area. He observed it move toward Sky Harbor and was trying to figure out what it was. It was at about 9,000 feet and was contrary to the local flight patterns. As it reached Sky Harbor it made a sharp 90-degree turn to the west and began to accelerate. At that moment, two military jets appeared, flying without their navigation lights and moved in the same pathway of the UFO in obvious pursuit. The jets also turned over Sky Harbor, but were unable to duplicate the 90-degree turn made by the object. The tail-end of the encounter was also observed by the witness's mother, who is a licensed pilot. Says the witness: "I've seen strange things in the sky before, but never with military jets following it."[207]

Tempe UFOs

On August 1, 2015, numerous witnesses in different locations around Tempe observed a group of red lights at low altitude moving in formation. One of the witnesses was driving south along Country Club Way when he saw the formation of lights. The witness has an engineering degree and was a former army intelligence officer who worked with NASA on the Apollo Program. He and his friend both followed the lights for about ten minutes until they moved out of view.

Meanwhile, unknown to the men, another car was traveling northbound on the 101 Freeway when they counted about eight to ten red lights moving in the same delta formation described by the other witnesses. At one point he drove directly underneath the objects. Says the witness: "[It was] very reminiscent of the Phoenix Lights back in 1997."[208]

Epilogue

Arizona has a history of UFO encounters stretching back more than 100 years, but there is some evidence that visitations have been occurring for many thousands of years. The Agua Fria National Monument, about forty miles north of Phoenix, contains 111 square miles and more than 450 archaeological sites, many of which contain petroglyphs. Some of these petroglyphs contain images that look startlingly similar to reports of UFO craft and ETs, including a lizard-like figure with a human-face.

It appears that the UFOs have been here for a very long time and they definitely show no signs of leaving. Arizona's UFO events have had a profound effect on the history of UFO events in the world. The Travis Walton abduction case remains one of the best-verified in history and continues to generate interest even today. The Phoenix Lights of 1997 was the state's most widely viewed sighting, and was the biggest sighting of the year, if not the decade. The Paradise Valley UFO crash was among the first UFO crashes ever mentioned, and today is among the best verified UFO crashes in the world.

Combining the statistics of MUFON and NUFORC, and adding in accounts from other sources, Arizona has been the location of several thousand encounters. While the majority of these are sightings, some of these cases—as we have seen— involve landings, face-to-face encounters, onboard experiences and, of course, UFO crashes. Arizona is number six on NUFORC's list of most active states. Something about Arizona is very attractive to UFOs.

Arizona's geography might well be a factor. The state has more copper mines than any other and is also rich in silver and gold. And, as we have seen, there are several cases in which UFOs have been seen over mines. Arizona also has vast undeveloped areas, with plenty of places for UFOs to hide undetected. The state also has several important military bases, such as Luke AFB and Davis-Monthan, both of which have been implicated in multiple UFO cases. The multiple sightings, landings, and one contact case at the Childs Hydroelectric Plant also deserve to be mentioned.

It appears that UFOs have different agenda and visit for different reasons. While ET miners do seem to be particularly common in Arizona, the state also has a high number of landings and onboard cases. These seem to follow the same basic pattern as reported in other areas.

As far as sightings, the Phoenix Lights dominates all other cases by far. While there were a few waves here and there, no other case comes even close. The only other big Arizona sighting story would be the ongoing sightings at Sedona. The Sedona area is perhaps Arizona's UFO hotspot, and remains a Mecca for New Age seekers across the world. The area contains a vortex, which apparently UFOs can use as a type of portal, or according to other explanations, it allows them to become visible. Whatever the reason, the area is definitely a high producer of UFO reports.

When it comes to landings, not many Arizona cases received national media coverage, and none became very well-known. Despite this, there are a large number of high-quality cases.

Regarding onboard experiences, the Walton case, with a five-day-long abduction is definitely an outlier, and no other case in Arizona has reached its notoriety. The Walton case, however, is not unique. Another case in Arizona involved missing time of three days among a large group of ranchers and their families. This case received no publicity at all. A few have attracted attention. The cases of Paul Solem and Brian Allan Scott both became fairly well-known. The vast majority, however, seem to slide under the mainstream media's radar.

Some of Arizona's cases are beyond bizarre. Reports of flying humanoids and pterodactyls are not unique to Arizona, but they certainly seem to fit into Arizona's mystique.

UFO crashes are among the rarest and most difficult to confirm. Despite this, Arizona has a long list of UFO crash events. Again, most of these have received little or no publicity, but they do show that UFOs are not infallible.

The state has also produced some of the world's most prominent and influential researchers. Jim and Coral Lorenzen and James McDonald pioneered UFO research not only in Arizona but across the United States. Thanks to their efforts, UFOs were studied scientifically and they set the model for future researchers and UFO investigative groups.

The trend continues to move towards government disclosure and open official contact. When this will take place is impossible to say, but as the number of UFO witnesses grow—as the UFO database becomes larger—it becomes increasingly difficult to maintain the cover-up and officially deny the UFO presence. In fact, Arizona's Fyfe Symington is one of very few state governors to actually admit to seeing a UFO.

Today, Arizona has its own MUFON chapter, which investigates the encounters on an ongoing basis. With Arizona's history of producing high-profile UFO cases, it's only a matter of time before another case occurs that is too explosive to be ignored by the mainstream media. Whether it's another case like Travis Walton, or another fly-by like the Phoenix Lights, it's going to happen again.

If you want to be on the cutting edge of UFO activity, Arizona might be good place to investigate.

Appendix

Case Number	Date	Location
Case 95	October 14, 1947	Phoenix, AZ
Case 361	April 28, 1949	Tucson, AZ
Case 384	May 9, 1949	Tucson, AZ
Case 1127	May 17-18, 1952	Yuma Test Station, AZ
Case 1163	May 27, 1952	Yuma, AZ
Case 1310	June 19, 1952	Yuma, AZ
Case 1812	August 4, 1952	Phoenix, AZ
Case 1964	August 24, 1952	Tucson, AZ
Case 2038	September 3, 1952	Tucson, AZ
Case 2048	September 6, 1952	Tucson, AZ
Case 2105	September 17, 1952	Tucson, AZ
Case 2388	February 4, 1953	Yuma, AZ
Case 2542	April 18, 1953	Tucson, AZ

Endnotes

1. Lorenzen, 1966, 20–21; NUFORC.
2. Andrus, July 1985, 3–10; Dolan, 31; Hall, Michael David, 56–58, 67; Hamilton, 2001, 32–33; Hesseman & Mantle, 8; Lorenzen, 1966, 17, 19–20; www.nicap.org .
3. Andrus, September 1984, 14; Hall, Michael David, 84, 125; www.nicap.org; Maccabee PhD, 102; Smith 9.
4. Dolan, 81; Johnson & Thomas, 48–49; Scully, 202.
5. Edwards, 1966, 44–45; Hall, Michael David, 134.
6. Hall, Michael David, 155.
7. Davenport, 66; Dolan, 100; Druffel, 42–43; Gribble, June 1992, 17–18; Hall, Richard, 1964, 30-31, 35; Hynek, 1977, 109–112; www.nicap.org/bluebook/bluelist.htm; www.nicap.org/bluebook/unknowns.htm.
8. Dolan, 2009, 15; Lorenzen & Lorenzen, 1968, 188–191.
9. Davenport, 135; Fuller, 137–138; Hall, Richard, 1964, 22, 35, 51–52; www.nicap.org/bluebooks/unknowns.htm; Stevens & Roberts, 222–223.
10. Druffel, 7, 19–20; Hall, Richard, 1964, 70; Van Velzer, 1.
11. Hall, Richard, 1964, 153.
12. Van Velzer, 1.
13. Steiger & Steiger, 116.
14. Hall, Richard H., 1964; Lorenzen, 1969, 80–81.
15. Druffel, 20.
16. NUFORC.
17. Druffel, 20–34.
18. Van Velzer, 1.
19. NUFORC.
20. Ibid.
21. Druffel, 34.
22. Hall, Richard, 1964, 68-69.
23. Lorenzen, Jim & Coral, 1968, 114–118.
24. www.nuufors.com/Jamie_Farr.htm; www.mufonohio.com/mufono/klinger.html.
25. NUFORC.
26. Van Velzer, 1.
27. NUFORC.
28. Ibid.
29. Davenport, 128–129; Hynek, 1972, 82–83; Keyhoe, 259–260.
30. NUFORC.
31. Ibid.
32. Burt, 320; NUFORC.
33. NUFORC.
34. Ibid.
35. Ibid.
36. Ibid.
37. Ibid.
38. Ibid.
39. Lorenzen, 1976, 51.
40. NUFORC.

41. MUFON CMS.
42. Ropp, 9.
43. MUFON CMS.
44. NUFORC.
45. Lorenzen, Coral, APRO Bulletin, February 1975, 3–4.
46. MUFON CMS.
47. NUFORC.
48. Spaulding, 6–7.
49. NUFORC.
50. Ibid.
51. Ibid.
52. Dolan, 2009, 223; Dongo, 78; Haines, 128; Hamilton, 2001, 54–55; NUFORC; Ropp, 9–10.
53. Filer, 14, December 2011, #524; NUFORC.
54. Hamilton, 2001, 43.
55. NUFORC.
56. Ibid.
57. Hamilton, 2001, 49–50.
58. MUFON CMS.
59. Hall,Richard, 1988, 316.
60. Dongo, 84–85.
61. NUFORC.
62. Harvey, 5; Hamilton, 2001, 50.
63. Steiger & Steiger, 48.
64. Doerter, 5.
65. Gribble, December 1992, 18; Ropp 10.
66. Hamilton, 2001, 50; Johnson, March 1994, #311, 4.
67. Kimball, 9.
68. Synnott, 56.
69. Hamilton, 2001, 2; Kitei MD, 3–11,18–19, 47.
70. Miller, 8.
71. Allen, 28–29; AP; Barks, 2–3; Butler, 59–64; Byrnes & Burt, 15; CNN News; Fiscus, 3; Greer, 163–166; Hamilton, May 1993, 3, 6-14; Hamilton, 2001, 1–40; Kitei MD, 2, 15–19, 40, 43, 47, 54–55, 57–58, 63, 65, 68, 70, 72, 88–89, 101, 132–133, 199; Maccabee, 3–7; Marrs, 191–203; Miller, July 3, 1998, 7; Motzer, 3-6, Murphy, 1; Rapp, 12–15; Steckner, 11; Wilson, 8.
72. Kitei, 88–92.
73. Kelly, February 2000, 13–17; Sylvester, 15–16; Wright, January 1999, 19.
74. Lorenzen, 1966, 17–18.
75. Bowen, 159–161; Lorenzen, 1967, 129.
76. Lorenzen, Jim and Coral, 1968, 118–120; Van Velzer, 1.
77. Clark & Coleman, 215.
78. NUFORC.
79. Ibid.
80. Ibid.
81. Ibid.
82. Ropp, 10.
83. Renzi, 5.
84. Johnson, November 1993, 15.
85. NUFORC.
86. MUFON CMS.
87. Harzan, 1.
88. MUFON CMS.
89. NUFORC.
90. Dongo, 67–68.
91. NUFORC.
92. Ibid.
93. Dongo, 57.
94. Dongo, 62–63.
95. Quinn, 2–3.
96. NUFORC.
97. Ropp, 9.
98. MUFON CMS.
99. Ibid.
100. Ibid.
101. Ibid.
102. Filer, November 2000, 12.
103. Filer, December 1998, 11.

104. Kelly, December 1999, #380, 12–13.
105. NUFORC.
106. Ibid.
107. Ibid.
108. MUFON CMS.
109. NUFORC.
110. Ibid.
111. Ibid.
112. MUFON CMS.
113. NUFORC.
114. MUFON CMS.
115. NUFORC.
116. MUFON CMS.
117. Marsh, September 29, 2014, 1.
118. MUFON CMS.
119. NUFORC.
120. MUFON CMS.
121. NUFORC.
122. Coleman & Clark, 213–222.
123. Hamilton, 2001, 19–31, 39.
124. http://thecid.com/ufo/ufo9/uf1/091035.htm.
125. Hamilton, 2001, 43; http://thecid.com/ufo/uf19/uf6/196031.htm.
126. Hamilton, 2001, 43.
127. Dongo, 31–34.
128. Barry, 1978; Clarke, Ric, 2; Connolly, 18–19; Dolan, 2009, 102–108; Nelson, 8; Randles, 1988, 148–149; Ryberg, 7–10; Walton, 1978; Walton, 1993.
129. NUFORC.
130. Ibid.
131. Ibid.
132. Hamilton, 2001, 33–36.
133. Hamilton, 2001, 44.
134. Hamilton, 2001, 45–48.
135. Hamilton, 2001, 56–57.
136. MUFON CMS.
137. NUFORC.
138. Ibid.
139. MUFON CMS.
140. Jensen, 5.
141. NUFORC.
142. Ibid.
143. Ibid.
144. Ibid.
145. Dongo, 66–67.
146. Boylan PhD, 119–125.
147. Dongo, 83–84.
148. Dongo, 67.
149. Ropp, 9.
150. Cox, 24–27.
151. MUFON CMS.
152. Ibid.
153. NUFORC.
154. MUFON CMS.
155. NUFORC.
156. MUFON CMS.
157. NUFORC.
158. Ibid.
159. Ibid.
160. MUFON CMS.
161. NUFORC.
162. Ibid.
163. MUFON CMS.
164. Ibid.
165. Ibid.
166. Casteel, 15–17; Hamilton, 2001, 35, Ropp, July 6, 1997, 3.
167. Hamilton, 2001, 39; Steinman, 350.
168. Beckley, 1989, 129; Birnes, 181; Davenport, 33; Dolan, 134; Greer, 2001, 384–385; Hamilton, 2001, 35–38; Kasten, 71–80; Randle, 1995, 57–68; Randles, 71–73; Scully, 136; Steinman, 371.
169. Steinman, 493–497.
170. NUFORC.
171. Ibid.
172. Filer, Feb 2004, 14.
173. Schwarz MD, 536; Steinman, 482–482.
174. NUFORC.

175. Ibid.

176. Ibid.

177. Filer, January 2001, 8.

178. Connelly, August 2001, 8.

179. Filer, December 2001, 16.

180. NUFORC.

181. Filer, May 2002, 17.

182. Filer, May 2003, 14.

183. Filer, November 2003, 14.

184. Filer, August 2004, 14; Filer, December 2004, 15; Filer, June 2004, 14, Filer, March 2004, 14; Filer, May 2004, 17; Filer, September 2004, 19.

185. MUFON CMS.

186. Filer, June 2005, 13.

187. MUFON CMS.

188. NUFORC.

189. MUFON CMS.

190. Renzi, 5.

191. Filer, April 2007; Schubert, 3.

192. Filer, December 2007, 19.

193. Filer, Septmber 2008, 18; email interview with the author (August 2015).

194. Filer, August 2009, 18.

195. Marsh, Jan 2012, 9; MUFON CMS; www.examiner.com.

196. MUFON CMS.

197. www.examiner.com.

198. Strong, September 15, 2010, 9; Strong, September 24, 2010, 8; Strong, Se 25, 9.

199. Filer, February 2012, 14; Kimball, 6-7.

200. Coffman, 4-7; Marsh, Jan 2012, 8-9.

201. Taylor, 6.

202. NUFORC.

203. Harzan, 1.

204. NUFORC.

205. Ibid.

206. MUFON CMS.

207. Ibid.

208. Ibid.

Sources

Books

Barry, Bill. *Ultimate Encounter: The True Story of a UFO Kidnapping*. New York: Simon & Schuster, 1978.

Beckley, Timothy Green. *MJ-12 and the Riddle of Hangar 18*. New Brunswick, NJ: Inner Light Publications, 1989.

Birnes, William J. *The UFO Magazine UFO Encyclopedia*. New York: Pocket Books, 2004.

Birnes, William J., and Harold Burt. *Unsolved UFO Mysteries: The World's Most Compelling Cases of Alien Encounters*. New York: Warner Books, Inc, 2000.

Blum, Ralph, and Judy Blum. *Beyond Earth: Man's Contact with UFOs*. New York: Bantam Books, 1974.

Bowen, Charles, ed. "A Survey of Worldwide Reports of Landings of Unconventional Aerial Objects and Their Occupants." Chicago, IL: Henry Regnery Company, 1969.

Boylan, Richard J., and Lee K. Boylan. *Close Extraterrestrial Encounters: Positive Experiences with Mysterious Visitors*. Tigard, OR: Wild Flower Press, 1994.

Burt, Harold. "Flying Saucers 101." Los Angeles, CA: *UFO Magazine*, 2000.

Butler, Edwin R. "The Phoenix Lights: A New Perspective." *Uncensored UFO Reports*. New York, vol. 1, #7, pp 58-64, 1997.

Clark, Jerome, and Loren Coleman. *The Unidentified: Notes Toward Solving the UFO Mystery*. New York: Warner Books, Inc., 1975.

Connelly, Dwigh, ed. "Arizona Object Puts on Show for Witnesses." *MUFON UFO Journal*. Aug 2001, #400, P8.

Davenport, Marc. *Visitors from Time: The Secret of the UFOs*. Tuscaloosa, AL: Greenleaf Publications, 1992.

Dennett, Preston. *UFO Healings*. Wild Flower Press. Mill Spring, NC, 1996.

Dolan, Richard M. *UFOs and the National Security State: Chronology of a Cover-up, 1941–1973*. Charlottesville, VA: Hampton Roads, 2002.

——. *UFOs and the National Security State: The Cover-up Exposed, 1973-1991*. Rochester, NY: Keyhole Publishing, 2009.

Dongo, Tom. *The Alien Tide: The Mysteries of Sedona, Book Two*. Sedona, AZ: Hummingbird Publishing, 1990.

Druffel, Ann. *Firestorm: Dr. James E McDonald's Fight for UFO Science*. Columbus, NC: Wild Flower Press, 2003.

Edwards, Frank. *Flying Saucers—Serious Business*. Secaucus, NJ: Citadel Press,

1966.

Greer, Steven M. *Disclosure: Military and Government Witnesses Reveal the Greatest Secrets in Modern History.* Crozet, Virginia: Crossing Point, 2001.

——. *Extraterrestrial Contact: The Evidence and Implications.* Crozet, Virginia: Crossing Point, 1999.

Haines, Richard F. CE-5: *Close Encounters of the Fifth Kind.* Naperville, IL: Sourcebooks, 1999.

Hall, Michael David. *UFOs: A Century of Sightings.* Lakeville, MN: Galde Press, 1999.

Hall, Richard H. ed. *The UFO Evidence.* National Investigations Committee on Aerial Phenomena, c1964 (1997, Barnes & Noble Books).

——. *Uninvited Guests: A Documented History of UFO Sightings Alien Encounters and Coverups.* Santa Fe, NM: Aurora Press, 1988.

Hamilton, William F. *The Phoenix Lights Mystery.* Merrimack, NH: Write-to-Print, 2001.

Hesseman, Michael, and Philip Mantle. *Beyond Roswell: The Alien Autopsy Film, Area 51 and the US Government Coverup of UFOs.* New York: Marlowe & Company, 1997.

Hynek, J. Allen. *The UFO Experience: A Scientific Inquiry.* New York: Ballantine Books, 1972.

Johnson, Dewayne B., and Kenn Thomas. *Flying Saucers over Los Angeles: The UFO Craze of the 50's.* Kempton: IL: Adventures Unlimited Press, 1998.

Kasten, Len. *Secret Journey to Planet Serpo.* Rochester, VT: Bear & Company, 2013.

Lorenzen, Coral. *Flying Saucers: The Startling Evidence of the Invasion from Outer Space.* New York: Signet Books, 1966.

Lorenzen, Coral, and Jim Lorenzen. *Encounters with UFO Occupants.* New York: Berkley Publishing, 1976.

——. *Flying Saucer Occupants.* New York: Signet Books, 1967

——. *UFOs: The Whole Story.* New York: Signet Books, 1969.

Lorenzen, Jim and Coral. *UFOs over the Americas.* New York: Signet Books, 1968.

Maccabee, Bruce. *UFO FBI Connection.* St. Paul, MN: Llewellyn, 2000.

Marrs, Jim. *Above Top Secret.* New York: Disinformation Company, 2008.

Randle, Kevin. *A History of UFO Crashes.* New York: Avon Books, 1995.

Randles, Jenny. *Abduction: Over 200 Documented UFO Kidnappings Exhaustively Investigated.* London: Robert Hale, 1988.

——. *UFO Retrievals: the Recovery of Alien Spacecraft.* London: Blandford, 1995.

Schwarz, Berthold E. *UFO Dynamics: Book II.* Vernon Hills, IL: Rainbow Books, 1983.

Scully, Frank. *Behind the Flying Saucers.* New York: Henry Holt and Company, 1950.

Steiger, Brad, and Sherry Hansen Steiger. *The Rainbow Conspiracy.* New York: Windsor Publishing, 1994.

Steinman, William, and Wendelle Stevens. *UFO Crash at Aztec.* Tucson, AZ: UFO Photo Archives, 1986.

Stevens, Wendelle, and August Roberts. *UFO Photographs Around the World,* vol. 2. Tucson, AZ: UFO Photo Archives, 1989.

Walton, Travis. *Fire in the Sky.* New York:

Marlowe & Company, 1990.

——. *The Walton Experience*. New York: The Berkley Publishing Group, 1978.

Magazines/Newspapers/Periodicals

Allen, Floyd. "The UFO Candidate." *Fate*, vol. 51, #9, Issue 582, September 1998, pp 28–29.

Andrus, Walt. "Air Intelligence Report No#100-203-79." *MUFON UFO Journal*. Seguin, TX, July 1985, #207, pp 3–10.

——. "Daylight Discs Seen in Phoenix." *MUFON UFO Journal*. September 1986, #197, pp 14–15.

Associated Press. "Arizona is Abuzz over Reports of Lights in the Sky." *Journal-Bulletin*. Providence, RI. June 21, 1997. (See UFONS: July 1997, #336, p7).

Barks, Cindy. "Eyes on the Sky." *Daily Courier*. Prescott, AZ, March 9, 2006.

Brilliant, Gregg. "Of a Fire in the Sky." *MUFON UFO Journal*. February 1993, #298, pp 3–5.

Casteel, Sean. "Arizona Crashed Disc Legend Resurfaces." *UFO Universe*. New York: GCR Publishing Group, Inc. Winter 1997, vol. 7, #4, pp 15–17.

Clarke, Ric. "'Walton Experience' Continues to Defy Skepticism." *News Tribune*. Tempe, AZ, March 6, 1989. (See UFONS #238, May 1989, p2).

Coffman, Frank. "Case 29703: Orbs Follow Woman's Car." *MUFON UFO Journal*. January 2013, #525.

Connelly, Dwight. "Ufology Profile: Travis Walton." *MUFON UFO Journal*. August 1998, #364, pp 18-19

Cox, Gem G. "Contact in Southern Arizona." *UFO Journal of Facts*. Tucson, AZ, April 1991, vol. 2, pp 25–27.

Doerter, Dr. James. "Fire Lookouts See Anomalies." *MUFON UFO Journal*. June 2003, #422 p5.

Filer George. "Filer's Files: Another Arizona Triangle—Arizona Backyard Sighting. Arizona Formation of Triangles." *MUFON UFO Journal*. January 2001, #393, p8.

——. "Filer's Files: Arizona." *MUFON UFO Journal*. December 1998, #368, p11.

"Filer's Files: Arizona Cigar." *MUFON UFO Journal*. June 2005, #446, pp 12–13.

——. "Filer's Files: Arizona Detective Sighting." *MUFON UFO Journal*. March 2004, #431, p14.

——. "Filers Files: Arizona Disc-Shaped Craft Witnessed by Police." *MUFON UFO Journal*. December 2011, #524, p14.

——. "Filer's Files: Arizona Flying Triangle." *MUFON UFO Journal*. December 2004, #440, p15.

——. "Filer's Files: Arizona Object Throws Sparks." *MUFON UFO Journal*. June 2004, #434, p15.

——. "Filer's Files: Arizona Orbs and Dark Rounded Shape." *MUFON UFO Journal*. May 2002, #409, p17.

——. "Filer's Files: Arizona Triangle." *MUFON UFO Journal*. November 2003, #427, p14 and Feb 2012, #526, p14.

——. "Filer's Files: Arizona UFOs Caught on Videotape in Storm." *MUFON UFO Journal*, September 2008, #485, p18.

——. "Filer's Files: Arizona Unknown

Object Filmed." *MUFON UFO Journal*, April 2007, #468, p15.

——. "Filer's Files: Arizona Video of Disc. *MUFON UFO Journal*. August 2009, #2009, #496, p18.

——. "Filer's Files: Arizona Web Cams Keep Photographing UFOs. *MUFON UFO Journal*. December 2007, #476, p18 (See: www.phoenixvis.net/came1/indext.html).

——. "Filer's Files: Cigar Shapes in Arizona. *MUFON UFO Journal*. February 2004, #430, p15.

——. "Filer's Files: Hooded Figures in 1996 Arizona Encounter. *MUFON UFO Journal*. November 2000, #391, p12.

——. "Filer's Files: Light on Wing in Arizona." *MUFON UFO Journal*. May 2004, #433, p17.

——. "Filer's Files: Lights in Arizona." *MUFON UFO Journal*. August 2004, #436.

——. "Filer's Files: Numerous Orbs in Arizona." *MUFON UFO Journal*. September 2004, #437, p19.

——. "Filer's Files: Object Just above Road in Arizona." *MUFON UFO Journal*. April 2003, #420, p14.

——. "Filer's Files: Reflective Sphere in Arizona." *MUFON UFO Journal*. March 2004, #431, p13.

——. "Filer's Files: Sphere Makes 90-Degree Turn in Arizona." *MUFON UFO Journal*. May 2003, #421, p14.

Fiscus, Chris. "Barwood Pushes UFOs in Bid for State Office." *Arizona Republic*. Phoenix, AZ, January 13, 1998. (UFONS, February 1998, #343, p3).

Gribble, Robert. "Current Cases: Log #921908W." *MUFON UFO Journal*. December 1992, #296, p18.

——. "Looking Back: April 1952. *MUFON UFO Journal*. April 1992, #288, p17.

——. "Looking Back: June 1952." *MUFON UFO Journal*. Jun 1992, #290, p18.

Hamilton, William F. "Mass Sighting in Arizona." *MUFON UFO Journal*. May 1997, #349, pp 3–6,14.

Harvey, T. "Latest UFO in Cloud Photo." *UFO Journal of Facts*. Tucson, AZ, September 1991, vol. 3, p5.

Harzan, Jan. "What Hath God Wrought?" *MUFON E-Journal*. www.mufon.com/directors-message/what-hath-god-wrought.

Jensen, Edythe. "Alien Creature Guides AJ Writer." *Sun*. Phoenix, AZ, December 25, 1995. (See UFONS, March 1996, #320, p5).

Johnson, Jerold R. "Current Cases: Log #930618C." *MUFON UFO Journal*. November 1993, #307, p16.

——. "Current Cases: Log #931201J." *MUFON UFO Journal*. March 1994, #311, p15.

Kelly, Jim. "Arizona Family Sees Diamond-Shaped UFO—Case of the Month." *MUFON UFO Journal*. December 1999, #380, pp 12–13.

——. "Police Helicopter Interacts with Strange Green Light." *MUFON UFO Journal*. February 2000, #382, p13.

Kimball, Richard W. "UFOs Spotted over Prescott Valley." *Daily Courier*. Prescott, AZ, November 18, 1994. (see UFONS, January 1995, #306, p9).

Lorenzen, Coral. "UFOs over Arizona," *APRO Bulletin*. vol. 23, No 4,

January–February, 1975, pp 3–4.

Maccabee, Bruce. "Phoenix Lights Revisited." *MUFON UFO Journal.* February 1999, #370, pp 3–8.

Marsh, Roger. "Comparing Case Elements: Studying Multiple Reports May Reveal Clues." *MUFON UFO Journal.* January 2012, #525, pp 8-9.

———. "Could Disappearing Arizona House Have Been a UFO?" *Open Minds UFO News and Investigations.* www.openminds.tv/disappearing-arizona-house-ufo/30206.

———. "Triangles 2011." *MUFON UFO Journal.* February 2012, #526, pp 7-8.

Miller, Jay. "Arizona UFO Second to Roswell." *Daily Record.* Roswell, NM, July 3, 1998. (See UFONS, August 1998, #349, p7).

Miller, Steve. "UFO Sightings Being Reported." *San Pedro Valley News Sun.* Benson AZ, December 25, 1996 (See UFONS; March 1997, #332).

Motzer, Richard F. "The Phoenix Lights, the Real Investigation." *MUFON UFO Journal,* July 1997, #351, pp 3–6.

Murphy, Michael. "UFOs Invade Barwood Race." *The Arizona Republic.* Phoenix, AZ, June 14, 1998 (See UFONs, March 1998, #344).

Nelson, Willard D. "A Note on the Travis Walton Experience." *MUFON UFO Journal.* Seguin, TX, May 1981, #159.

Price, Richard. "Arizonans Say the Truth about UFO is Out There." *USA Today.* Arlington, VA, June 18, 1997 (See UFONS: July 1997, #336).

Quinn, Ron. "E.T.—A Summer Visitor at Ruby?" *Southern Arizona Trails.* Tumacacori, AZ, December 13, 1988. (See UFONS #234, January 1989, p2)

Renzi, Steve. "MUFON." *Desert Leaf.* Tucson, AZ, July/August 2006. (See UFONS, August 2006, #445)

Rapp, David. "Lasers and the Phoenix Lights." *MUFON UFO Journal.* October 1998, #366, pp 12–15.

Ropp, Thomas. "Forget Roswell; Arizona's UFO Hotbed." *Newsday.* Melville, NY, July 6, 1997.

———. "Star Tripping: UFO Fans Look to Arizona for UFO Encounters." *Arizona Republic.* Phoenix, AZ, July 4, 1993.

Ryberg, Bill "Then and Now: High Prices for Walton's Story Spark Renewed Interest in 1975 Abduction Experience." *MUFON UFO Journal.* April 2011, #516, pp 7-10.

Schubert, Rebecca. "Leupp Residents Report Another UFO Sighting in Nighttime Sky." *Navajo-Hopi Observer.* Flagstaff, AZ, January 31, 2007 (see UFONS, March 2007, #452, p3).

Smith, Kim. "Legend Has Kingman as Alien Crash Site." *Mojave Daily Miner.* Kingman, AZ, June 25, 1995. (See also: UFONS, September 1995, #314, p9).

Spaulding, William H. "Arizona Patrol Officer Reports EM Effects." *Skylook.* December 1975, #97, pp 6–7.

Steckner, Susie. "Object Seen over State a Puzzle—Was It a UFO?" *Arizona Republic.* Phoenix, AZ, March 18, 1997 (see UFONS: May 1997, #334, p11).

Steiger, Sherry Hansen, and Brad Steiger. "Sedona, Arizona: Gateway to Another Dimension. *UFO Universe.* New York: Condor Books, 1990, vol. 1, No 5.

Strong, Cherlyn Gardner. "KGUN 9 Employees in Tucson Capture UFO Image." *The Tucson Citizen*. Tuczon, AZ, September 15, 2010 (see UFONS, November 2010, #496, p9).

——. "Strange Lights over Tucson." *The Tucson Citizen*. Tucson, AZ, September 24, 2010.

——. "UFO Sighting in Tucson Sparks Dozens of Calls to Newsrooms." *The Tucson Citizen*. Tucson, AZ, September 23, 2010. (see UFONS, November 2010, #496 p9).

Sylvester, Bob. "Police Helicopter Case Report Review." *MUFON UFO Journal*. February 2000, #382, pp 16–17.

Synnott, Kenneth. "True Mystic Experiences: UFO over the Zoo." *Fate*. Lakeville, MN: January 2003, vol. 56, #1, Issue 633, p56.

Taylor, Erin. "UFO Sighting? Kingman Lightshow Defied Logic, Photographer Says." *Daily Miner*. Kingman, AZ, August 7, 2011 (see: UFONS, August 2011, #505).

Van Velzer, Ryan. "15 Arizona UFO Stories from the Project blue Book." AZ Central. January 22, 2015. www.azcentral.com/story/news/local/arizona/2015/01/23/arizona-ufo-stories-from-project-blue-book/22131391/.

Walton, Travis. "The Walton Experience Revisited." *MUFON UFO Journal*. February 1993, #298, pp 6–8.

Wilson, Steve. "Phoenix Lights Witnesses Credible, Hard to Dismiss." *Arizona Republic*. Phoenix, AZ, March 11, 1998.

Wright, Dan. "Case of the Month." *MUFON UFO Journal*. January 1999, p18.

Documentary Films

I Know What I Saw: Government and Military Officials Reveal the Truth about UFOs (Written and directed by James Fox), 2009

Websites

www.examiner.com
www.mufon.com
www.nuforc.com
www.nicap.org
www.prestondennett.weebly.com
http://sedonanewagestore.com/sedona-visitors/ufo-tours/ufo-research-center/
www.ufoevidence.org

Index of Place Names

Agua Fria National Monument178

Ahwatukee, 59, 61

Alamo Lake, 49

Albuquerque, NM119

Apache Junction, 87, 113, 168

Apache Lake, 47

Apache Mountains, 52

Aravaipa Canyon, 67

Benson, 14

Bisbee, 23, 46, 84–85

Bradshaw Mountains, 57

Bullhead City, 164

California, 6, 15, 19, 34–35, 85, 163

Camp Verde, 121

Carswell AFB, TX15

Casa Grande, 56, 124–125, 161, l73

Catalina Mountains13, 54–55, 98

Cave Creek, 57, 60, 136, 147, 150

Chandler, 48, 61, 76, 140, 175

Childs, 39, 103, 121–122, 178

Chino Valley, 60, 105

Cochise, 60

Colorado River, 7, 23, 35

Congress, 170–171

Cordes Junction, 60

Cottonwood , 33, 52, 136

Dallas, TX, 34

Davis Dam , 23

Davis–Monthan AFB 12, 13, 15, 17, 21,
    42–43, 48, 54, 64–65, 69, 86, 106,
    172–173, 175, 178

Dewey, 60, 138

Douglas, 10–11, 21, 42

Fish Creek, 129

Flagstaff, 7, 13, 106, 174

Fort Defiance, 176

Fort Huachuca (see Huachuca)

Fossil Creek Canyon, 103

Gila, 61, 167

Gila Bend, 59, 61, 64, 137, 166

Gila Indian Reservation, 61, 176

Gilbert, 159

Glendale, 29, 32, 48, 61, 173

Globe, 85, 102, 141, 151

Golden Valley, 173

Grand Canyon, 6–7, 21, 98

Hamilton Field, CA9

Havasu, 7, 21, 32, 99, 170–171

Highway 8, 50

Highway 40, 35, 141

Highway 60, 164–165, 168

Highway 61, 157

Highway 80, 19

Highway 87, 134

Highway 89, 90–91, 93, 156

Highway 347, 176

Holbrook, 43

Holloman AFB, NM44

    Hoover Dam, 23

Hotevilla, 86

Howe, ID, 112

Huachuca, 36, 42–43, 130, 155–156

Interstate 8, 166, 173

Interstate 10, 53, 63, 100, 103–104, 142,
    146

Interstate 17, 61

Interstate 40, 108, 157, 169

Interstate 93, 108

Jakes Corner, 132
Joseph City, 22
Kayenta, 90
Keams Canyon43
Kingman, 7, 37, 108, 141, 144, 153–154, 160, 169, 173, 175
Klondyke, 93
Lake Havasu (see Havasu)
Lake Powell, 92
Las Vegas, NV37, 58, 82, 119, 140, 157, 171
Laughlin, NV, 23
Leupp, 174
Loy Butte, 51, 115
Lukachukai, 89
Luke AFB, 20, 29–30, 40, 44, 48, 58–61, 64–65, 98–99, 132, 144, 161, 175, 178
Marana, 103
Marana AFB, 14
Maricopa, 72, 82, 87, 176
March AFB, CA15
Mesa, 24, 26, 48, 52, 78, 115, 122, 141, 143, 166, 168
Mexico, 6, 21, 23, 29
Mingus Mountains, 33
Mongollon Rim39, 52, 55, 116
Morenci, 46–47,
Morgan Ranch, 131
Nogales, 10, 21, 25
New Mexico, 6, 13–14, 44, 126, 149, 152, 154
Page, 92, 146
Papago Indian Reservation, 28
Paradise Valley, 98, 124, 149, 151–152, 155, 178
Parker Dam, 23
Parker, 105, 125
Philadelphia, PA113
Phoenix, 4–5, 7, 9, 11, 17, 24–25, 29, 39, 40–41, 44–45, 48, 53, 54–55, 57–72, 74, 78, 80, 86–87, 90, 98, 100, 104, 111, 114, 121–122, 124–125, 127, 129, 133–134, 140, 143, 147–148, 152, 161, 163, 165–168, 175, 177–180

Pima, 36, 89, 97, 112, 173
Prescott, 20, 22, 57, 60, 88, 93, 112, 128, 176
Prescott National Forest, 44
Quartzite, 104, 162–163
Saint Johns, 164
San Carlos Indian Reservation, 40–41, 163
San Manuel, 89
Santa Rita Mountains, 21
Secret Canyon, 156,
Sedona, 7, 51–53, 55, 74, 76, 93, 95, 97, 104–105, 107, 115, 125, 134, 136, 156, 165, 179
Seligman, 157
Scottsdale, 39, 47, 60, 63, 88, 102, 127, 137, 151
Show Low, 94, 157
Snowflake, 7, 38, 116, 118–119, 139
Sitgreaves National Forest, 116
Sonora Desert, 78, 167
Squaw Peak, 4, 61, 70
Strawberry, 103
Sunflower, 159
Tempe, 60, 63, 76, 165, 177
Tombstone, 16, 60, 74
Tonopah, 144, 146
Tonto Rim, 8, 102
Tortilla Mountains45
Tucson, 10, 12–13, 17, 20–23, 26, 28–30, 32, 36, 38, 41–42, 54–56, 64, 85, 101, 103, 106, 110, 120, 130, 142, 162, 167–168, 171–173, 180
Verde River, 39, 51
White Tank Mountains, 40, 123
Williams AFB, 26, 87–88
Willcox, 60,
Winslow, 8, 119, 168
Wright–Patterson AFB, OH9, 93, 153–154
Yavapai County, 128
Yucca, 104
Yuma, 7–8, 10–11, 14, 19–20, 48, 50, 71, 82, 91, 190